Howard Risher and Charles Fay:
The Performance Imperative: Strategies for Enhancing Workforce Effectiveness

New Strategies for Public Pay

Howard Risher

Charles H. Fay

and Associates

New Strategies for Public Pay

Rethinking Government Compensation Programs

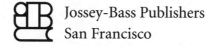
Jossey-Bass Publishers
San Francisco

Substantial discounts on bulk quantities of Jossey-Bass books are available to
corporations, professional associations, and other organizations. For details and
discount information, contact the special sales department at Jossey-Bass Inc.,
Publishers (415) 433–1740; Fax (800) 605–2665.

For sales outside the United States, please contact your local Simon & Schuster
International Office.

Jossey-Bass Web address: http://www.josseybass.com

 Manufactured in the United States of America on Lyons Falls Turin Book. This
paper is acid-free and 100 percent totally chlorine-free.

Library of Congress Cataloging-in-Publication Data

Risher, Howard W.
    New strategies for public pay: rethinking government compensation programs/
Howard Risher, Charles Fay, and Associates
        p. cm.—(Jossey-Bass public administration series)
    Includes bibliographical references and index.
    ISBN 0–7879–0826–6
    1. Civil service—Salaries, etc. 2. Compensation management. I. Fay, Charles H.
II. Title. III. Series.
JF1661.R57 1997
352.6'7—dc21   96–53433

FIRST EDITION
HB Printing   10 9 8 7 6 5 4 3 2 1

The Jossey-Bass
Public Administration Series

Consulting Editor
Public Management and Administration

James L. Perry
Indiana University

Contents

⟞ᴡ⟞ Preface

New Strategies for Public Pay was developed to support the mushrooming interest in reinventing government. The wage and salary programs in the public sector have seen only superficial change since the end of World War II. The most widely used model has its origins in an earlier era of federal reinvention following World War I. The current federal program as well as the programs in many state and local government units still reflect this vintage model. There are a few recently introduced exceptions, but public pay programs can only be characterized as dinosaurs in an era of rapid organizational change.

This is in direct contrast to the trend in the private sector. Here there seems at times to be a race to discard the old and introduce new program concepts. In hindsight, traditional pay program concepts never did have strong top management support. Somehow they were tolerated as "another personnel program," but they were never really understood. Now, however, reengineering initiatives open the door to and encourage the critical rethinking of practices and methods. That has prompted the recognition that traditional programs are not meeting organizational needs nor are they consistent with emerging management thinking.

The goal in the private sector now is to move to program concepts that support the organization's business strategy and contribute to its performance. The traditional model, with its emphasis on time-consuming analyses and organizational hierarchy, is incompatible with the need for flexibility and quick response. The traditional model is also out of sync with the delegation of accountability to lower-level managers for their unit's performance. Corporations are simply unwilling to commit the resources necessary to administer a traditional program or to allow the administrative bureaucracy to get in the way.

Significantly, there is wide recognition that financial rewards affect employee performance. Rewards can benefit an organization if they are tied to important organizational goals, or they can have an adverse impact if they motivate the wrong behaviors. Recently, for example, reengineering and quality management experts have concluded that one of the reasons these initiatives often do not generate expected gains is that people are still being rewarded for old behaviors, which makes them reluctant to adopt change. Organizations that want to change the way workers approach their job need to consider the potential use of rewards.

Even in government, where financial rewards are deemphasized, people know how to behave so that it is in their best interest. Management may not promulgate a formal reward policy but every organization has a reward system. People know what they need to do to be promoted, to earn special privileges, or to stay out of trouble. Every time a supervisor smiles at a subordinate, the interaction serves as positive recognition that the employee is viewed favorably. Organizations that do not by policy reward good performance are inadvertently encouraging people to stay at minimal performance levels. Managers who want to maintain the status quo or to avoid rocking the boat know how to send this message to their people. They may not rely on cash but they know how to manage rewards.

For government reinvention initiatives to be successful requires providing managers with tools that can provide the motivation needed to accept change and new work behaviors. Financial rewards are certainly not the only consideration, but if existing programs are not reconsidered, employees may continue with business as usual. There is no inherent reason to preclude a shift to financial rewards linked to successful reinvention results.

AUDIENCE

This book is not a technical or academic personnel volume, nor is it a how-to manual. It was planned and developed as a resource for anyone who may be asked to play a role in rethinking a pay program. The goal is to balance the more conceptual and strategic side of program planning with adequate coverage of program design issues. In this regard the book could be useful at the policy level as well as the program administration.

The field of compensation has until recently been dominated by a cookie-cutter mentality: every new program looked like every other, with only minor arcane differences that had little if any impact on compensation decisions. The importance of reengineering and the logic of process redesign is rapidly changing the field. In the future compensation will not be a closed and carefully guarded function. Increasingly, pay systems will be redesigned by committees that may or may not include a technical specialist. Committee members will likely know little about the nuances that have dominated compensation conferences for the past decade or more, meaning there is no longer a reason to expect programs to reflect a universal model.

Traditional thinking also treated pay systems as having a life of their own, independent of organizational needs and human resource policies. For reasons that have never been documented, public pay systems have been sacrosanct and unchanged in some jurisdictions for decades. The underlying body of knowledge has been handed down from generation to generation, with only a small number of technical gurus—the so-called classifiers—trusted to guard the secrets. In reality, classifiers are often the only people who understand the program.

But members of the old guard are now viewed as part of the problem. If their knowledge and the standard model have lost credibility, perhaps no one working in government has the accepted expertise to redesign a pay program. This book was written for people who may have no prior experience in the field. It is intended to prompt the questions and raise the issues that need to be addressed by policy makers.

The book should also be useful to students of government at all levels. Individuals who want to understand public personnel management will undoubtedly take at least one course in compensation management; this book is not a text but its general framework is similar to many textbooks in the field. It could serve as a supplementary text for courses in public personnel management.

A reality of compensation management is that the problem is essentially the same in every government in every nation: wage and salary costs are often the single largest budget item. That means there is a universal need for effective systems. Moreover, employee compensation is universally important as a determinant of lifestyle and status. There are cultural differences that need to be considered in program design, but the problem is essentially the same around the world. This book should be useful to public officials outside the United States.

OVERVIEW OF THE CONTENTS

Our objective in planning this book was to develop a single resource for people who may be asked to play a role in rethinking government compensation programs. There are number of textbooks on compensation management written for technical specialists in the field, but most of them reflect the philosophies, values, and people management strategies typical of the corporate world. The political reality that dominates the culture in the typical government organization prompts important questions regarding the efficacy of corporate programs as they apply to government service. This book focuses on the problems associated with planning new programs in the public sector, and it may be unique in that regard.

The introductory chapter, by Howard Risher and Charles Fay, discusses the growing interest in rethinking compensation programs in the context of the new work management paradigm and the initiatives to reinvent government. In the corporate world compensation programs are increasingly viewed as management systems that can provide the incentive to improve organizational performance. The role of compensation programs in the public sector is one of the fundamental and unresolved questions this book attempts to address.

Part One provides an overview of the decision-making systems that are, in effect, the structure of salary management programs. These systems focus on the questions of how much a job is worth and how much must be paid to recruit and retain adequately qualified personnel. The chapters in Part One discuss the methods and systems developed to provide answers to these questions.

The author of Chapter One, Barbara Wamsley, came to understand the strengths and the weaknesses of the federal pay system as a line manager. Shortly before she left public service she played a lead role in several personnel studies conducted by the National Academy of Public Administration; one evaluated the broad-banding concept as an alternative to the federal salary structure. Her chapter is based on problems with the federal program, but realistically they are prevalent in virtually every public pay program.

Chapter Two by Howard Risher looks at the framework for making wage and salary decisions—the salary structure or schedule. The grades and ranges used to guide or control decision making in a traditional salary program are the heart of the program. The chapter also discusses the newer alternative, broad or grade banding. Banding moves a pay program away from the control orientation that was so important in the traditional model and introduces considerably more flexibility for managers and supervisors to manage staff salaries.

In Chapter Three, Charles Fay discusses the importance of and problems associated with aligning pay programs with prevailing labor market pay rates. In the private sector, where payroll is a significant issue in determining how a company's operating costs compare with its product or service competitors, this is a significant business concern. Government has not typically devoted as much time or as many resources to understanding market pay rates. The alignment does, however, affect every employer's ability to recruit and retain qualified personnel.

Chapter Four looks at the role of classification systems. These systems have been an integral component of public personnel systems for over a century. They have been criticized as too rigid and bureaucratic; according to the critics, they should be eliminated. The authors of this chapter, Lyn Meridew Holley and James O'Connell, have extensive experience with the federal classification system. O'Connell has been the point person for the federal Office of Personnel Management on initiatives to automate the classification process. The chapter looks at the applications served by classification and at the prospects for improving these systems.

One of the basic questions in salary management is the fairness and equity of the pay-setting process; most employers rely on job evaluation systems as the basis for making these decisions, but such systems did not receive much attention until the late 1970s, when feminists focused on the pay equity argument. That prompted widespread interest in the development of more valid and reliable systems. These problems are discussed by Howard Risher and Lois Wise in Chapter Five along with the efforts to develop automated versions of such systems.

Chapters Six, by Nina Gupta, and Seven, by Howard Risher, look at newer concepts in salary management: skill-based and competence-based pay. In the emerging work management paradigm, the traditional concern with determining the value of a job is replaced with a focus on the value of the individual. With skill-based pay, employees are paid for the specific skills they can perform. With competency-based pay, employee compensation is based on an assessment of competence. With either, the more individuals can do the more they are paid.

The final chapter in Part One is about executive salary management. For jobs below the executive level, the salary planning process is somewhat mechanical and based on practices that balance the relative internal value of a job with the need to remain competitive in the marketplace. At the executive level, political reality makes it impossible to be fully competitive with pay levels for similar jobs in the private sector, even though senior jobs in government, including those of elected and appointed officials, carry significant responsibility that demands competent management talent. Chapter Eight, by Howard Risher, sets forth a framework for making decisions about senior management salaries.

Part Two considers the controversial issues involved in pay-for-performance practices. Performance improvement is currently a top management concern in every sector. In corporations, a primary goal in redesigning compensation systems is strengthening the linkage between performance and rewards. The chapters in this part of the book examine the potential for and the constraints against using compensation systems as an incentive to improve performance in the public sector.

Chapter Nine discusses the problems with and established practices in the management of employee performance. Doris Hausser and Charles Fay provide an overview of the practices that have proven effective in government. Hausser is the chief of the performance management staff of the U.S. Office of Personnel Management. In this capacity, she leads the federal government's efforts to improve its performance management systems.

Merit pay has proven to be one of the most controversial and difficult problems in public personnel administration. In corporations, merit pay is deeply entrenched and generally has the strong support of top management. In a few (typically smaller) government organizations, merit pay has a similar status. But in other and larger government agencies, merit pay is a complete failure and resisted by supervisors and employees alike. Chapter Ten, by Howard Risher, Charles Fay, and James Perry, explores the theoretical and practical rationale for merit pay and the basic approaches developed to enable managers and supervisors to make the difficult decisions regarding it.

Chapter Eleven considers alternative ways of rewarding the performance of groups. One of the most important trends in the compensation field over the past few years has been the creative work done to develop group incentive plans. The original concept, often referred to as gainsharing, has recently been redefined and expanded to include new plan concepts. The author, Ronald Sanders, was the chief of the Department of Defense civilian personnel staff and as such was responsible for implementing and evaluating several group incentive plans at federal work sites. This hands-on experience makes him well qualified to discuss the potential use of these plans in a government work environment.

In Chapter Twelve, Brigitte Schay looks at the overall federal experience with special demonstration projects designed to test pay-for-performance practices. For the federal government, new program concepts must be tested before they can be broadly adopted; Schay has been responsible for completing the testing. She based her assessment on a series of criteria for practices set forth by Edward Lawler, a prominent researcher in the field of compensation. The results of these analyses confirm that it is quite possible to have effective pay-for-performance practices in government if they are carefully planned and managed.

Part Three examines two issues related to the prospects for the public sector to rethink its pay programs. In Chapter Thirteen, Bonnie Bogue discusses the role of unions and collective bargaining in addressing compensation problems. Unions and employee associations are important stakeholders in the public sector; though the importance of unions has been steadily declining in the private sector over the past decade or two, they have lost little of their power in government. The law varies from state to state, but when employees are represented by a union or similar association, the issues are basically the same.

Chapter Fourteen looks at trends in selected developed countries throughout the world. The author, Anke Freibert, is on the Organization for Economic Cooperation and Development (OECD) staff that keeps track of developments of this nature. Significantly, the push to reinvent government and rethink public pay programs is a worldwide phenomenon.

The concluding chapter, by Howard Risher and Charles Fay, considers the future of compensation management. The traditional salary management model was conceived in a past era for organizations that are now things of the past. Virtually all employers, public and private, are moving along a continuum of change that makes old ideas ineffective and obsolete. The emerging work management paradigm is very different from the old. Pressures to reinvent government have prompted a broad interest in introducing new programs more compatible with the new paradigm and new expectations.

April 1997   HOWARD RISHER
Radnor, Pennsylvania
CHARLES H. FAY
Highland Park, New Jersey

⎯⌇⎯ The Authors

Howard Risher is senior fellow and adjunct professor of human resource management in the Wharton School, University of Pennsylvania. He received his B.A. degree (1965) in psychology from Pennsylvania State University and both his M.B.A. degree (1968) in human resource management and his Ph.D. degree (1972) in labor relations and economics from the Wharton School.

Risher has twenty-five years of experience in the areas of workforce management, compensation system design, and employee research. He previously managed consulting practices for two international consulting firms. He served as the project director for the study that resulted in federal pay reform and the enactment of the Federal Employees Pay Comparability Act (FEPCA) in 1990. He has served as a consultant to federal and state government agencies, to hospitals, to colleges and universities, and to major corporations.

Risher is a member of several associations and serves as an instructor for certification courses in compensation management. He is also a member of the advisory board for *Compensation and Benefits Review*. He is the coeditor with Charles Fay of the recent book, *The Performance Imperative: Strategies for Enhancing Workforce Effectiveness* (Jossey-Bass, 1995). He has authored or coauthored more than twenty articles and book chapters on human resource topics.

Charles H. Fay is director of the graduate program in human resource management and associate professor of human resource management at the School of Management and Labor Relations at Rutgers University. He received his B.A. degree (1961) from New York University in English and history, an M.B.A. degree from Columbia Graduate School of Business (1963), and a Ph.D. degree from the University of Washington (1979) in organization and management theory.

Fay is a former member of the Federal Salary Council, a presidential council that advises the Federal Pay Agent on salary issues concerning white-collar employees. He is the coauthor or coeditor of several books, including *Compensation Theory and Practice, The Compensation Sourcebook,* and *The Performance Imperative: Strategies for Enhancing Workforce Effectiveness* (Jossey-Bass, 1995). He is also editor of *Human Resource Planning* and serves on the board and the research committee of the Human Resource Planning Society.

He teaches courses on compensation, human resource strategy, and human resource information systems. He has also taught human resource courses in the Executive MBA Program offered by Rutgers. He developed and directed a Masters in Human Resources program offered jointly by Singapore Institute of Management and Rutgers. He engages in research and consulting focused on compensation systems, performance management, performance appraisal, and human resource support systems. He served as chair of the Research Committee of the American Compensation Association.

Bonnie G. Bogue is an arbitrator and mediator of labor and employment disputes. Her familiarity with pay setting in the public sector stems from her experience arbitrating bargaining disputes in state and local government and her years as a research specialist in public sector employment and labor law with the Institute of Industrial Relations at the University of California, Berkeley. There she serves as director of the California Public Employee Relations Program and as contributing editor of the journal CPER. Her recent publications include *Pocket Guide to Public Sector Arbitration* and *Pocket Guide to Workplace Rights of Public Employees.* She is serving as chair of the Labor and Employment Sector Law Section of the State Bar of California for 1997–1998. She has been on the section's executive committee since 1993. She has also served on the State and Local Government Bargaining Committee of the American Bar Association's Labor Law Section. She is a member of the National Academy of Arbitrators and holds a J.D. degree from Boalt Hall School of Law, University of California.

Anke Freibert is a German senior civil servant and currently senior adviser for civil service issues and human resource management at SIGMA (Support for Improvement of Governance and Management in Central and Eastern Europe), a joint initiative of the Organization for Economic and Cooperative Development (OECD) CCET and European Community PHARE. In this role she works with governments in creating and implementing a legal framework to set up a professional civil service, including remuneration systems and related human resource management systems. Prior to joining OECD in 1995, she worked for five years as the focal point of public service issues at the International Labor Office, with special emphasis on labor relations and wage determination. Until 1990, she worked in the German federal ministry on a variety of human resource management issues. She holds a German law degree and an M.P.A. degree from the John F. Kennedy School of Government, Harvard University.

Nina Gupta is professor of management at the University of Arkansas in Fayetteville. Her research has focused on organizational compensation systems, employee absenteeism and turnover behaviors, and work stress. Her research has encompassed both traditional and innovative compensation systems, and she has published extensively in these areas. Gupta is one of the nation's renowned authorities on skill-based pay systems. She codirected the U.S. Department of Labor's national study of skill-based pay systems in 1984 through 1986, she codirected the Study of Skill-Based Pay Systems sponsored by the American Compensation Association, and is currently completing work on compensation systems in use in a cross-section of companies across the United States. Her work has appeared in numerous academic and practitioner outlets including *Academy of Management Journal, Journal of Applied Psychology, Compensation and Benefits Review,* and *ACA Journal.* Gupta received her Ph.D. degree from the University of Michigan. She conducted sponsored research in her areas of interest in Michigan and Texas for several years before joining the faculty of the University of Arkansas.

Doris Hausser is chief of the Performance Management and Incentive Awards Division of the U.S. Office of Personnel Management and is responsible for developing and administering governmentwide regulations, policies, and programs regarding performance management systems for the federal workforce, including performance appraisal, incentive awards, and pay-for-performance systems. She received her Ph.D. degree in organizational psychology from the University of Michigan, is a certified compensation professional, and has taught in the American Compensation Association Certification Program. Hausser has coauthored books and articles on survey research, organizational development, and public management. She has also been a consultant to the Executive Education Center of the University of Michigan Graduate School of Business Administration. She is a member of the Academy of Management, the American Compensation Association, and the International Personnel Management Association (IPMA) and serves on the board of directors of IPMA's Federal Section.

Lyn Meridew Holley is a job classification and compensation policy consultant to national and international public organizations. She has served as a classification policy expert in the United Nations International Civil Service Commission and directed programs encompassing job classification in three U.S. federal agencies, one at the cabinet level. Holley was project director of the Volcker Commission's (National Commission on the Public Service) Compensation Task Force and is a past national president of the Classification and Compensation Society. Other professional associations include Public Employees Roundtable, American Society for Public Administration, and Pi Alpha Alpha Scholastic Honor Society. She is now working toward a doctorate at the University of Nebraska at Omaha.

James R. O'Connell is an independent consultant specializing in training and in automating human resource management processes. In 1996 and 1997, he developed job classification systems for the Office of the Civil Service Commission of Thailand. From 1990 to 1996, he was project manager for automated classification at the U.S. Office of Personnel Management. Prior to 1990, he worked in several federal government agencies in a variety of human resource management areas. He has served as an expert witness on position classification in federal court and holds advanced degrees in public administration and political science.

James L. Perry is professor in the School of Public and Environmental Affairs at Indiana University. He received his Ph.D. degree from Syracuse University in 1974. His research focuses on issues of public management, public personnel management, and currently, public service motivation. Perry is a leading authority on pay-for-performance systems in the public sector. His research has appeared in such journals as the *Academy of Management Journal, Academy of Management Review, Administrative Science Quarterly, American Political Science Review,* and *Public Administration Review.* He is editor of the *Handbook of Public Administration* (2nd ed., 1996). Perry is also the recipient of the Yoder-Heneman Award for innovative research from the Society for Human Resource Management, the Charles H. Levine Memorial Award for Excellence in Public Administration, a Fulbright Fellowship, and a National Association of Schools of Public Affairs and Administration Fellowship.

Ronald P. Sanders is associate professor of Public Administration with the George Washington University School of Business and Public Management. Previously, he held the faculty position of Eminent Professor of Public Administration Practice at the Syracuse University Maxwell School of Citizenship and Public Affairs, where he also founded and headed Maxwell's Center for Advanced Public Management in Washington, D.C. Sanders is a career member of the Federal Senior Executive Service (with presidential rank) and has over twenty-five years of experience in public sector human resource management. From 1991 through 1995 he served as Director of Civilian Personnel for the U.S. Defense Department, where he managed DOD's historic civilian drawdown. He was also founding director and CEO of the Defense Civilian Personnel Service, a $42 million DOD agency responsible for human resource management business operations worldwide. Sanders has been published in numerous books and professional journals; most recently he coauthored *Civil Service Reform: Building a Government That Works* (1996).

Brigitte W. Schay is a senior research psychologist at the U.S. Office of Personnel Management's Personnel Resources and Development Center. From 1990 to 1995 she directed the evaluation of federal personnel management demonstration projects and other human resource innovations. She was the principal author of the Office of Personnel Management's study of federal broad-banding experiments and has published numerous articles on broad-banding and performance management issues. She received her Ph.D. degree in social/organizational psychology from George Washington University and is a member of the American Psychological Association, Society for Industrial and Organizational Psychology, and the International Personnel Management Association.

Barbara S. Wamsley is the principal of LNA International, an association of international experts on organizations and management. She teaches and lectures as Fellow of the Maxwell Center for Advanced Public Management at Syracuse University and of the Center for the Study of American Government at Johns Hopkins. She holds a Master of Public Administration degree from Harvard University's John F. Kennedy School of Government and is also a Littauer Fellow of that institution. In 1996 Wamsley was inducted as a Fellow of the National Academy of Public Administration (NAPA). Wamsley's thirty-year experience as a manager with the federal government and her research for the NAPA on managing human resources provides her with insight into public sector management issues that is broad in scope and focus. She sees traditional management systems (human resource systems in particular) as aids to management rather than rule-driven impediments. She was project director of the NAPA 1991 publication *Modernizing the Federal Classification Systems: An Opportunity for Excellence* and the NAPA 1993 publication *Leading People in Change: Empowerment, Commitment and Accountability.* Both studies were extensively cited in the President's National Performance Review (NPR) report. The 1991 NAPA approach to broad banding was adopted by the NPR as the basis for reform. Her knowledge of the American system of government and democracy keeps her occupied as a frequent lecturer and adviser to foreign visitors to the United States.

Lois R. Wise is associate professor of policy and administration in the School of Public and Environmental Affairs, Indiana University, Bloomington. Her research focuses on public management reform and human resource management. She has authored and coauthored numerous articles and book chapters pertaining to central and local government employment policy and practice in the United States and other countries. She has served as an adviser on questions related to job evaluation, pay policy, and management reform to local, state, and central government organizations in the United States and abroad. She is recipient of a Fulbright Fellowship for research and the Jubilee Prize for International Scholarship from the Swedish Institute, Stockholm.

New Strategies for Public Pay

Rethinking Government Compensation Programs

Howard Risher
Charles H. Fay

—∿∿— There is a growing consensus that compensation programs for employees in the public sector are not working. Workers get
paid, but reward programs often do not meet the needs of their
employers, a problem that has not been an issue in the past. But with
mushrooming interest in reinventing government, cutting costs, and
enhancing public sector performance, those who believe in initiating
change—the leaders of the revolution—have come to realize that pay
programs can either be part of the problem or a tool in its resolution.

In the Report of the National Performance Review[1] (NPR), the federal government acknowledged that its rewards program is part of the
problem in rewarding public employees. The report's first chapter recommends that the government "dramatically simplify the current classification system" and allow agencies to "design their own performance
management and reward systems, with the objective of improving the
performance of individuals and organizations" (p. 25). This report put
the federal government solidly behind a commitment to reinvent government that is shared by many at the state and local levels, where
groups similar to the NPR are being formed across the country to
improve government operations. Employee pay programs are only one

1

of the concerns voiced by these groups, but a rethinking of what until now have been staunchly defended practices is becoming common.

This trend is consistent with the tidal wave of change affecting industry. The way work is organized and managed is in the middle of a transformation that goes far beyond anything contemplated even a decade ago. Management practices and the norms of work and organizational design have relied on the so-called principles of scientific management for the last century. American industry was still in its infancy when Frederick W. Taylor developed and gained broad support for this approach to organizing work, which is reflected in virtually every organization in the world. His thinking had its genesis in the reality of the 1890s and the early part of this century. But that era is rapidly coming to an end as companies are forced by competitive pressures to become more productive and responsive to customers.[2]

The organizational problems that affect government are essentially the same as those that have prompted changes in private sector organizations. A corporation may have to approach its competitive situation as a survival issue, but the bottom line, to use an important phrase from industry, is the need for organizations to be more productive, more flexible and responsive, and more focused on meeting the needs of customers. Meeting this goal involves people management issues common to and pervasive in both the private and public sectors. Lester Thurow, a prominent expert on management issues, has argued that in the future people will be the only sustainable source of competitive advantage.[3] His argument is as relevant to government as it is to industry, even though government organizations of necessity view competitive advantage from a very different perspective.

COMPENSATION AS A MANAGEMENT TOOL

A central consequence of changing the way work is organized and managed is the need to rethink reward systems. Conventional wage and salary programs were designed for conventional organizations. The basic premise has been that jobs can be defined by a job description that consists of a set of fairly static task sets and the specifications (knowledge, skills, and abilities) to perform those tasks. Each job, thereby, is a box on an organization chart that will be stable for some period of time. The hierarchy of jobs is important to the management of such an organization and thus the "org" chart is important too.

Conventional programs, in effect, set a price for labor by focusing on jobs. Each job has a starting rate; as incumbents gain experience, their rate goes up. In concept, when some aspect of the job requirements change, the rate should be reviewed and (possibly) adjusted as well. The rates are aligned internally to be equitable, and maintaining this equity is often an important program objective. The job evaluation systems used to manage this originated in the 1930s and 1940s and are based on industrial engineering principles.

The earliest systems for evaluating jobs were developed to administer pay for manual workers and reflect efforts to engineer activities to maximize the ergonomic efficiency of each worker's body mechanics. The level of detail documented by the engineers covered every movement involved in performing the job. This "science" made it possible to manage work activities closely. The goal was to make the entire production operation run like a well-oiled machine.

This thinking carried over to the growing white-collar occupations after World War II, and although industrial engineers lost control of the systems to personnel specialists there was little change in the approach to program administration. The amount of information collected in job analysis might have been somewhat reduced, but today it is still possible to find job descriptions that run on for pages.

The industrial engineers' purpose was to enhance control and supervision. In some situations the focus of analysis was at a level of minutia, all to ensure efficiency and minimize errors. Management knows best, said the predominant theory, and because it is accountable for results it needs control. This approach provides for narrowly defined jobs and constrained decision making, so workers have little discretion. What decisions they do make must be reviewed, often by two or more levels of management. This reflects an implicit lack of trust that in some organizations comes close to paranoia. This philosophy is slowly being supplanted but is still dominant.

Despite policy statements that make individual merit important, salaries have been managed in a lockstep manner. Government pay programs have been the most rigid, but even the most aggressive corporate programs rarely give meaningful recognition to outstanding employees in the management of salaries. Over time the better workers in industry can expect to be paid more, but small differences in annual salary increases must compound over many years before their salaries are significantly higher than those of their poorer-performing coworkers.

The concern with control and documentation has led to bureaucratic and paper-intensive administrative systems. Although computers have assumed some of this burden in recent years, salary management programs still commonly require heavy time commitments by job incumbents, supervisors, and human resource specialists. Whenever a job changes, new job information needs to be generated and evaluated to determine if changes warrant a change in salary. Even with computerized systems, this process can take weeks (or even months!) before the decision is finalized. Needless to say, this administrative mechanism is burdensome and costly.

Much of this has begun to change, at least in the private sector. Organizations are rethinking their approach to management and their expectations of workers. The principles of scientific management fail to take into account that workers can think and make decisions. In the new paradigm, workers are expected to perform their jobs with less—in some cases no—oversight review and approval. Many organizations are changing so rapidly that it is impractical even to try to generate written job documentation. The phenomenon is affecting organizations in every sector, but the number of anecdotal stories of surprisingly high performance by less-supervised employees is mushrooming.

This new world of work is very different from the environment that existed when conventional wage and salary programs were conceived. Such programs are now problematic; they were designed not to accommodate and support rapid organizational change but rather to reinforce the stability of work and organizational relationships characteristic of the traditional scientifically managed organization. The administrative burden of this approach is more than most employers are now willing to accept. The pressure to change comes from outside the human resource function, and human resource specialists are now in the awkward position of defending ideas that are seen as outdated.

Nevertheless, there is a widely shared belief that pay is a motivator. There are different perspectives on what pay motivates; some argue that pay programs trigger more harm than good. All agree, however, that pay influences employee behavior. It is not the only source of motivation, but workers react to the way they are paid and usually behave in a manner they believe will maximize their economic return. Probably the only people who do not react to the way they are paid are volunteers!

Corporations are beginning to rely on pay programs as a tool to drive organizational change. Until recently the assumption was that changes in pay programs should be introduced after organizational change. Changing pay programs was seen as too politically sensitive and potentially disruptive. Moreover, the changes have largely been driven by experts outside of the human resource field who assume that people will see the advantage of the changes and quickly get onto the bandwagon, or who focus on technical issues and ignore the people side of the equation.

These change initiatives are kicked off with high expectations, including the belief that workers will feel good about their new roles and improved performance. This will (in theory) generate intrinsic satisfaction and the motivation to change behavior to support the new approaches to the way work is organized and managed. The reality is that actual performance may improve but often fails to reach expected levels. Returns on investments made in quality management and reengineering as well as in reinventing government have frequently been disappointing, rarely reaching their potential.

Unfortunately, people tend to resist change; they stay with established behavior patterns until motivated to change. Intrinsic job satisfaction is important but not likely to support new behavior if old behavior is still rewarded. Conventional pay systems—or from this perspective, any element of the reward system triggered by success in old behavior patterns—will be an impediment to change.

The stage is now set for changing pay programs. Many pay programs in government have been unchanged (other than in details) for twenty years or more. If any employer were to design a salary program for a greenfield operation today, it is safe to assume that employer would not end up with a program that resembles the typical government program.

At the very least, reward systems need to be able to respond to and accommodate changes in the structure of the organization. Conventional job evaluation systems and salary structures can be an impediment to reducing the number of organizational levels and downsizing if managers are rewarded for the size of their staff. Moreover, the need for extensive documentation and centralized control not only requires a significant time commitment but also tends to prolong the time required for decision making.

New ideas like self-managed teams will undoubtedly be adopted by every employer, private as well as public, over the next few years. The salary system has to accommodate and support these changes. When we acknowledge that these changes are coming, it makes sense to assess current policies and practices to see if they will support the transition or become part of the problem. It also makes sense to look several years into the future to anticipate changes and to plan for future organizational needs. The problems associated with changing a salary program mean that it could easily require two or three years for full implementation. It also means employers need reward programs that have the flexibility to adapt to predicted work and organizational changes.

One of the more important policy issues for government is whether to use compensation as an incentive for improved performance. There has been a deep-seated reluctance to make merit pay an important issue in managing compensation, reinforced by the writings of W. Edwards Deming, a staunch critic of merit pay practices. Despite the Deming criticism there is little evidence that corporations are ready to eliminate programs that reward performance, or merit. To be sure, they are being reconsidered, but with the goal of finding better ways to link pay to performance. There is no real expectation that industry is willing to return to and live with the consequences of general increase or step-increase policies.

The thrust in industry is to find ways to use pay to enhance employee and organizational performance. Cash incentives are a key focus; new salary-management concepts such as competency-based pay are hot. There is also a shift in decision making to give line managers and supervisors more control of pay programs, gradually turning human resource specialists into consultants rather than auditors and controllers. The goal is to give management the tools to help accomplish missions and operating goals. The recognition that pay programs have been part of the problem has triggered a quiet revolution.

MESSAGES, MESSAGES, MESSAGES

Workers rely on both what they are rewarded for and the way they are rewarded to understand what is important and what is not. The reward system in this context includes everything management controls that affects employees' organizational status and compensation over their careers. These decisions and the consequent rewards (and punishments) tell employees how well they are performing and whether they are behaving in a manner that pleases or displeases. Sometimes the messages involve tangible rewards; sometimes the rewards are intangible. Sometimes the message can be as private and informal as a supervisor's smile; sometimes it is as formal and public as an awards ceremony.

In addition there are other organizational rewards ranging from a colleague's congratulations to the intrinsic satisfaction realized from successful job performance. Realistically, employees are on the receiving end of numerous rewards throughout the work week.

Knowing what drives an employee's performance requires understanding the full range of rewards available from all sources, the employee's career and life goals, and the recent history of work-related events, all of which influence the individual's perception of current events. If we understand all this, we can begin to understand the person's motivation.

Workers have to decide what they want to achieve in their jobs and then determine how they can best accomplish their goals. They look to their supervisors and to organizational communication to guide their behavior. If, for example, they want to be considered for promotion, they need to understand how best to prepare for the new role and to establish a favorable track record. Where there is a merit pay policy, they need to understand how their supervisor makes these decisions.

Reward systems can and do influence employee performance. Management may make repeated statements about organizational values and what an employee should do to succeed, but actions speak far louder than words. Reward systems, along with promotions and other forms of recognition, make it clear to everyone what an employee has to do to be successful in the organization. They also make it clear what supervisors actually want employees to do and not do, regardless of what they may say. If supervisors want subordinates to be proactive in solving problems or dogmatic in attending to every detail, the message is sent by who gets rewarded and who does not. If the organization's priorities change, that message is communicated by changes in how rewards are distributed. If management wants the staff to resist change, it will communicate the fact through a compensation system that continues to reward those who persist in old behavior patterns.

This concept is central to the success of organizational change programs. Whatever the initiative—quality management, reengineering, and the like—if management sincerely wants it to happen and to be successful, it has to be supported by the reward system. Teams, for example, are never going to be fully productive if rewards continue to be tied solely to individual performance. If the system continues to reward "business as usual," everyone may give lip service to a new initiative but likely will behave in ways that minimize chances for its success. This is especially true of rewards in the form of compensation. Reward systems can speed up change, or they can slow it down or even prevent it through the messages that they communicate to staff.

How salaries are managed is certainly an element of the reward system, but at least in government, the salary program has not been as important as the textbooks contend. If anything, government salary programs too often suggest that if you stay out of trouble and help keep your supervisor out of trouble, you will get your pay increase. More than a few corporate supervisors have the same personal policy. It is the easier road to follow, but over time it leads to a culture that no one feels good about or anticipated being part of when he or she started a career.

When management decides to rethink its pay program, the issue of messages should be an underlying concern. This is the time to decide how the reward system is going to be tied to performance. For better or worse, it is impossible to sever the tie between performance and rewards. Considered in this broader context, organizational rewards are inevitably going to influence performance. Management needs to decide if it wants to use the compensation program as a tool to influence employee performance. That policy consideration is a theme of this book.

THE TOTAL COMPENSATION CONCEPT

The focus of surveys is generally on base salaries or, for occupations where incentives are common, on cash compensation, defined as the total of salary and annual incentive awards. Many employers have implemented long-term incentive programs for employees other than executives (for whom they have long been common). In addition virtually every employer maintains a package of paid time off and benefit plans; the combination of these and cash compensation is referred to as *total compensation*.

The cost of paid time off and benefits is typically in the range of 30 to 45 percent of salary. According to the widely cited U.S. Chamber of Commerce survey, the average for 1993 (the latest data available) was 41 percent of salary, but there is substantial difference from industry to industry.[4]

By tradition, base salaries in government are lower than in the private sector, but the value of benefit packages is higher. Although it would be difficult to confirm that this pattern is anything more than rumor, it highlights the importance of benefit plans. Some workers would willingly trade higher cash compensation for job security—another government tradition—or for improved benefit plans. At one time the focus was probably on pension benefits, but with the rise of the two-income family, health benefits and particularly required employee contributions have become important considerations in selecting a job.

From the employer's perspective, one of the differences between the public and private sectors is the tax deduction available to corporations. Company contributions to benefit plans are fully deductible as a business expense, thus reducing their after-tax cost. For example, if a company contributes $100,000 to a pension fund and its corporate tax rate is 35 percent, the company's tax liability is reduced by $35,000 and its net income by $65,000. In effect, the federal tax system is funding a portion of the cost. Public employers obviously do not have this advantage.

The tax laws also provide another advantage to corporations that fund qualified retirement plans. Under ERISA (Employee Retirement Income Security Act), companies have to keep their plans adequately funded. The money goes into a trust where the capital is invested and any gains accumulate tax free. In contrast, public employers do not have the same funding requirements. Moreover, pension benefits are a future cash outlay that elected officials can pass along to future generations. Consequently, public pensions are often underfunded; the typical corporate pension plan costs between 5 and 8 percent of covered salaries, whereas public sector pensions are often two or more times as expensive in terms of the cash outlay to pay benefits.

Even with this cost advantage, there is an important trend in industry to shift from a defined benefit pension plan to a defined contribution plan. With the latter, the company commits to match a portion of an employee's contribution. Most of these plans require employee contributions so both the company and the employee are saving for employee retirement. For example, the employee might contribute 4 percent of salary, with the company matching 50 percent of that amount. The cost to the company may only be 2 or 3 percent of the payroll, as some employees make less than the maximum allowable contribution or decline to participate at all. Many larger corporations maintain both a defined benefit and a defined contribution plan.

The differences in program design make it difficult to compare costs across employers. Not only do the plans differ but the ways companies finance the benefits differ. There is enough discretion in the funding of retirement income plans to make this a senior management concern. Firms with fully funded pension plans may not have to make a contribution every year, so there is no cost on their financial statements. For health and welfare plans, insurance carriers play the lead role in setting annual premiums so their financial condition can influence year-to-year costs.

Benefit costs are also related to the age and years of service of employees. Companies with older, long-service workers normally have higher costs for paid time off and for benefits. In companies with low turnover, the aging of the workforce can be a significant cost issue.

The problems in precisely comparing benefit costs in the private and public sectors are significant but do not make the issue less important. The fact is that benefit costs in the public sector are high and government has not tried to manage and control them as aggressively as industry has. This is not to suggest that government should start cutting benefits but simply to note that payroll costs are significant to government operations, and if costs are too high, pay programs represent a trade-off that affects those operations.

PAY DETERMINATION IN THE PUBLIC SECTOR

Labor economic theory argues that wage and salary levels are determined by the relative supply of and demand for specific skills. When demand exceeds supply, pay levels rise; when supply exceeds demand, pay levels fall. This theory is supported by trends over time in the private sector, where pay levels for occupations requiring college education—the knowledge jobs—have risen since the post–World War II era relative to pay levels for unskilled and semiskilled occupations. This phenomenon has driven up pay for information technology specialists for the past three decades as new languages and hardware make some workers obsolete and others heavily recruited commodities. It also drove up pay for registered nurses until demand began to fall as health care reform forced some health care providers to close down operations and use less highly trained personnel.

Some corporations carry this understanding of labor markets a step further by paying above-average compensation to enable them to attract and retain above-average personnel. They are convinced that the adage "you get what you pay for" also applies in competing for high-caliber workers. There is a distribution of pay levels (that is to say, some people are paid more than others) for every job and occupation. The differentials reflect such factors as industry, location, and individual years of experience. Companies that operate this way are willing to pay more for highly qualified individuals, suggesting that Harvard graduates command more than the graduates of schools with lower standards.

Most corporations have a policy of paying everyone at the market median or average, but a few pay at (for example) the 75th percentile. The rationale for paying above-average salaries is that it will facilitate the recruiting and retention of above-average employees.

Linkage to prevailing pay levels is a strategic issue. The expectation is that above-average employees will help the company improve its performance. If the assumption is reasonable, elevated salaries are best viewed as a business decision. The company may in fact pay some employees above average and others by policy at average levels. For example, a company in a high-tech field might pay the specialists in its core business at the 75th percentile, but support staff at the 50th percentile.

Although pay policies are not precisely determined, there is an underlying business rationale. Companies understand that the caliber of the workforce is a business consideration. The argument that people are the only sustainable source of competitive advantage makes this a central strategy issue. Where payroll costs are a significant percentage of operating costs, relative labor costs can be an important competitive issue. Few companies, however, try to compete on the basis of a below-average pay policy.

Public employers tend to maintain a general alignment with market pay levels but do not appear to place as much emphasis on market analyses. Clearly, relative pay levels are not going to drive government out of business. There is an unstated assumption that average starting or entry-level salaries, or close to average salaries, will make it possible to recruit adequately qualified new hires. However, there does not seem to be any willingness to discuss what steps could be taken to attract above-average candidates.

Larger public employers, with employees spread over large geographic areas such as states, often try to pay all incumbents in a job based on a single salary range. This in effect ignores labor market differentials that might exist across the area. The federal government's recently adopted locality-pay policy is a notable exception to this, although the plan is to pay differentials to make up for cost-of-living disparities between large urban areas. Another exception is Virginia, which maintains a modest differential for employees working in the counties close to Washington, D.C. Policies of this type are, however, rare in the public sector.

The federal government can adopt special rates when an agency finds it difficult to recruit needed personnel because of below-market pay levels. Prior to pay reform this provision was used routinely in a few areas across the country, such as Los Angeles and New York, where the federal General Schedule (GS) rates were ridiculously low.

One notable difference between the public and private sectors is the reliance on single salary structures. Corporations almost universally maintain separate structures for hourly, clerical, and professional and managerial personnel; commonly there are separate hourly and clerical structures for each work location. This practice is driven by labor market considerations. The trend for several decades has been for prevailing hourly and clerical pay levels to go up more slowly than professional and managerial rates. The year-to-year differences are not significant, but compounded over time professional and managerial salaries have pulled significantly ahead. The separate structures make it possible to accommodate these differences and to manage salaries relative to labor market trends.

Salary programs that rely on a single structure or a single structure for white-collar jobs (such as the GS program) cannot be aligned with market pay levels. The effect in most government organizations, particularly of the federal government, has been to flatten the salary curve relative to private sector organizations, resulting in pay that is well above market for the lowest-level employees and far below competitive levels for senior professionals and managers. As there are far more lower-level employees than senior-level professionals and managers, this policy unnecessarily inflates the payroll, makes it difficult to attract and retain competent professional and managerial employees, and shifts funds away from other government operations. The policy has been justified as being a matter of equity—the labor market may discriminate against the women and minorities who hold many of these lower-level jobs, but government has a responsibility not to; senior professionals and managers should not make more than elected officials or political appointees who run departments and agencies—but this has to be balanced against the cost of a higher total payroll and the existence of a cadre of professionals and managers willing to work for considerably less than they would in the private sector.

The pay determination process also differs between government and industry because of the importance of unions. In the corporate world, the unionized proportion of the workforce has fallen steadily to less than 20 percent, with the higher concentrations in basic manufacturing and regulated industries. In sharp contrast, in some states the majority of government employees are represented by unions. Although the unions' role in wage setting varies from state to state, they clearly represent employee interests and lobby for enhanced pay and benefits. Where unions do have the right to bargain over wages, the collective bargaining process is similar to that of the private sector, but the threat that payroll increases could drive the employer into bankruptcy barely exists. This changes the economic considerations at the bargaining table. A second key difference is that employees in a private sector organization rarely form a large organized voting bloc that could theoretically deprive senior executives of their jobs in the next election. In the public sector, especially local government, a candidate's support of government employee unions can make the difference between winning and losing an election.

Wage and salary determination in government is driven more by political than economic considerations. The need to remain loosely aligned with prevailing market levels is honored in policy statements, but realistically, annual pay increases are controlled by the political consequences and the need to raise taxes or cut services to fund the increase. Though government's need to compete for talent is given lip service, in relatively few instances has a public agency been unable to fill jobs. (Prior to federal pay reform, agencies such as Social Security with operations in Manhattan did find it virtually impossible to find even minimally qualified job candidates for some openings.) At the management level, where government has little need to compete for executive personnel, there is an unstated ceiling on pay levels that defies labor market trends.

PLANNING FOR NEW PAY PROGRAMS

In the context of initiatives to reinvent government, conventional pay programs should be seen as part of the problem. Conventional classification and compensation programs were not conceived or intended as a tool to facilitate and enhance government operations. The static and bureaucratic nature of these programs makes any reorganization difficult and time consuming. It is completely fallacious to argue that government pay programs represent a management system.

When there is a preliminary decision to revamp a pay program, it may make sense to start with an assessment of the current program. In keeping with the logic of reengineering, an assessment probably should start by asking the customers of the program if it is working. Employees may be the largest group of customers, and their opinions are clearly relevant, but the organization itself and the managers who are accountable for mission accomplishment are also customers. Their viewpoints need to be considered in the program planning process.

Also, in keeping with the work steps common to reengineering projects, it will be useful to identify the basic processes involved in program management and to determine how much time is spent by line managers and human resource specialists in each process. The likelihood is that the time requirements will be surprising. Another issue in this review should be cycle time (that is, the time needed to complete an administrative action). This provides a basis for estimating the administrative costs and for assessing improvement if the program is changed.

The individuals who speak for an agency should be heavily involved in goal setting. We cannot realistically tell if something is broken unless we know what it is supposed to do. Many government pay programs have their origins far enough back in history that it is now difficult if not impossible to understand the original goals and the thinking that governed program design. The goals for a new program should be as specific as possible.

In today's climate one of the most important strategy considerations is the process employed to gain the input of key decision makers. If one starts from the premise that the pay program is a management tool, the opportunity to be involved in program planning will effectively co-opt skeptical managers. A useful analogy is the train pulling out from a station. Everyone who will be involved in program administration needs to understand and buy into the planned changes.

In this regard it may make sense to survey employees or to conduct focus groups of employees. However approached, the questions to employees should focus on program effectiveness. "Are you properly paid?" is a question that may have to be included, but as most people think their jobs should pay more, it often is not a very useful one. The more pertinent questions relate to the credibility of the processes and the employees' perceptions of how the overall program fits the organization and its current needs. In today's environment, with its shift to empowerment and recognition of the employee's role in organizational improvement, it would be a mistake to deny employees the opportunity to play a role in reengineering the compensation program.

If the decision is made to replace or modify the existing program, the project plan needs to be carefully conceived. There is probably no other change initiative (with the exception of a force reduction) that triggers as much anxiety and is as potentially disruptive. The program changes will to some degree upset the perceived job hierarchy; some employees are bound to feel like winners and others like losers. In government, any plan that adversely affects employees has the added complication that they know they can turn to one or more elected officials for protection. This makes it important to develop a plan to secure final approval for the program changes even before the changes are completely developed. This reality is unique to government.

The planning phase should address several basic philosophical and practical policy issues:

- Will the planned changes support and facilitate anticipated organizational changes? Is reinventing government an important goal? How does this change employee performance expectations?

- What does the organization hope to achieve in changing the program? Can the benefits be measured? Is it possible to quantify them?

- How does the anticipated program differ from the existing program? Are the changes a response to recognized organizational problems? Can the planned changes be fully justified as benefiting the organization?

- What are the intended messages to employees? How will the program changes reinforce organizational priorities? Is performance improvement an explicit goal?

- Do the planned program changes reflect current thinking in compensation planning and management? Have the pros and cons of alternative program concepts been fully evaluated?
- How will the new program be aligned with prevailing market pay rates? Will the new program be fully competitive? How do benefit plan costs affect the pay strategy?
- Will the new program maintain the existing job hierarchy? What is the rationale for determining internal value? How does the value of the individual influence pay planning?
- Has the impact on employees been fully considered? Do the planned changes adversely affect specific employee groups? If so, can the changes be justified and defended?
- Does the project plan include a strategy for securing approval for the new program? Does the plan recognize the need for buy-in and approval by stakeholders and political leaders?
- Have the political ramifications of the planned changes been fully considered?
- Will the organization be able and willing to commit the resources needed to administer the new program? Do current budgets include adequate funds for training and communication?

These are largely process, not technical, issues. The planning and design of new pay programs involves numerous technical considerations; these issues at one time would have been the primary concern in project planning. The era when pay studies were treated behind closed doors has effectively ended in both the private and public sectors. The basic goal has to be to benefit the organization either by reducing costs or improving performance. However the benefits are defined, the project plan should anticipate and account for the inevitable reactions of employees and managers. These reactions should be anticipated and the project planned to provide a good chance that the projected benefits will be realized; reactions are the key to realizing full benefits.

Notes

1. National Performance Review, Vice President's Report, *From Red Tape to Results: Creating a Government That Works Better and Costs Less* (Washington, D.C.: U.S. Government Printing Office, 1993).

2. For a description of these changes, see Howard Risher and Charles Fay, *The Performance Imperative: Strategies for Enhancing Workforce Effectiveness* (San Francisco: Jossey-Bass, 1995).

3. Lester Thurow, *Head to Head: The Coming Battle Among Japan, Europe, and America* (New York: Morrow, 1992).

4. U.S. Chamber of Commerce, *Employee Benefits: 1993* (Washington, D.C.: U.S. Chamber of Commerce, 1994).

Understanding Salary Management

Wage and salary management involves two types of decisions repeated over and over throughout the organization. The first decision governs the basic pay level of an employee hired or promoted into a new job. That rate of pay needs to be high enough to induce the individual to accept the job (in other words, competitive in the labor market) while remaining in line with the pay levels of other employees in related jobs. The second type of decision governs periodic pay adjustments, increases over time. As the funds for such adjustments are typically provided in a single line item in an operating budget, an allocation problem arises: for Sally to get an above-average increase, other employees must receive smaller increases. Pay adjustment decisions are made either by or with input from supervisors across the organization. The discussion in Chapters Three through Nine relates to these decisions. Together these chapters cover the body of knowledge that is the foundation for salary management.

These decisions are not made in a vacuum, of course. An overriding reality of salary management is that, in the aggregate, base salaries represent the single largest expenditure of most government agencies.

Salaries and salary costs are closely scrutinized and, in the public sector, are a subject for public debate. Another reality is that every employee is interested in compensation and can be expected to react to proposed changes. The rollout of a new pay program can be very disruptive; people may get angry about changes in the way they are compensated. When an organization decides to change its pay program, both of these realities tend to dominate and influence the planning discussions.

Yet another reality, sometimes not acknowledged in the debate over pay planning in government, is the impact of money on employee behavior. This is far more complex than the simple carrot-on-a-stick analogy. It is safe to argue that people behave in the ways they think will be in their best interests. That involves pay but also encompasses many noncash elements of the reward system, such as acceptance by coworkers. It is also safe to argue that pay can result in negative as well as positive behavioral consequences. On the negative side, one of the deeply entrenched problems in government is the psychological feeling of entitlement and its impact in an era of tight budgets. It boils down to the need to understand and consider the impact of the pay system on employee performance and organizational performance. This is inevitably an issue in salary management. Pay affects employee behavior and the anticipated impact needs to be considered in program planning.

In the past few years, pay has become a hot-button issue in initiatives to change organizations. One argument is that traditional pay programs are an impediment to change. They were designed for the work management paradigm that emerged between World War I and World War II, an era of close management control and hierarchical organizations. The methods that drive pay decisions, such as job evaluation systems, reflect the scientific management thinking of that era. The argument now is that though the traditional salary management model serves to reinforce and perpetuate the thinking appropriate to the old paradigm, organizations that want to move to a new paradigm (perhaps including, for example, self-managed learning) will be stymied in the attempt by a traditional salary program.

Employee motivation is also an issue. Continue to reward old-style behaviors, for example, and it is less likely that employees will embrace new ideas requiring new behaviors. Pay programs send subtle messages to employees. The program's design and administration—that is to say, day-to-day decisions—tell employees what is expected from them and what they can expect from the organization. For example, continued reliance on general or step increases sends the message that pay is unrelated to and not affected by performance. It also tells employees something about the organization's value system. One of the reasons "empire building" is a problem in government is the tendency to reward managers based on the size of their organizations. That can be a real impediment to downsizing.

This is one reason many organizations are now rethinking their compensation systems as part of organizational change initiatives. Quality management and reengineering have been adversely affected by traditional compensation programs; both initiatives require new thinking, new behaviors, and the acceptance of new values. If the reward system is tied to the old work paradigm, these changes are less likely to occur. Some leaders of change initiatives expect people simply to accept their thinking because it will lead to a more successful organization. That, however, assumes that the rational mind drives all behavior. But, to be repetitious, continuing to reward old behavior most likely encourages the old behavior. That is one of the reasons Michael Hammer, the guru of reengineering, is currently espousing the reconsideration of reward systems.

How people react to the way they are paid is largely based on how they perceive their base salaries compared to those of coworkers and others in similar jobs in other supposedly comparable organizations. Such perceptions may or may not reflect reality, but they are a key consideration in salary management. The mechanism for assessing internal comparisons is a job evaluation system. The external comparisons are based on the analysis of salary survey data.

When salaries are aligned with prevailing labor market pay rates, it is often referred to as a market-based salary program. Under this philosophy, jobs are assigned to a salary range that provides for "competitive" salaries. At one extreme, internal comparisons are essentially ignored. At the other extreme, internal comparisons are the primary concern. The phrase *internal equity* signifies the goal of an internally focused program. Federal white-collar jobs, for example, are assigned to salary ranges based exclusively on internal considerations. The textbooks would argue that the balance between internal and external alignment is a basic policy issue. The general practice is to blend the two perspectives, although over the past few years the concern with labor costs has prompted greater concern with external competitiveness.

The framework for managing these issues is the salary structure, which is a series of overlapping grades and ranges. Individual salaries are managed within the ranges. Because each job and each incumbent represents a somewhat different problem, concerns about fairness and equity are always present.

One of the most important considerations for the public sector is the rationale for awarding salary increases. Corporations almost universally rely on assessment of individual performances and merit pay increases. Government has been more likely to rely on job tenure or service, general increases, or cost-of-living increases, but the push to reinvent government and improve government performance has prompted wide interest in moving toward policies that give greater emphasis to performance. Merit pay has its critics, however, including W. Edwards Deming, who listed performance appraisal and merit pay as one of the "deadly diseases" of management. Moreover, though merit pay is deeply entrenched in some corporate cultures, there is a general recognition that the policy is not completely effective; it is important to note that many corporations have long-standing commitments to the pay-for-performance philosophy that makes merit pay more acceptable. Unions in the public sector, of course, also have a history of opposition to merit pay. For these reasons public employers have not rushed to embrace merit pay.

Salary management is currently in a period of significant transformation. The high level of interest in rethinking organizations has triggered a reconsideration of base pay concepts. Traditional salary programs focus on jobs as the basis for planning and managing salaries. The push for more flexibility and responsiveness is now the impetus for new concepts that shift the focus to individuals and the value of their capabilities. The concepts known as *skill-based pay* and the newer *competency-based pay* are more compatible with the way work and the workforce will be managed in the future. One type of more flexible salary structure is referred to as *broad banding*.

When these concepts are brought together, the result is a new model for salary management. It is both conceptually and practically a radical departure from the traditional model. In a shift away from traditional tight-control and arguable "scientific" methodologies, the new model is based on a different set of values and was conceived as a response to, and intention to support, the new work management paradigm. One of the important differences for government is the delegation of program management responsibility to managers and supervisors. At the same time, it is compatible with the way jobs are often defined and careers managed in the public sector. The new model represents a viable alternative for agencies that have concluded that their traditional programs are impediments to change.

CHAPTER ONE

Are Current Programs Working?

Views from the Trenches

Barbara S. Wamsley

The Report of the National Performance Review[1] (NPR) in 1993 reaffirmed the need for reinventing the federal government's human resource management systems and processes. It proposed "dramatically simplify[ing] the current classification system, to give agencies greater flexibility in how they classify and pay their employees" (p. 24). Yet I am not optimistic that any major reform of the current system for classifying federal work will occur soon. Several reasons account for this pessimistic outlook. First, Congress has considered no legislative reform recently. Second, the administration's draft reform met with resistance from managers and union leaders alike. Management representatives argue that it gives too much say to the unions over how people and work are managed, and the union representatives argue that it gives managers too much discretion over hiring and firing workers.

The 1996 elections passed with the reform of civil service (including classification) never approaching the top of the congressional and presidential agenda. So managers continue using a job classification system that, as James Colvard, former deputy director of the Office of

Personnel Management (OPM), says, "errs [by] allowing managers to be precisely wrong, rather than roughly right."

Although major legislative reform of the federal personnel system is unlikely, it does not mean that we should or will have the choice of continuing to manage people as we have in the past. Today, managers have little choice but to become better managers of their people—and a key management tool is job classification.

Over my thirty-three-year career I have occupied positions classified in many ways: management analyst, program analyst, staff assistant, budget analyst, executive assistant, senior counsel to the deputy secretary. During that time I also managed a diversity of professional staffs—lawyers, accountants, secretaries, and management, program, regulatory, and facilities engineering analysts, to name a few. Through the years I have managed large and small staffs. I have written job descriptions, developed career development and performance plans, worked with personnel to classify new jobs. Yet I have never been classified as a human resource manager or called one. During an almost four-year tour at the National Academy of Public Administration (NAPA), I directed two major studies of the current federal system for managing human resources. The first, *Modernizing Federal Classification: An Opportunity for Excellence,*[2] was used by the NPR in setting its framework for the subsequent NPR report on classification reform. Likewise, the second NAPA study I directed, *Leading People in Change: Empowerment, Commitment, and Accountability*[3] (which reemphasized the need for reform in a more comprehensive look at how people are managed), was also quoted extensively in the NPR report.

So although I have managed human resources (people), I have never been a human resource manager as defined in the job classification arena. Yet I have found plenty of reasons to give much time and attention and thought to this thing called job classification.

JOB CLASSIFICATION

What does *job classification* mean? It is the backbone to defining and assigning work, recruiting and hiring staff, and paying and rewarding employees. This is a lot to expect from a system that is only vaguely familiar to most managers, who view it with suspicion at best and disdain at worst. Yet organizations could not exist without the actions of building and retaining a qualified workforce. Without work classifications, a manager would not know what work has to be done, and so would not know the types of people needed to do the work, and thus would not know who should be hired. Without some form of job classification, managers would have no one to manage.

Different organizations approach classification in different ways. Some say they have no classification system, but if a method exists for ranking pay according to either position or work, then classification is occurring. Other organizations classify according to position title; for example, some state governments have more than five thousand classifications, and the federal government employs two million people using 484 job classifications.

Not much has changed about the federal classification system since it was designed in 1949. All work of the government is classified into fifteen levels or grades. All pay can be associated with those fifteen grades and the ten interim steps within each grade. Part of the design is systems for ranking work; the rank or grade determines the pay level. A new science was born: position classification. Managers write a description of the job, and classifiers in the personnel offices evaluate the work and classify the job.

It appears simple enough—except that it errs in trying for too much precision when organizations need greater flexibility. In 1949 and for many years after, the systems rigidly and precisely defined types of work—clerk typist, budget analyst, and program analyst are a few examples—with very precise qualifications for each job. This precision and rigidity served the useful purpose of screening out most applicants for federal jobs. Over the last decade, however, many government jobs have had too few applicants, not too many.

Should a system designed to meet the needs of 1949 be expected to meet the needs of today? Strangely, it never really served well. By the time the 1949 Classification Act was enacted its design was out of date; the need to find better ways to manage employees was already evolving.

Ask yourself, or any manager, what your most important organizational asset is. Overwhelmingly the answer will be people. But though we may believe that to be true, it is not demonstrated by how we treat and manage these assets.

People are the only assets for which we compete at or near the market rate but that once acquired usually increase in cost while often declining in value. A bold statement, but think about it:

- We have entitlement features in our pay system that continue to increase pay, above cost-of-living increases, without any tie to increased skills or proficiency of performance.

- We hire people for particular skills, but technology changes skill requirements. Employees are not provided training and learning opportunities to remain current; instead, the lack of employee skill is used to justify hiring contractor help.

- During budget cutbacks, managers are forced to choose between cutting training and cutting staff. Training investments invariably lose.

- Special systems or policies, such as pay setting, classifications, and employment ceilings, force managers to look at bottom-line numbers, which often bear little relationship to improving the efficiency of their operations.

- Employment ceilings and classification rules obscure the issue of whether an organization has too few or too many resources or the right staff skills to do its job.

Managers seeking to save money and improve services by replacing high-graded staff with more journey-level staff will quite likely be unable to do so. Restrictions on the number of staff or staff grades will impede the task. A manager's own salary level or grade may even be jeopardized; reducing the grade level of people under the manager's supervision can result in the manager's own job being classified to a lower grade level. In the existing system, managers have few incentives to find more efficiency in their operations; many see plenty of disincentives.

THE NATIONAL PERFORMANCE REVIEW

The National Performance Review recognized the need to reinvent how we manage, value, involve, and develop our employees as assets. Its report *From Red Tape to Results: Creating a Government That Works Better and Costs Less: Reinventing Human Resource Management*, cited at the beginning of this chapter, summarizes the problems with the current classification system as lack of mission focus, low credibility, complexity, inflexibility, hierarchical orientation, and fragmented accountability.

Lack of Mission Focus

Supporters of the current system argue that both the system and its classifiers are needed to ensure that internal equity exists in how people are compensated for the work they do. As the NPR report states (p. 20), "Over time, the ideal of internal equity has emerged as the supreme goal of the system, instead of being viewed as a means to attaining the larger goals associated with effective government." If internal equity means that people within an organization doing the same work should get paid the same, ironically the current system does not provide that type of equity. It does ensure equal pay for an equal grade, but in no way does it guarantee people that if they do similar or equal work, they will receive equal pay.

The primary objectives of the classification system set up by the Classification Act of 1949 were to base pay on the principle of equal pay for substantially equal work, and to preserve differences in pay in proportion to the differences in difficulty, responsibility, and qualification requirements of the work performed and to the contribution of the employee to the efficiency and economy of the organization.

The act tied the classification system to a uniform pay plan. The automatic progression through steps within the pay schedule based on time and satisfactory performance leads directly to different pay for people doing the same work. One who has been at a job for five years will get paid more than another who has been doing substantially equal work for fewer years, even if the less tenured person is doing better work. Pay tied to time on the job moves away from the act's intent of internal equity. I am not arguing against longevity increases, but when pay increases are granted on something other than what work is being done, internal equity is jeopardized, strictly speaking.

Another flaw in the current system that works against the principle of internal equity is that it sets too much store on precision in defining differences in the work performed. The designers failed to recognize the role human judgment must play in classification. Classifiers are not all-knowing. They have to make a judgment based on information before them. It is understandable that two classifiers could classify the same job differently, and they do. Based on my experiences in 1985, here is an illustration of inequity in the system:

The Department of Health and Human Services (HHS) employs analysts to write regulations on cash payment welfare policy. The

Department of Agriculture (DOA) also employs analysts to write regulations on food stamp welfare policy. The two agencies occasionally issue joint policies that were also developed jointly for consistency in positions taken with state governments. In HHS the journey level was classified at grade 14 and in unusual circumstances at grade 15. In DOA the journey level was classified two grades lower. My attempt to fill a division director position with a person from DOA was futile. Though he was already a comparable division director over policy development, he was two grades below the position I was trying to fill, and one full grade below the people he would be supervising at HHS.

Low Credibility

Because of many situations like the one just described, employees have very little faith in the fairness of the current system, especially when they experience its inequities firsthand. A 1992 survey by the Office of Personnel Management found that only 31 percent of employees agree that their pay is fair considering what other people in their organizations are paid. As the NPR report states (p. 20), "Ironically, it appears that the more precision sought in job evaluation, the more likely that the measurements of equity will be incomplete and open to criticism."

In a 1991 survey by the National Academy of Public Administration, more than 65 percent of personnel directors and classifiers felt the system did not give anyone fair and equitable results. That rose to more than 83 percent when administrative officers and managers were asked the same question.

The example of a three-legged stool has been used to describe complex interrelated systems, functions, or issues: if any leg is missing, the stool topples. Looking at the credibility of the current system, it appears that not just one leg is missing but all three. The people who manage the system, the managers who use it to manage people, and the employees themselves have low regard for the system's fairness and equity. Can a system like this be patched to resemble a three-legged stool again, or will it still be wobbly at best? Credibility will improve when everyone gets involved in constructing a new stool that all must stand upon.

Complexity

As noted by the NPR report the classification system is difficult to understand and use. It discourages managers from assuming the primary role in classifying jobs and being accountable for results. Instead, "the system is largely run by OPM and agency personnel specialists with classification expertise. Its complexity promotes excessive paperwork and slow, cumbersome administrative procedures" (p. 21). A report by the National Academy of Public Administration[3] concluded, "In an era of growing pressures for efficiency, productivity, flexibility, customer satisfaction and goal-directed results, the classification system is mired in expensive, time-consuming rule driven complexity" (p. 38).

As project director for the 1991 NAPA study on modernizing classification, I participated in focus groups with managers and employees about the current system. Some managers proudly told us that although they disliked the current system they had found ways to manipulate it and get what they wanted. When offered a model of a more responsive and less complex system, one manager said, "Please, no; better the devil I can manipulate than a new one I don't know."

In an office that administers block grants to state and local jurisdictions, a grievance was filed by two grade 13 program analysts who alleged that they did work identical to that of four grade 14 analysts and therefore should be promoted to grade 14. In response, a classifier was called in to review both the grade 13 and 14 positions in the office. To the horror of the grade 14 employees, the classifier determined that everyone was doing only grade 13 work, a decision that pleased no one. The employees then vented their dissatisfaction to their managers, who were made uncomfortable by this unseemly situation and the resulting conflict. The result? The position descriptions of the grade 14s were modified with weighty phrases, such as "work had national scope," to support and solidify their grade 14 status. The two grade 13 employees were promoted to grade 14. Everyone went away happy. But was the actual result two people being appropriately upgraded, or six people being overgraded?

An early lesson learned by many managers in getting the system to classify jobs at higher grades is that adjectives are very important. In setting up a new office with hierarchical grade structures such as junior, journey, and senior expert work, the position descriptions for grades 5 to 9 would emphasize some supervision; at grades 11 to 13 for journey level work, supervision would change to almost none; and the senior expert at grades 14 and 15 would give supervision but receive none. The system is complex and can be unresponsive unless one is aware of the tricks of the trade. But should responsiveness depend on manipulation?

Inflexibility

The NPR report criticizes the one-size-fits-all rigidity of the classification and pay system. It quite bluntly challenges the current system, saying it "must not be so immutable that it cannot respond to new ways of designing work, the changing value of jobs, or changes in the work itself" (p. 21). The report also quotes the Merit Systems Protection Board as noting that "the grade level criteria have become viewed as 'cast in stone'. . . resulting in virtually fixed and therefore unresponsive standards" (p. 22).

More than 73 percent of the respondents to the previously mentioned 1991 NAPA survey found that the standards for classifying jobs were too inflexible and that the overly rigid job hierarchy principles of the system could not change with new structures. Among the respondents, more managers and administrative officers (close to 90 percent) felt this way than personnel directors and classifiers (more than 60 percent).

The Social Security Administration (SSA) runs the world's largest administrative hearing system, providing hundreds of thousands of hearings each year that lead to even more formal decisions on claims for Social Security benefits. About 1,000 administrative law judges (ALJs) hold the hearings and decide cases at SSA's 132 hearing offices across the country. To help, SSA employs *decision writers,* staff whose primary responsibility is to draft the written decisions for the ALJs.

The basic function of decision writing can be successfully done by either an attorney or a nonattorney (a paralegal specialist). Indeed, to become an effective decision writer an attorney with no knowledge of the basic Social Security program and underlying law would need extensive training to become an effective decision writer, whereas minimal training on case law would be needed by a paralegal specialist who had worked in a Social Security office and knew the program. Therefore, in choosing whether to hire an attorney or a paralegal specialist, hearing offices would consider many factors. Is immediate production critical to handle backlogs? Will decision writing be the sole task or is there more strictly legal work to be done (coordination with the local U.S. Attorney's office)? Which is more immediately available on the labor market, attorneys or paralegal specialists? Are the ALJs in the local office comfortable with nonattorneys or do they demand that decision writing be done by attorneys only?

As hearing offices answered these questions differently over the years, the positions were filled with a mix of attorneys and paralegal specialists. However, the Office of Personnel Management noticed this fact when SSA tried to upgrade the position and invoked the classification principle that qualification requirements for a position should be the minimum necessary. Thus if a nonattorney could do the work the position could not be classified as an attorney position.

What was the practical result of OPM's decision? Extremely unhappy hearing offices that could no longer advertise decision-writing vacancies as attorney positions at precisely the worst possible moment—when workloads were skyrocketing and cases were becoming increasingly backlogged. Without the flexibility to offer either (or both) attorney or paralegal specialist positions, recruitment was often disrupted and slowed dramatically. Those hearing offices and ALJs who preferred hiring attorneys were irate at the decision.

Hierarchical Orientation

Although organizations are looking to streamline through delayering organizational structures and oversight positions, they are confronted with a system that rewards hierarchical models when defining grade and pay values of work.

Previous case examples in this chapter illustrate the impact of this thinking. The grade 13s became 14s and the grade 14s retained their grade by emphasizing the national scope of their work. Should it be assumed that someone working in Washington always has a more difficult, demanding, complex job than someone in the field working at the front lines? If this was ever true, it is not today; more organizations are delegating more authority and responsibility for program outcomes to field components.

With the help and full knowledge of my personnel office I manipulated the system to beat the hierarchical rules. In the early 1980s, Congress mandated that our department conduct a major study of the quality control systems of the welfare programs. I was given responsibility for pulling the right people together to get this $1 million effort accomplished. A grade 15 from one program was recognized in and out of the department as an expert on these systems. He was willing to transfer to my office to oversee a team of experts from around the department to do the study. He also would be the contracting officer for a Brookings Institution companion study, also mandated by Congress. This job would be long-term in that it included ongoing functions for quality control that had never been staffed.

The initial outcome was that the classifier told me I could not hire this person as a grade 15 because he would not be supervising any staff. The fact that he would be directing a team of more than twenty people around the department carried no weight. The conclusion to this story is that I created (wrote) three job descriptions: a grade 15, and a grade 14 and grade 13 reporting to the 15. All jobs were classified and the expert was transferred to the new grade 15. I never filled the other two positions and never had intended to; I had no personnel ceiling or payroll money to do so. Still, I met the hierarchical rules of the personnel system, got the right person (who did an exceptional job), and lost all respect for the validity of the classification system.

Fragmented Accountability

It is clear that the system we have does not work well for anyone. Surveys taken by NAPA and others show that both the managers and the customers of the system are dissatisfied. So who is accountable? It reminds me of the many lectures I have heard about the first hurdle to overcome to make real change in organizations or systems. That hurdle is where everyone agrees that things should change, yet no one associates that needed change with him- or herself. It is always the other guy.

Accountability for classification follows that pattern. Very few managers think they are responsible if a position is overgraded when a job audit occurs. Of course, it must be the fault of the rigid classification rules. Could it be that the manager did a poor job of describing the work that needs to be done or of keeping that description current?

To their credit, classifiers often feel that they are the guardians against bad and unequal treatment of people being hired and promoted by managers. Managers have given them reason enough to feel this way. Nevertheless, classifiers only encourage poor behavior by managers when they continue to approach legitimate problems with rules and reasons why management needs cannot be met, rather than with innovative solutions that both meet management needs and preserve equal treatment.

I grant you, these statements are broadly drawn. There are good managers of people who work well with good classifiers and reach results acceptable to everyone. The statistical surveys, however, clearly point toward the generalization that it does not work.

Accountability will always be fragmented in public sector organizations. However, it should still be approached as shared. Managers are ultimately responsible for their employees, the personnel office is accountable to management, and employees must make sure the necessary tools they need to do the job are in place and working. All public servants are accountable to the public for integrity, commitment, and positive results. Thus, when a system is not working, it is the responsibility of everyone to find a solution to make it work.

CHANGE MUST HAPPEN

At the beginning of this chapter I said that the prognosis is poor for any relief from the rigid rules and structures of the current system through legislative reform. By now the reader may think I have made the case for muddling along with what we have and maybe even for special classes for management on how to bend the rules. That is not what I recommend to anyone.

Instead, I recommend that managers become more knowledgeable and accountable for the process and products of the classification system. They have little choice. Factors are driving people to be better managers of their human resource assets. Whether or not we see a revolution in classification systems, we are experiencing an evolution in management in the public sector:

• The partnership of labor and management, started in the private sector, involves partnering with employees through their union representatives. This is proving beneficial to the organization, its employees, and its customers. Unions are having more of a say in how work is structured, how employees are brought into decision making, and how organizations plan for strategic improvements. They are being invited by management to participate. Adversarial roles of the past are seen by both labor and management as counterproductive to good business.

• Organizations must compete for the best and brightest for their workforce. In the public sector, we often compete against ourselves. Yet with changing expectations of employees, it is the organization that recognizes the need for flexible approaches to assigning work that will attract the best staff. Employees are looking for broad and varied opportunities, not jobs that pigeonhole them early in their career into a specific narrow occupation.

• Total Quality Management (TQM) and business process reengineering (BPR) are spreading widely throughout organizations. Quality management initiatives will only succeed if there are systems and tools that match rather than contradict quality principles. TQM and BPR rely on team and group work. Yet our work design systems (classification) narrowly target people into jobs, and our performance management systems rate and reward individuals instead of teams. There is flexibility in the current system to make the classification system responsive, but it takes teamwork and communication between the personnel community and management. Managers must have union representatives and the personnel office on their TQM or BPR team.

CREATING A NEW SYSTEM

Designers of a new system have an advantage not apparent to the designers of the current system. Much is known about what is not working, about mistrust of the present system by nearly everyone, and about some excellent experiments, such as the Navy's China Lake project, that offer alternatives. Still, some essential problems must be addressed before any discussion takes place about constructing a new three-legged stool.

The first problem to overcome is attitude. Managers must stop grousing about a system that is not responsive to their needs and stop proudly finding ways around it. Each time a detour around the system is found, classifiers redouble their effort to protect the system.

The second problem is communication. Managers, employees, and classifiers must learn to share their common frustrations with the current system and work out solutions agreeable to all. They must look for and find the flexibilities together.

The third problem is management accountability. Managers must recognize that they are accountable for the performance outcomes of their organizations. To achieve the results they want, they have to become proactive managers of their people rather than blaming systems that are there to support them. It is management's responsibility to change archaic systems into tools, not hindrances, in the move toward organizational effectiveness.

Here are six basic criteria for a new system that builds on communication and results in credibility and accountability:

- Provide for a quality workforce.

  Recruit for diversity.

  Retain and develop employees to meet their potential.

  Support the workforce with a competitive pay system.

- Support getting the job done.

  As work changes, be flexible in how the system recognizes, assigns, and rewards work.

  Classify work, not positions, recognizing the trend toward teamwork versus individual work.

  Clarify what is meant by *internal equity,* and place individual competency into an organizational and system design philosophy that recognizes individual abilities.

  Provide for quick recognition and removal of incompetent workers.

- Anticipate and act on needs for change. As in any system redesign, the job is never over.

  Methods to decide whether changes work and whether the system is still appropriate for today's needs should be employed.

  Methods for evaluating the current system—obtaining opinions from users, managers, and systems administrators—should be in place and operating.

  Timely modifications to the system should be based on this feedback.

- Link the system to the business strategy. One major impediment to all the improvements that human resource managers have attempted at all levels of government is the failure of leaders to bring human resource management into corporate strategic planning and management. Many progressive companies inside and outside government are recognizing that they cannot survive without considering their people equally with other resources crucial to the organization's ability to carry out its mission.

- Try to create a collegial system. No better example than the current system exists of why you should not design a system without involving the users. Not only in designing the system but in operating it, people must learn to work across organizational lines.
- Insist on accountability. Leadership has to remember the three-legged stool. Behavior will follow accountability. If only the personnel community is held accountable for outcomes, the organization is placing human resource management alone on a one-legged stool.

FEATURES OF A NEW SYSTEM

Fortunately, because of experiments in the Navy, the National Institute of Standards and Technology, the Central Intelligence Agency, the General Accounting Office, and other major innovators, much is known about how to do things differently. From these experiments and from studies by NAPA and the NPR, certain changes are evidently warranted:

1. Move to a broader system of classification, reducing the number of occupational families and using grade and pay banding.
2. Base the design of the system on describing work, which changes, not on job descriptions that are too rigid.
3. Link performance expectations with teamwork while also recognizing individual contributions.
4. Link pay to performance of the organization, team, and individual, especially allowing for recognition of individual competencies.
5. Link employee development to performance, potential, organizational and career goals, and succession planning.
6. Define the work trends as part of organizational strategic planning, coupled with workforce abilities, workforce needs, and investment needs.

CONCLUSIONS

I am not the first among humankind to find us a funny lot. We believe in equity but usually only when we do not think we have it. Should we build any system on a negative? Instead, let us consider a system that recognizes that inequities will always exist in our society. We can be proud of all our equal employment opportunity programs for the opportunities they gave many of us, including me. Still, no system will ensure equity because human judgment, bias, and prejudices are involved. So let us not preserve a system that has mistakenly waved the banner of equity long and hard as the reason why it should not and could not change. Instead, we should look for a system that builds on something different: fairness and equal opportunity. Couple this with building a new breed of managers that treat people as assets and are held accountable for maintaining, investing in, and increasing their value.

Why not think toward the day when managers' human resource management performances are measured based on their abilities to increase their staffs' competitive position in the marketplace? This may appear outrageous, but when you think about it, why?

The purpose of this chapter is not to give a new model for classification; I think that is more than adequately addressed in other chapters of this book and in other publications such as the 1991 NAPA report *Modernizing Federal Classification.* Major reform of the current system does not seem likely to occur soon, but there are plenty of problems with the current system that can be fixed without major reform. However, sometime soon we must start building a new system, not continue patching the old one.

Notes

1. National Performance Review, Vice President's Report, *From Red Tape to Results: Creating a Government That Works Better and Costs Less* (Washington, D.C.: U.S. Government Printing Office, 1993).
2. National Academy of Public Administration, Panel Report, *Modernizing Federal Classification: An Opportunity for Excellence* (1991).
3. National Academy of Public Administration, *Leading People in Change: Empowerment, Commitment, and Accountability* (1993).

CHAPTER TWO

Salary Structures

The Framework for
Salary Management

Howard Risher

T he heart of a base pay program is the wage or salary structure. A conventional salary structure is composed of a series of overlapping grades and ranges. Although there are subtle differences in the structures typical of the private and public sectors, the similarities make it difficult for all but human resource specialists to tell them apart.

All salary management decisions are made within the framework of the salary structure. Each job is assigned to a grade based on its relative value. Jobs assigned to the same grade are considered to be roughly equal in value. Each grade in turn has an assigned range of salaries, from a minimum to a maximum. In a typical salary program the minimum salary is generally treated as the appropriate salary for a new employee with minimal qualifications. As individuals gain job experience or enhance their skills, their salary is increased—they gain a merit or step increase—and over time their salary progresses through the range. This general approach to salary management is almost universal in both the private and public sectors.

COMPARISON OF PUBLIC AND
PRIVATE SECTOR PRACTICES

The nuances make the difference. The typical private sector salary program is based solidly on merit pay principles; government programs commonly rely formally or informally on time in position as the rationale for salary increases. On paper the programs may look similar, but the underlying philosophy is different, and this is reflected in program administration.

Corporate salary structures (see Figure 2.1) are typically based on a range of 50 percent from the minimum to the maximum. At the executive level the spread is often larger, to as much as 60 or 70 percent. For hourly and clerical support positions the spread is smaller, 30 to 40 percent. Government ranges tend to be smaller; rarely are they as much as 50 percent. The federal General Schedule ranges are effectively 30 percent.

The typical corporate salary range has a midpoint—halfway between the minimum and maximum—that is communicated as the competitive pay level for a fully performing employee. When the salary structure and ranges are developed, the midpoints are aligned with competitive pay levels for the jobs assigned to each grade. Each year new salary surveys are analyzed to determine how prevailing pay levels have changed over the year, and the grade midpoints are adjusted to maintain the planned alignment. This approach provides a simple but effective basis for managing the program relative to labor market pay levels.

Corporations typically manage salaries relative to the range midpoints. Toward this end, compensation specialists may calculate a *compa-ratio,* defined as an individual's salary divided by the range midpoint, as a way to track how well employees are paid relative to the midpoint and indirectly relative to the labor market. For example, a compa-ratio of .90 means the individual's salary is 10 percent below midpoint. The purpose in mentioning this practice is only to emphasize the corporate focus on maintaining competitive salaries.

Beyond this, many corporations divide the ranges into quartiles (or other segments) and provide for differentiated merit increases within the quartiles. To illustrate, the possible merit increases in the first quartile might be 8 percent; in the second quartile to the midpoint, 6 percent; in the third quartile (above the midpoint), 4 percent; and in the

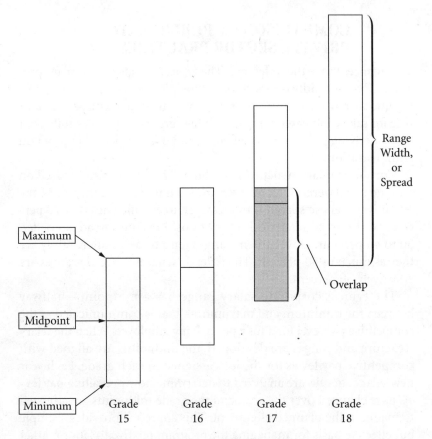

Figure 2.1.   Example of Salary Structure.

fourth quartile to the maximum, 2 percent. Such a distribution provides more rapid salary progression for employees who are low in the range while slowing increases for employees above the midpoint, as they are already paid above the market level. The increase pattern resembles a learning curve that is probably appropriate for employees as they become competent in their jobs. This practice reinforces the importance of the range midpoints.

The importance of individual performance is often recognized by linking merit increases to both position in range (via the compa-ratio) and to performance appraisal conclusions. There are many variations on this practice but it effectively establishes caps or limits within each range. To illustrate, workers whose performance is rated average (for example, 3 on a 5-point appraisal scale) cannot receive a salary increase above the range midpoint; their salary cannot progress above the average market pay level. In this example, only an outstanding worker rating 5 on the 5-point scale could expect increases to the range maximum. This practice has become more prevalent in the past few years.

It would be unusual for a public employer to manage salaries this way. Government salary ranges may be adjusted annually, but the adjustment factor is likely to be a general across-the-board increase. Moreover, it is unusual to manage salaries relative to range midpoints. The corporate practice carries with it a commitment to pay competitive salaries and to adjust salary ranges regularly to keep them competitive. Policies that slow down increases above range midpoints keep salaries in line with competitive levels, but government programs are not as tightly tied to prevailing market rates.

Surveys of corporate salary practices all show that merit pay is pervasive in the private sector, at least for white-collar occupations. Although the surveys tend to focus on larger companies, they indicate that 95 percent or more of the respondents rely on merit pay; for professional and managerial occupations it may be universal. In smaller companies, which tend to be private and often family owned, the salary program may be informal, but individual performance is still the basis for granting salary increases. Surveys show that reliance on merit pay principles has actually increased over the past decade or so.

The corporate philosophy is based solidly on the understanding (though it is rarely stated in corporate policies) that an individual's value depends on performance. Pay increases are warranted under this philosophy only when and if the individual demonstrates enhanced performance. But there is a gap between philosophy and typical corporate practice: the same surveys show that at least 95 percent of employees in the typical company get a merit increase, although some receive more than others. The underlying merit philosophy is solidly entrenched and reinforced by frequent policy pronouncements, but the typical private sector employee can expect an annual salary increase with almost as much certainty as the typical public sector employee.

The emphasis on individual performance and individual value is the basis for defining the corporate range spread. The spread for management-level positions—as much as 70 percent—is ostensibly because the incumbents and their performance can have a significant impact on the value of the job. But in clerical and blue-collar jobs the incumbents cannot significantly increase the value of the job, so the spread is appropriately less. For the few remaining jobs where output is controlled by machines, individual performance has no potential impact and a single flat pay rate is the logical answer.

Very few corporations have automatic step increases built into their wage or salary programs. Increasingly, corporate concerns about competitive pay translate into strong opposition to any form of entitlement; the only exceptions are programs covering unionized workers or those where that is a possibility. The step increase concept is not compatible with the merit philosophy, so it likely will never be much more prevalent than it is today. This corporate reality may not have a direct impact on government pay programs, but it helps explain why the public is critical of government practices.

The emphasis on the value of the individual also justifies a starting salary above the range minimum when circumstances warrant it. By the logic of this philosophy, new employees with above-average credentials and prior experience have enhanced value that should be reflected in the starting salary. It is not uncommon in corporations for individuals to be offered a starting salary as high as the range midpoint. This would not be permitted in the typical government salary program.

DESIGNING A CONVENTIONAL SALARY STRUCTURE

The design principles for a conventional structure are surprisingly limited. Aside from the somewhat abstract merit principles, there is no underlying theory. Salary structures tend to be very similar because they follow accepted practice—that is to say, most adhere to a similar framework because they are designed to replicate other programs. Virtually all private and public salary structures are based on the same rules of thumb.

The use of the word *conventional* is important because in the past few years there has been mushrooming interest in a new concept referred to as *broad banding* or *grade banding*. The level of interest is high in both the public and private sectors, although the number of employers of any type that have adopted the concept is still relatively small. The concept is important enough, however, that the National Performance Review report recommends it for the federal salary program. The concept is discussed in a later section of this chapter.

In designing a conventional structure only four decision points exist, and when three are defined the fourth is automatically determined:

- Number of grades and ranges
- Range spread (minimum to maximum)
- Progression, or difference between ranges (usually expressed as a percentage)
- Overlap from one range to the next

The overlap occurs because the spread of the ranges means some portion of a range covers the same salaries as the ranges above and below. The decisions are interrelated; for example, the range spread decision affects the degree of overlap. Figure 2.1 illustrates a conventional salary structure and the decision points.

If the pay program is to be based on step increases, the size of a step and the number of steps must be decided. That essentially defines the range spread. For example, if the steps are 3 percent and there are ten steps, the range from step 1 to step 10 is slightly more than 30 percent (with compounding).

The range progression is normally expressed as a percentage; in a conventional structure it typically varies between 5 and 10 percent, although for executive salary grades the difference is sometimes larger. Increasing the percentage effectively increases the importance of job evaluation and salary grade assignment decisions. When the progression is only 5 percent, the difference in pay between one grade and the next is less significant and therefore less likely to be a source of contention between line managers and human resource specialists.

When the progression between grades is 5 percent, however, there are twice the number of grades as in a 10 percent structure. The larger number of grades means that any change in job content could affect job value enough to warrant a grade change (going from grade 5 to grade 6, for example). Doubling the number of grades means more reasons to argue for a grade review. Although any change in the way a job is defined should trigger its reevaluation, when the difference between grades is relatively large it is less likely that new duties will warrant a grade change and therefore less likely that the supervisor or incumbents will be willing to fight for the grade change. In other words, the percentage difference between grades appears to be of little consequence, but it does have administrative implications.

Salary programs that combine an internal job evaluation system with a linkage to market pay rates often base the salary structure on a so-called policy line. Figure 2.2 shows jobs plotted on a graph where the X-axis scale is job evaluation points and the Y-axis scale is market salary level. The policy line through the points is determined with regression analysis. The midpoints of the grades are on the policy line, with the minimums and maximums calculated around the midpoints.

The policy line concept is simple to communicate and to maintain. It makes sense, however, only when there is a commitment to keep the program aligned with the labor market. That means adjusting the structure and budgeting the salary increase amount needed to remain competitive.

If the market drives up pay levels for all jobs at roughly the same rate, it is easier to live with than when some occupations are going up faster than others. The reality is that salary increase rates differ across job families and industries. In the post–World War II era, prevailing rates for managerial and professional jobs have been going up faster than clerical and hourly rates. With market pay levels for higher-paid jobs going up more rapidly, the slope of the policy line changes to the benefit of the holders of higher-paid jobs. Adopting a constant structure adjustment (that is, a fixed percentage) across all jobs means

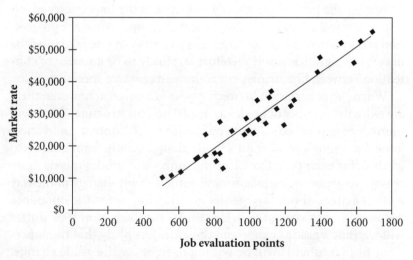

Figure 2.2.   Job Evaluation Points Versus Market Rate with Policy Line.

either the lower-level jobs will pay more than market levels or higher-level jobs will fall behind the market.

This raises another prominent difference between private and public sector practices. Corporations base their salary increase budgets and the annual structure adjustment on a competitive market-based philosophy. Numerous surveys are conducted each year that track salary-increase trends and salary-increase budgets. Few if any corporations rely in today's business climate on cost-of-living increases as the rationale to plan salary program adjustments. Increases in the Consumer Price Index are monitored, but the annual program planning cycle is based on labor market trends, not cost-of-living increases. This effectively bases salary adjustments on the changes in the cost of labor.

THE BROAD-BANDING ALTERNATIVE

Banding is simple in concept: what would have been three, four, or five salary ranges in a conventional structure are combined and treated for administrative purposes as a single broad band. This means that the traditional and almost universal range spreads of 30 to 50 percent are doubled or even tripled, often to 100 percent or more. More important, banding represents a shift in the underlying administrative philosophy away from mechanistic control and toward enhanced flexibility.

Banding was first introduced in 1980 at two Naval federal research facilities at China Lake and San Diego, California. Frustrated with the rigid federal job classification system and facing increasing difficulties recruiting and retaining top-quality scientists and engineers, these labs designed a new compensation and classification system to give their managers the flexibility they needed to be more competitive with the private sector. The new program was closely scrutinized and periodically assessed for the next decade. The program concept introduced at the federal facilities has now been adopted by the private sector and is sometimes cited as the next model for salary management.[1]

Since then a number of other federal agencies have experimented with grade banding. Agencies that have implemented a version of banding include the National Institute of Standards and Technology, an air force base, the Government Accounting Office, and the Central Intelligence Agency. It is also a high-priority recommendation for reinventing government in the 1993 National Performance Review report.

The state of Washington recently introduced a new compensation system based on a banded salary structure for the Washington Management Service. Under the new program all state managers are assigned to one of four bands. The bands are illustrated in Exhibit 2.1. The band decision is based on a simplified job evaluation process that considers three factors: decision-making environment and policy impact, nature of management (defined in terms related to organizational level), and scope of management accountability and control. The factors are displayed in a matrix format that makes job evaluation as simple as selecting the most appropriate cell in the matrix.

The underlying reason for considering banding in both the public and private sectors is a desire to get away from the bureaucracy of a conventional program. Organizations are moving toward a very different environment and have different management problems than existed when the conventional salary management methods were introduced in the years before and after World War II. The methods developed and introduced then, such as the point factor job evaluation plans, were designed for use in essentially static organizations where jobs were defined in terms of a listing of ongoing duties. With a conventional program, when a job is changed a human resource specialist works with the incumbents and the immediate supervisor to document the changes and to measure the change in the job's value. This environment also places heavy emphasis on centrally controlled policies and administrative procedures. This philosophy evolved when the emphasis of wage and salary management was still on control and there was concern that program differences across the organization could be disruptive.

The banding concept emerged as a response to the following organizational problems:

•   The recent emphasis on reorganization, downsizing, and delayering triggers an ongoing and intensive effort by compensation specialists to reevaluate newly created or redefined jobs. This opens the door to confrontations and "games" involving affected employees who want to avoid having their jobs downgraded. This resistance to organizational change often impedes and reduces the expected benefits of the reorganization. Banding diminishes the prospects for downgrading (as well as upgrading) as a result of a reorganization. By reducing the time needed to address job value questions, it also reduces dramatically the level of administrative effort needed to support a reorganization.

Band and Salary Levels	Types of Positions Typically Assigned to Bands
Band IV $67,000–$96,000	Top officials in small agencies (for example, comptroller, director, children's services)
Band III $54,000–$80,000	Functional directors at agency level (for example, prison superintendent, finance director)
Band II $42,000–$64,500	Managers of technical or professional positions (for example, manager, legal library, budget manager)
Band I $32,000–$52,000	First- and second-level supervisors (for example, correctional captain, accounting manager)

Exhibit 2.1.   Washington State's Broad-Band Salary Structure for Management Positions.

• The downsizing and diminished prospects for organizational expansion translate into fewer promotional job openings. To provide new job challenges and personal growth opportunities, organizations are relying more often on lateral transfers to new assignments. The traditional structure and job evaluation logic would require an analysis of each job change to determine if it warrants a higher or lower salary grade. Needless to say, employees are always going to be reluctant to accept a transfer to a lower-rated position even if it will at some point enhance their career prospects. The banding concept facilitates lateral job changes.

• Similarly, the increasing emphasis on flexibility and responsiveness means that job incumbents need to be able to react to changing circumstances. The traditional job description and the job evaluation logic are premised on the expectation that job duties can be specified and remain static over at least some period of time. By the traditional logic, any change in job content, even if temporary, should be assessed to determine if it affects the salary grade. Banding places less emphasis on changes in job content and thereby introduces increased flexibility.

• Flexible job duties are incompatible with traditional administrative mechanisms. Companies moving in this direction often begin to emphasize the value of the individual rather than the value of the job. The move to banding is compatible with this philosophy and can be introduced concurrently with a shift to skill- or competency-based pay.

• The traditional job evaluation process has focused on and served to formalize the job hierarchy. Employees certainly know that at least an informal hierarchy exists, but the knowledge that their job has been evaluated and points assigned makes them decidedly more sensitive to their place in the hierarchy. They also appreciate why the evaluation points are important and understand that it is to their benefit to develop a personal strategy to justify an increase in points. More important, they develop greater sensitivity to the relative ranking of other positions. In some organizations job evaluation points become a basis for assessing individual status. This attention to the hierarchy can hinder working relationships. The banding concept reflects the conclusion that strict adherence to the job hierarchy is out of sync with the new paradigm and the emphasis on responsiveness.

• The current interest in total quality management has triggered a high level of interest in team performance and cross-discipline cooperation. Realistically, the ability and willingness of workers to function as a team is affected by differences in status and perceived power, which in turn are affected by job evaluation distinctions. The banding concept alone cannot facilitate team cooperation but it can help to create an appropriate environment. A conventional salary program is seen as an impediment.

• The conventional process is the responsibility of designated compensation specialists. They normally have considerable authority to evaluate and assign jobs to salary grades. In many organizations they are the detective, the judge, and the jury. Their role involves enough win-lose confrontations with line managers that they can easily fall into disfavor. Banding minimizes these confrontations and the inevitable ill feelings that result. From a different perspective, a conventional job evaluation system forces supervisors and job incumbents to devote more than a few hours to completing the paperwork required to provide requested job information to ensure that jobs are properly evaluated. This can represent a dramatic reduction in the time and resources needed to maintain a wage and salary program.

Experience with banding is still preliminary. In addition to the federal agencies, an increasing number of prominent corporations such as General Electric and Xerox[2] have made the transition to a banding program. However, no organization (other than the Naval research labs) has enough experience to determine whether banding is meeting its needs. More experience is necessary before formulating recommended strategies or approaches; it will be several years before we understand what works and what does not. At this point some of the early programs have bands that range up to 200 percent from the bottom of a band to the top. Every organization is going to have to develop a program concept that appears to fit its needs.

This initial experience does, however, confirm that grade banding represents a sound way to simplify salary administration practices and support organizational change initiatives. Banding makes sense if it supports a strategy to decrease the layers of management or to diminish the administrative burden. It makes fewer distinctions than traditional work classification systems and gives managers more discretion to define subordinate roles as needed to respond to changing circumstances.

Banding places greater emphasis on the management of individual salaries. The traditional practices governing salary progression to the midpoint and above are no longer applicable. There is no grade midpoint! The minimum of a band may be the competitive entry level rate for a few positions but is likely to be too low for most. Similarly, the maximum will be too high for all but the most outstanding performers in high-paying occupations.

This makes it important to establish decision rules and guidelines for managing individual salaries within a range. It also makes it important for supervisors to assume greater responsibility for these decisions, as centralized administration is less practical in broad banding than in traditional salary structures where pay is monitored relative to the range midpoints. With banding it is impractical to rely on a strict time-in-grade approach; no organization could rationalize annual step increases for a band that could easily be 60 percent or more from the first to the last step.

Within the public sector there will almost certainly be a need for program controls or guidelines to ensure consistent administration over time and across agencies. If one of the reasons for moving to banding is increased flexibility, the two goals will need to be balanced in the program's design. This is a philosophical and political question related to the role of managers and supervisors and their accountability for managing their unit.

WHOSE PROGRAM IS IT?

Traditionally, the human resource function has "owned" the wage and salary program. The increasing emphasis on merit pay over the past twenty years and the concomitant decreasing reliance on general or cost-of-living increases is gradually shifting program management from human resource specialists to line managers and supervisors. Managerial discretion is, however, still constrained by policies and procedures controlled by the human resource function. Managers who may have the authority to spend thousands or even millions of dollars once the budget is set cannot grant a subordinate an extra 10 percent without securing human resource approval.

With the trend to delegate day-to-day operating decisions to the lowest management level, it may be inevitable that line managers will want, and possibly demand, an expansion of their role in salary management and the introduction of new work unit incentive systems. If they are accountable for their unit's performance, they need to control the tools that influence employee behavior.

(Concomitant with this trend has been a reduction in human resource staff in both the private and public sectors. Cutting such staff makes it difficult if not impossible to manage a salary program with traditional administrative methods. Thus reduced control and, at some point, delegation of authority are the only recourses as the program management staff are reduced.)

Managers and supervisors also have a better understanding of the situation in their units and of their subordinates' individual circumstances, career aspirations, and relative contributions to the unit's success. The employee relations philosophy in government (at least as it is reflected in classification and compensation programs) has not been changed in any significant ways for decades. The importance of control and consistent treatment is obviously an overriding concern. The interest in defining a broader role for managers is beginning to permeate government; if they are accountable for the performance of their unit, it will be difficult to deny them a broader role in managing payroll and making compensation decisions.

Realistically, it makes little sense to maintain centralized control of the rewards if the plans and programs are soundly designed and budgeted at appropriate levels. In this era of "nanosecond management," day-to-day program administration is best delegated to managers and supervisors who fully understand local organizational needs. When managers understand the program objectives and are adequately trained in making decisions, they should be fully capable of managing the pay of their subordinates within budget constraints. Human resource or personnel specialists can continue to play what is essentially a consulting role to help managers deal with pay problems, but the final authority needs to remain with line managers.

CHOICES AT THE CROSSROAD

The choice between a conventional salary structure and a banded one represents a significant difference in program philosophy. The choice needs to be the right one today and for the foreseeable future. If past experience is an indicator of the future, public employers should expect to live with the new program framework for years to come. That means it has to be compatible with future initiatives to reinvent government and with the way work is organized and managed.

Employers both public and private are reluctant to move to a new salary structure. The structures are adjusted annually (or periodically) but the same grades and ranges are used for program management. Continued reliance on the same structure provides stability and gives employees a sense of where they stand in the hierarchy.

The key is the number of salary grades. When the number changes, some jobs move up in the hierarchy (because they are now grouped with different higher-level jobs) and others move down. The impact of the changes will be problematic; regardless of how it is handled, some employees will be dissatisfied. It is not possible to know what problems will arise, but it is probably inevitable that some people will feel they are losers. This makes the decision to introduce a new structure important to the organization.

The possible choice of a simplified, banded structure is normally associated with other initiatives to change the organization. It needs to be evaluated in light of its prospective impact. The new program concept will contribute to and facilitate new management styles and send different messages to managers and employees.

In deciding on a new salary structure, the parameters depend on the answers to the following questions:

- How many organizational layers or tiers need to be accommodated by grade distinctions? Within the organizational hierarchy, how great are the differences between tiers? Is there a need to downplay the hierarchy?
- What are the planned career ladders? The structure needs to

accommodate the number of rungs in the ladders. For most nonexempt job families there are typically three career levels; for most professional and technical job families there may be up to four levels, but any more would involve artificial job distinctions. Are employees transferred between job families?

- Is it important to the culture to treat all occupational groups similarly? Is the compensation philosophy the same? Would separate salary structures serve a valid purpose?

- Has the organization made a commitment to multifunctional teams? Do team members typically have similar skill levels? If not, are members performing similar or different roles?

- Is the most important organizational priority to introduce quality management? To reduce the bureaucracy? To increase flexibility? To reinvent government?

- How are annual salary increases going to be handled? Are increases based on merit or time in grade? Is there a sense of entitlement? Do increases need to reflect team performance? Is there a policy or plan to manage salary progression relative to prevailing market levels?

- How much influence do managers and supervisors have to manage payroll? Are they expected to plan the composition and job structure of their staff? Are they accountable for operating results? Do they receive adequate training in making these decisions?

- How important is the existing structure as a determinant of status and organizational importance? Are any perquisites or privileges tied to current grades? Is it important to perpetuate these status indicators?

- What is the appropriate role of human resource or personnel specialists? Is the administrative staff adequate to maintain the program? Do the administrators have the confidence of senior management? Do they have the technical expertise to handle program changes?

The choice of a new salary structure establishes the framework for the program. It needs to be consistent with plans for managing the workforce. The answers to the questions should help to evaluate the alternatives and to understand the administrative process that the structure needs to support. The answers will also serve to highlight administrative concerns that need to be accommodated in the salary program.

SUMMARY

A salary structure is normally taken for granted until there is a decision to change it. That decision is typically triggered by officials outside the human resource function who are convinced that the existing structure is an impediment to management initiatives. Their reasons are generally unrelated to the nuances that differentiate conventional structures. Realistically, their concerns prompt a choice between a conventional structure and a banded structure. This places the individuals responsible for choosing the new structure squarely at the crossroads.

The potholes that may be encountered when moving along the road to a new structure are significant. There will be winners and losers. From this perspective, a new program has to be planned so that it has broad-based support and remains viable for several years. This makes it important to look into the future, to the degree that this is ever possible, and anticipate how program administration may change over the next few years.

There is an apparently high level of interest, although this may not be fully articulated in many government agencies, in providing more flexibility in pay program administration. There is also support for giving managers and supervisors more of a role in managing the payroll and the salaries of their staff. If these goals are relevant, it prompts a move away from conventional structure concepts.

It is important to appreciate that the new structure should not, and in some respects cannot, depend on adhering to accepted practice. We simply do not have adequate experience with new structure concepts to formulate rules of thumb. For those who have become accustomed to mimicking the practices in other organizations, that may be a problem. However, if those responsible for conceiving program changes start with an understanding of internal needs and assess design considerations in light of those needs, there is no reason to expect a new structure to look like those in other organizations. The structure is nothing more than a framework to facilitate decision making. Those decisions relate to important workforce management concerns. That makes it important to develop the structure to support internal goals, regardless of the practices in other organizations.

Notes

1. For a discussion of federal experience with grade banding, see Howard Risher and Brigitte Schay, "Grade Banding: The Model for Future Salary Programs?" *Public Personnel Management,* Summer 1994, *23*(2), 187–199.
2. Other companies that have implemented some form of banded structure include Aetna, AT&T, Bausch & Lomb, Chrysler, Citicorp, Control Data, Data General, Johnson & Johnson, Marriott, Merck, Monsanto, Navistar, Northern Telecom, RJR Nabisco, and Steelcase.

CHAPTER THREE

Aligning Pay Levels with Prevailing Labor Market Rates

Charles H. Fay

P ay levels of government employees have been of great concern to politicians and taxpayers throughout the history of the United States. Discussion of appropriate pay level is almost always couched in terms of comparison with relevant private sector pay. Alignment of government pay with private sector pay is a major goal of most government human resource units (although parity is rarely expected). At the federal level significant legislation has been enacted attempting to make this alignment, the latest of which is the Federal Employees Pay Comparability Act of 1990 (FEPCA).

The importance of achieving some degree of market comparability lies in the consequences of not doing so. If a government organization pays noncompetitively (that is, below prevailing market rates), then better workers will tend to leave government service for the private sector. The remaining government employees will be either those dedicated to public service or those who are less attractive to private sector employers because of outlook or incompetence.

Similarly, if a government organization pays more than prevailing market rates, it incurs unnecessary salary expenses, as the workers it hires would be unlikely to find jobs elsewhere at the same salary levels. (It may seem strange that a government might pay wages above those in the private sector, but there is considerable evidence that this does occur at lower job levels. Justification for such practice is usually based on arguments that lower-level jobs are occupied primarily by women and minorities and that market wages for these jobs are artificially low due to discrimination; government organizations have a responsibility to avoid such discrimination as a matter of public policy.)

Under any circumstances, government organizations are not immune to market forces and must accommodate them implicitly or explicitly. This chapter focuses on an explicit strategy for government organization alignment with market wage and salary levels, describes current practice with respect to implementing alignment strategies in both the private and public sectors, and discusses emerging challenges to current practice, along with approaches that may help overcome the problems resulting from these challenges.

STRATEGIC ISSUES IN MARKET ALIGNMENT

Six issues relative to market alignment must be addressed, whether explicitly or implicitly. These issues are summarized in the following questions:

- How closely will the organization tie jobs to the market? By following an internal labor market strategy the organization can weaken links of most of its jobs to external markets, thereby making alignment less of an issue.

- What positioning strategy will be followed? Will all jobs be tied to the same level of the market (such as the 50th percentile), or will different jobs be tied to different levels?

- What competitive level will the organization choose?

- How will markets be defined? That is, in which labor markets does the organization compete?

- Which parts of the compensation package are to be aligned with the market? Will the organization seek market alignment for base salaries? For incentive payments? For benefits? For total compensation? Will it seek the same mix of reward system components that prevails in the market?

• Will the organization follow the same market alignment strategies across all (local or regional) geographic areas in which it operates?

Labor Market Strategy

Organizations that pursue an external labor market strategy hire new employees (potentially) into any job in the organization. This makes the organization especially sensitive to market alignment, as the applicants it recruits are likely to be familiar with the salary levels being offered by other organizations and, presumably, making acceptance decisions at least in part based on the salary offers they receive. (In earlier years, when government benefits levels and degree of job security were higher, starting salary is likely to have played a smaller part in job acceptance decisions.)

The opposite of the external labor market strategy is the internal labor market strategy. Organizations following this strategy hire from the outside market only into a limited number of "portal" positions; other jobs are filled by promotion from within. Government organizations have traditionally followed an internal labor market strategy. To some extent this is a matter of necessity. The military forces of the U.S. Army provide a good example. There are not too many jobs in civilian labor markets that provide the training and experience required for most senior enlisted or officer positions; the Army hires in at the recruit and second lieutenant level and then provides the specialized training and experience required for more senior jobs.

One consequence of following an internal labor market strategy is that a majority of jobs are insulated from the marketplace. Even though incumbents may be highly qualified for jobs in other organizations, the salary may deviate from market rates quite widely before any incumbent feels compelled to seek another employer. Internal wage comparisons, vested benefits, and other factors affecting job satisfaction may outweigh any external wage comparison incumbents may make.

Positioning Strategy

An organization may choose to pay all jobs at a certain level with respect to the market. This is an across-the-board positioning strategy. Under this strategy, all jobs might be paid at market rates (that is, the median or average wage paid to workers) or at some other point in the market distribution (such as the 65th percentile).

A different strategy, a selective positioning strategy, would pay different jobs at different levels with respect to the market. An organization pursuing this strategy would determine which jobs provide competitive advantage and pay them more relative to market than jobs not related to the core technology. The justification for this approach is that it is crucial to get the best people available for critical positions, and relatively high salaries will help do that. For noncritical positions average applicants will do, and the money saved by paying incumbents of these jobs less can be used to fund the higher salaries of those in critical positions, with no overall increase in the cost of labor.

Most government organizations follow a different version of the selective positioning strategy. Market-level differences are not a function of core technology but of organizational level. Lower-level jobs in most government bodies are paid more relative to market levels (frequently well above market) and more senior jobs are paid less relative to market (usually well below market). The impact of this is that total payroll is higher than it need be (as there are many more employees in lower-level jobs) and it is difficult to recruit and retain higher-level employees.

Competitive Level

A government organization may choose to pay below market, at market, or above market. Stated government policy (when there is one) usually refers to market *comparability.* Under FEPCA, for example, federal employees are supposed to receive pay rates comparable to those in the private sector in the localities in which they work. The actual formula designed to close the pay gap allows for a 5 percent differential to remain between federal and private sector salaries; under the alternative pay plans advanced by the President the pay gap has widened in most localities since FEPCA rather than decreased. (Implicit and explicit policy frequently differ in both the public and private sector.)

Market Definition

Traditional compensation practice has defined labor markets almost entirely in terms of geography. The relevant labor market for lower-level jobs (blue-collar and most clerical and other pink-collar jobs) has been the local labor market, defined in terms of probable commuting patterns. The Federal Wage System (FWS) under which blue-collar jobs are paid divides the contiguous forty-eight states into a series of local labor markets for wage determination purposes.

For higher-level jobs there are regional labor markets. Many administrative, technical, and lower-level professional jobs exist predominantly within regional labor markets. Most MBAs, for example, get their first jobs in the region in which their degree is granted. More common is the notion of a national labor market, particularly for professional and managerial jobs.

The federal government has (until FEPCA) operated on the assertion that professional, administrative, technical, and clerical jobs have a national market, and each of them (all are General Schedule, or GS, jobs) has had a single national rate. Other government units operating in the United States (with the exception of some multistate compact organizations) have not had to cope with national or even regional markets, although state governments have had multiple local markets to deal with.

As private sector organizations have become more integrated into the global economy, there has been less emphasis on geographically determined labor markets and more emphasis on product- or service-market competitors as the appropriate labor market for comparative purposes. If I am an automobile manufacturer, what other employers in my geographic area pay is of much less importance than what other automobile manufacturers in Europe and Japan pay. My labor cost of doing business is the critical issue, and if I pay higher wages than my competitors for employees who operate at the same level of productivity, I will be at a significant competitive disadvantage.

Government organizations have traditionally been immune to product- or service-market competition because governments have been in a monopoly position. The trend toward outsourcing and privatizing what have traditionally been government functions creates a new impetus for government organizations to redefine the labor markets in which they compete.

Compensation Package Alignment

Compensation in most private sector organizations used to consist solely of base pay for nonexecutive and nonsales jobs. The mix of pay has been expanded as private sector organizations have introduced both short-term and long-term incentives. Private sector organizations have moved toward a total compensation perspective in which the cash compensation portions of the total reward package are integrated with benefits. As employers consider rewards policies they think in terms of the total compensation received by each employee and about the mix of reward system components that is most suitable to organizational goals and culture.

This emphasis on total compensation raises several issues for market alignment strategies. Senior management, clearly interested in the total labor cost of doing business, focuses on aligning total compensation costs with the appropriate market. Unfortunately, most market alignment technology (such as the wage survey) provides information either on base wages received by employees or on target total cash compensation received (base salary plus the expected value of long- and short-term incentives). Very little market data is available on the value of benefits received.

Not only the level of each component of total compensation received is important; the mix may be equally or even more important. A total cash compensation package of (for example) $50,000 in base wage with no incentive pay opportunities is very different from a package of $40,000 in base wage and a target bonus of $10,000 that may range from nothing to $25,000, depending on organizational, unit, and individual performance. The two packages will attract and retain different kinds of employees and motivate different behaviors in incumbents. Mixes that include at-risk components are likely to attract and retain proven higher performers who will make more under these systems.

Thus organizations must determine not only the level of total compensation at which they will compete but how they will compete using mixes. Most government organizations still focus most (and in many cases all) cash compensation on base pay, but an increasing number are experimenting with or implementing at-risk and variable pay systems. Even those government units paying all base pay still compete in labor markets against private sector organizations that use sometimes bewildering mixes of pay programs, so that the comparison problems still exist.

Constancy of Market Alignment Strategies

The final aspect of alignment strategy is the degree to which the organization will pursue the same market alignment strategies across all geographic areas, local or regional, in which it operates. For example, should the federal government be equally competitive in all the major metropolitan areas in which it operates? Should it be more competitive in urban areas than rural areas? Similar policy issues exist for many state governments. Aggressive competitive pay policies for protective service employees in major urban areas might be justified, but not for similar workers in rural or suburban areas. Alternatively, mix policies might be pegged to markets in major urban and suburban areas and state employees in rural areas might have the same performance-based earning opportunities even though no other employer in the area provides any form of cash compensation other than base pay.

TECHNICAL ISSUES IN
MARKET ALIGNMENT

A number of technical issues are faced by government organizations seeking to align pay levels with market rates. These generally are related to one of two broad areas: market survey technology and technologies associated with relating market rates to internal valuation processes. The second set of issues are largely beyond the scope of this chapter, but a limited set of these issues directly impacting market alignment is addressed here.

Survey Technologies

The goal of any compensation survey is the development of an estimate of prevailing market pay levels. It is important to keep this goal in view whether developing a compensation survey or considering purchasing one. The imprecision inherent in any measure of job value (whether internal or external) requires a balance between survey cost and estimate usefulness.

WHY PAY VARIES   An understanding of labor market characteristics leading to different wage or salary levels provides a useful guideline to determining survey development. These characteristics include the following:

• Locational factors. Pay levels vary across geographic areas. Differences in wages between the Northeast and the deep South are generally recognized. There is less awareness that wage rates for a job within a local labor market may vary due to desirability of work site, ease of commuting, and distance from residential areas.

•   Industry factors. Industries vary in ability to pay, degree of unionization, the total mix of jobs (association with more highly paid jobs is likely to raise the salary of a given job), age of industry, centrality of a given job to core technologies, and other factors that affect wage levels.

•   Organizational factors. Larger organizations tend to pay more, as do unionized organizations. Other organizational impacts include ability to pay, organizational reward policies and practices, organizational culture, geographic dispersion, and organizational demographics.

•   Job factors. Though a surveyed job may be fairly similar across all organizations, there will actually be significant differences in the duties and responsibilities, specifications (incumbent requirements), and working conditions for the same job in different organizations, and even for different positions but the same job within an organization.

•   Incumbent factors. If an organization is populated by more experienced employees who are uniformly high performers, wage rates are likely to be high compared to rates in organizations populated by junior employees who are lesser performers.

•   Interaction of factors. A difficulty in adjusting for these factors is that there is an unknown degree of interaction. In some cases the factors reinforce each other (for example, an organization in Manhattan in a high-paying industry with a policy of paying at the 65th percentile has very high profits compared to others in the industry and has mostly senior employees who are high performers); in other cases they may cancel each other out (for example, an organization in the deep South in a low-paying industry with a policy of paying at the 65th percentile has high profits compared to others in the industry and has a mix of employees with respect to seniority and performance).

Understanding why pay may vary for the same job in different locations or organizations, or even within the same organization, suggests the factors the compensation specialist would like to control for when developing a survey. It is rarely possible to control for most of these factors, because to do so requires collecting extensive information from each survey participant. Given the downsizing of most organizations, there are fewer and fewer employees in a typical compensation unit available to provide survey information. Following standard survey guidelines will account for some pay variation factors and lessen the impact of others.

SURVEY GUIDELINES   The first guideline concerns who is to be surveyed. Federal government surveys are the only wage surveys that use a rigorous sampling technology to select survey units. Commercial surveys tend to use either clients of the surveying organization or a broad mailing of surveys to members of compensation associations, corporate human resource departments, or some other list of organizations or people thought to include appropriate survey targets.

Individual organizations developing their own surveys have tended to use convenience samples; that is, the compensation analyst simply contacts colleagues in other organizations thought to be cooperative and having similar jobs. Concerns for confidentiality and wage-fixing charges has decreased personal contact surveys of this nature. Such convenience samples also do not speak to control of the pay differential factors noted earlier.

A more useful approach is to construct a sample with the desired characteristics that will control for pay differential factors. For some jobs such a sample may be primarily of local organizations; for others a sample focusing on other organizations in the same industry of approximately the same size may be developed. A judgmental sample may be developed as an industry or local human resource organization project. To avoid wage-fixing and confidentiality issues, such a survey may be conducted through a third party who actually receives the salary data and provides reports to participants.

A second guideline concerns which jobs should be included in the survey. To some extent this depends on how important to the organization alignment with external labor markets (external equity) is as opposed to the alignment of the salaries of jobs within the organization (internal equity). If external alignment is paramount then market data on all jobs will be sought (but will not be found). Organizations pursuing a market-pricing strategy (where internal equity is determined solely by market rate) seem to hit a ceiling of finding market correlates for about 85 percent, although these jobs will probably account for 95 percent or more of all employees.

As internal equity concerns grow, the percentage of jobs for which it is necessary to get market rates drops. The jobs that are surveyed are known as key, or benchmark, jobs. They generally constitute 20 percent to 30 percent of the total number of jobs in the organization, although more of the employee population. Key jobs have several distinguishing characteristics. They should be well understood and readily definable. Key jobs must be common in the organizations who will make up the survey sample; there is little point in surveying jobs that no other organization has. Key jobs should vary on the factors used in the given job evaluation scheme, otherwise there may be some difficulty in combining job evaluation and salary survey results. Key jobs should reflect all salary levels of the organizations and pay mix should also reflect organizational pay mix policies. Key jobs should be relatively stable with respect to duties and responsibilities and to the knowledge, skills, and abilities required. Major entry-level jobs and jobs that are presenting recruiting and turnover problems for the organization are usually included with key jobs even if they do not otherwise qualify. Of course, not all key jobs will be surveyed in a single survey, and data for some jobs may be so plentiful from a number of sources that the organization will not survey them at all.

The third guideline concerns what information to ask for. Very simply, less is more—that is, the fewer data asked for the more responses are likely to be received. A listing of data of interest includes:

• Information on the Surveyed Organization. This information would include (aside from identification and contact information) the location, size, and industry of the organization, along with degree of union representation, workweek, and a copy of the organization chart noting the level of all surveyed jobs.

• Rewards policies. In the area of wages and salaries, information may include the job evaluation system in use, wage structure characteristics, merit policies, mix policy, and miscellaneous pay differentials. In the area of benefits this information would include pension and capital accumulation program policies, health and other employee welfare programs, policies concerning pay for time not worked, and major miscellaneous benefits.

• Individual job data. This information could include a job description (or the degree of match with a provided job description), job specifications, wage and salary data, perquisites and allowances, and job incumbent information such as seniority, performance levels, number of incumbents, and turnover rates. For a variety of reasons most organizations choose the median rate paid in the market for a job as the measure of the market. (The median is the rate paid at the middle of the salary distribution; half of the distribution receives less than the median rate, and approximately half of the distribution receives more. In most salary distributions the median is smaller than the average.)

Government organizations seeking data to implement market alignment face somewhat different problems than do private sector organizations. Making things somewhat easier is that public sector salaries are public information and thus data are more readily available. Public sector organizations have also lagged in designing and implementing short-term and long-term incentive programs, so that a focus on base wages is more justifiable if comparisons are to be limited to other public sector organizations.

Still, there are rarely more than a few public sector organizations operating in any specific area, and these organizations typically account for only a small portion of the total labor market. Many of the jobs in any public sector organization are unique to the public sector (tax agent, cooperative extension agent, and court bailiff, for example), and few have even distant correlates in private sector organizations.

A fourth guideline concerns the way surveys are constructed. As any market researcher can testify, survey instrument questionnaire construction is not work for amateurs. Poor wording can result in unanswered questions or, worse, plausible but inaccurate responses. Survey specialists exist in many organizations, including public sector organizations, and their assistance on instrument design can avoid poor response rates and inaccurate responses. Pilot studies are worthwhile for major surveys.

Given all the flaws inherent in the compensation survey process one might question why any compensation analyst would undertake one or trust data from those that are commercially available. The simplistic answer, of course, is that even questionable data are better than no data at all. Beyond this lie two reasons why surveys can still be useful. First, for most jobs there are multiple survey data sources, each with its own strengths and weaknesses. An experienced analyst can use compensation data from different sources and, recognizing the specific characteristics of each source, arrive at a reasonable estimate using experience and judgment.

More important, it is useful to remember that the goal of the survey process is to develop an estimate that allows alignment of salary levels with external markets, so that wages offered to applicants and paid to incumbents will be perceived as competitive. Applicants and job incumbents have a perception of the market rate based on a much smaller and less relevant sample than even the most casual organizational survey; employers need only an approximation of market levels in order to determine competitive salary levels.

Relating Market Rates to Job Valuation Results

Market surveys provide data that are more or less accurate estimates of the market rate for each job surveyed, but even with the best market data there is no guarantee that the organization will actually align its salaries with labor markets. This is because the ways the market data is used to price jobs within the organization can serve to distort market alignment. If pure market pricing approaches are used the problem does not arise, but few organizations in the public sector (or in the private sector, for that matter) use such an approach.

Briefly, such an approach involves paying the market rate for all jobs for which a market rate exists. Jobs for which a market rate does not exist are paid based on a pricing model, typically one that regresses wage rates on job attributes to provide a multiple regression equation that can be used to estimate what the market rate would be if the relationship between job attributes and wages holds for all jobs.

In most organizations some version of job evaluation is used to construct an internal value hierarchy. (Most common are point factor systems or classification systems.) This value hierarchy is divided into salary grades, and the market rates for jobs in each grade are used to price the salary structure. The process of pricing the structure involves several steps that distance the salary rate for a job from its market rate, and does so in a somewhat haphazard manner.

The first step in pricing a structure is to average the market rate of the jobs in each grade or class to get an initial midpoint. Depending on the jobs assigned to the grade, that average may be very different from the salaries many of the jobs are paid in the market. Compensation analysts usually shift outlier jobs to other grades in the structure or do not use outlier rates in computing the initial midpoint; this reduces but does not solve the problem.

Because market data is collected sometime before the salary structure is placed in service, it is necessary to estimate market growth and adjust initial midpoints based on that estimate. This "aging" of the data is only as good as the estimate of market growth. These estimates are rarely available for local labor markets, and the national rate is unlikely to reflect local differences.

Salary structure midpoints are usually adjusted a second time to take into account expected market movement during the period the structure will be used. Most organizations follow a *lead-lag* policy, in which the structure is adjusted to where market rates are thought likely to be around July 1 of the salary administration year. These adjustments suffer the same problem as the aging adjustments, amplified somewhat by the greater time into the future covered by the estimate.

The final adjustment to the structure is one which "regularizes" it. Typically, the initial midpoints, if plotted, would form a very irregular salary curve. Though salary structures in different organizations may have very different slopes, no organization will have a jagged salary curve. This smoothing, however, further separates salaries paid from the original survey data, and for many jobs alignment with market is questionable at best.

The consequence of the flaws of survey technology and the manipulation of survey data in the building of salary structures is that market alignment is difficult at best. It is critical that organizations who seek market alignment evaluate final salary levels for jobs against market survey results to be certain that alignment has in fact taken place.

FEDERAL GOVERNMENT APPROACH AND THE BLS

The federal government tracks wages through many different surveys (such as the Current Population Survey of the Bureau of the Census); two sets of surveys are used to benchmark federal government employee salaries.

The Occupational Compensation Surveys conducted by the Bureau of Labor Statistics (BLS) are used to benchmark General Schedule employees. Because these surveys are used for other government purposes (such as determining prevailing wages), the jobs surveyed cover a wide range of professional, administrative, technical, clerical, protective service (for example, police officer), maintenance and toolroom, and material movement and custodial jobs.

Some 142 jobs are tracked by BLS. Included among them are several job families that may include several levels of an occupation, such as Secretary I through Secretary V; thus fewer than 142 distinct occupations are tracked. Not all jobs are tracked in all surveys. Because the

BLS has very stringent data quality standards, many of the jobs tracked may not have published data for many of the surveys in which they are included.

BLS surveys are unquestionably the best salary surveys available. They are the only major surveys that use rigorous sampling procedures. Survey employees are more thoroughly trained than those of any other wage survey organization. Results are analyzed, and only those data that meet BLS quality standards are published.

A different set of surveys is used to benchmark blue-collar jobs. The function of the Federal Wage System (FWS) surveys is to provide a measure of local market wage levels for the purpose of assuring comparable pay for FWS (blue-collar) workers. Each survey is a product of the joint efforts of the principal federal agency employing FWS workers in the area (typically the Department of Defense, in some cases the Veterans Administration), the union representing the largest number of federal employees in the area, the Office of Personnel Management, and the Bureau of Labor Statistics. The local survey committee consists of equal numbers of lead agency and union members. FWS survey data do not always share the high esteem in which BLS survey results are held because the procedures used to collect and analyze the data are not as rigorous.

EMERGING PROBLEMS IN MARKET ALIGNMENT

Traditional market surveys and the way their results are used pose significant problems for market alignment. There are other developments in organizations that create even more difficulties and make traditional surveys even more problematic as a tool to achieve market alignment.

The first difficulty is one previously mentioned: the total compensation perspective being adopted by an increasing proportion of organizations. This perspective leads organizations to compete for labor on the basis of a package of rewards, including base pay, short-term incentives, long-term incentives, and benefits. In this context, alignment with market base rates is increasingly irrelevant. Alignment with total cash compensation has inherent problems, because a $50,000 guaranteed base salary is much different from a target compensation of $50,000 consisting of $40,000 guaranteed base plus a package of incentive payments with an expected value of $10,000. Differences in benefits packages amplify the problem.

Getting data for market alignment when survey respondents include organizations with a total compensation perspective presents additional problems. Most commercial surveys include measures of variable or at-risk pay, both targeted and received. The specific makeup of the variable pay package is not usually specified, and it is unclear whether (for example) a job incumbent received variable pay related to individual, group, or organizational performance.

When benefits are considered, the problem gets significantly more complicated. Very few surveys provide much information on benefits received. Most of the data indicate whether a specific benefit is received or not, but benefit level is provided by only a few surveys. Choosing a dollar value for a benefit is even more problematical. Two different organizations may have very different costs for a specific benefit, depending on employee demographics, administrative skill, and vendor choice, even when the value of the two packages to a given employee is the same.

However, the perceived value of any benefit to two employees will vary depending on their demographic characteristics and preferences. Flexible benefit plans with a given dollar value may have greater value to an employee because of the right to choose specific levels of preferred benefits than would a fixed package of the same dollar value. This is not to say these problems cannot be lessened; surveys are beginning to appear that provide actuarial estimates of the dollar value of a benefits package calculated on a common basis by the survey vendor.

A more complicated (and for the time being, less solvable) problem arises from the many efforts taking place in organizations to redesign work. Three forms of this work redesign present special problems to achieving market alignment. Organizations that are downsizing and delayering are creating hybrid jobs that consist of task sets previously associated with distinct traditional jobs. Many organizations are moving from individual jobs defined in terms of tasks to teams with outcome objectives. Finally, even many employees who still work primarily as individuals have their work defined in terms of outcomes.

Hybrid jobs create problems for market alignment; market data exists for each of the components of the hybrid, but there are no data available for the combination. One organization has merged three traditional plant maintenance jobs into a single hybrid job. Though market data exist for the jobs of the electricians, plumbers, and mechanics that form the basis for the hybrid job, it is not clear what the hybrid is worth. Clearly it is worth more than any of the individual jobs it comprises, but it is unlikely to be worth as much as all three jobs combined. As more hybrid jobs emerge there will be two impacts on market alignment efforts. First, organizations with hybrid jobs will have more jobs for which they can find no match in the market. This creates a problem for them, especially those that value market alignment (external equity) over internal alignment (internal equity).

A second impact, and one that affects all organizations, is that fewer and fewer organizations will be able to contribute meaningful data to compensation surveys. It may be that this is a temporary problem and that some inherent logic of job hybridization will result in a new set of jobs that are fairly standard across most organizations. Thus, instead of trying to get compensation data on plumbers, electricians, and maintenance mechanics, most organizations will need data on "plant maintenance workers."

Similar problems are arising because of the move toward teaming in organizations. The traditional job has been seen within the context of the assembly line, even in nonmanufacturing organizations. That is why many nonmanufacturing organizations have been referred to as "paper factories." The work process specifies expected and accepted worker tasks and duties. Technology has driven job design, and as most organizations have adopted similar technologies (the "one best way" espoused by F. W. Taylor and other early management experts) there has been a pool of jobs common across most of the economy. As other criteria for work design have been more widely adopted, and especially as teams have become a more normal way of designing work, the commonality of jobs has begun to disappear; in many organizations the traditional job has begun to disappear, replaced by ambiguous and unstable team roles. Workers operating under the new team-based job design, when asked what they do, reply not in terms of specific tasks or responsibilities, but rather "whatever it takes" or "do you mean last week or this week or next week?" In short, people who work on teams cannot be characterized easily by the job descriptions that typically define jobs in surveys. Even if their roles could be described, it is not clear that their wage is or should be equivalent to someone who matches the job description but works as an individual. Surveys of the future will need to address the teaming issue.

New approaches to base pay also create problems for benchmarking labor market costs. Many organizations are experimenting with skill-based and competency-based pay systems. These systems usually accompany a team-based or hybrid job design, but not always. When base pay focuses on the person rather than the job, traditional market referents are no longer sufficient to understand the benchmark data in the survey. An example in more traditional settings is the series job, such as Attorney I through IV. The various levels of the job do not necessarily have different tasks, but may have a different mix of the same task set, take on more complicated cases, and so forth. If the four levels of the job were not differentiated, the data received from the survey would be of little use in determining salary levels; the range would be too great, and the average salary would be inapplicable to most incumbents.

Any job with pay determined by a skill- or competency-based system is similar to the series job. Unless skill or competency levels are specified, survey data will be of little use. If all members of the survey sample of a job type were receiving skill- or competency-based pay and the skill or competency breaks were similar, benchmarking would be possible. At least in this time of transition, neither of these conditions holds true.

A second change in compensation practice creates problems in benchmarking salary structures. In the last ten years many organizations have adopted broad-banded salary structures; these have fewer salary grades than traditional structures and consequently much broader range spreads than traditional structures. Many market benchmarking surveys provide structure data, usually in the form of salary grade midpoints. Midpoints in broad-banded structures are irrelevant, and if survey results include midpoints of broad bands, the data are misleading and will distort any analyses using them.

NEW APPROACHES TO SURVEY DESIGN

The problems resulting from changes in work design and pay practices have had an impact on the usefulness of compensation surveys to the extent that some thought is being given to changes in approaches to survey design. These changes tend to move away from making whole-job matches and toward focusing on job factors or incumbent factors.

The human resource function at a major high-tech manufacturer provides an example of this approach. The organization had restructured its human resource group so that all were generalists. The organization had four levels of individual contributors and three levels of management in its human resource unit. In addition, it expected to service the human resource management needs not only of its own organization, but also provide consulting and administrative services to other organizations. No surveys available could be used to benchmark these jobs.

The organization contracted in 1993 with a team from the School of Management and Labor Relations at Rutgers University to research a different approach to benchmarking. Briefly, a series of job factors was developed that seemed useful in determining job value. Some of these factors looked much like job evaluation factors, such as financial responsibilities inherent in the position, kind of outside relationships, and so forth. Others, such as incumbent experience and education level, were characteristics of the incumbents rather than job requirements.

Any human resource management incumbent or job could be matched against the survey instrument, although it did take respondents more effort to complete the survey, in part because their organizational information systems are not geared to provide information in this format. Regression analysis was used to estimate the appropriate market rate of any specific combination of job and incumbent. This approach could be used to price hybrid and team jobs.

A recent BLS study[1] proposes a somewhat similar approach toward changing the surveys it does. The test surveys proposed would collect wage information for a random sample of jobs within each survey site, and for each job sampled would also get information on nine "leveling" criteria: knowledge required, supervisory controls, guidelines, complexity, scope and effect, personal contacts, purpose of contacts, physical demands, and work environment. Job family of the sample job would also be collected. BLS proposes to continue the broad job families in traditional use: professional, administrative, technical, clerical, protective services, and blue-collar.

Sample data could be used to estimate appropriate wages for each GS level in an area. Other estimates could be made as well. Although the outcomes of this project are not yet known, such an approach to compensation surveys could provide a model for future survey development.

SUMMARY

Wage and salary surveys have been a mainstay of compensation practice in the United States for many years. A survey technology has been developed that, though not meeting the standards of most marketing research surveys (with the exception of those surveys conducted by the BLS), still provides information of sufficiently good quality that most organizations feel confident in using it to benchmark their wage levels.

Changes in job design and compensation practice have made benchmarking problematic for many organizations. New approaches to survey design may solve many of the problems inherent in current surveys. Until such surveys are common, organizations will have continued difficulty in knowing what prevailing labor market rates actually are, and thus alignment will be questionable.

Note

1. Bureau of Labor Statistics, "Compensation 2000: Albuquerque, New Mexico and Allentown, Pennsylvania Test," *Federal Register,* Sept. 1, 1995, *60*(170), 45, 742.

CHAPTER FOUR

Job Classification
The Support System for
Personnel Decision Making

Lyn Meridew Holley
James R. O'Connell

For most managers, the job classification system is relevant to their role only when they want to hire or promote an employee. Then they are forced to take time away from normal duties to comply with the requirements of the system. The time required by the typical system is often seen by managers as unproductive and excessive. Moreover, managers anticipate that the experience could be frustrating and possibly disturbing. Job classification specialists typically have the authority to decide whether the new or revised job meets the requirements to be classified as the manager requests. The classification system is the domain of the personnel or human resource function and is sometimes managed with little if any concern about its impact on government operations.

Survey after survey at all levels of government show that managers perceive job classification as a stumbling block. Job classification does not make sense to managers, and job classification specialists often can't explain it fully. The few managers who do understand it know how to use the process for their own ends. Those who do not know how to play the game view the process as an impediment to achieving their goals. The interest in reinventing government has elevated interest in moving away from personnel systems that are seen as part of the problem. This chapter provides an overview of classification systems and raises questions about their future role.

WHAT IS JOB CLASSIFICATION?

Job classification is a process for sorting jobs[1] into types (a job series or family) and levels of work (signified generally by a salary grade and range), then assigning codes to each job that document its class. All positions with similar duties and responsibilities are treated as a job and assigned to the same class. Jobs in the class are assigned the same title and the class is defined by a brief class specification. Conceptually the process is very simple, but its outcomes permeate almost every aspect of personnel management.

A job classification process exists in some form in virtually every organization. When people are hired or moved from one job to another, someone has to consider their qualifications relative to the job's requirements. Someone also has to consider their salaries relative to others in similar jobs as well as prevailing pay levels in the labor market. In larger organizations these decisions are normally documented. However structured, if at all, this is effectively job classification.

Managers certainly can decide if they need a chemist or an accountant; they can also specify the basic prior experience and credentials a candidate needs to be considered for a job opening. However, they may need help in screening applicants and in determining the appropriate salary range for the job. As long as public policy continues to emphasize fairness and consistency, there will be a need to limit managerial discretion and to manage these personnel actions. Agency heads and legislators or board members need the assurance that personnel or human resource management is justified and defensible. Classification systems support this public policy objective.

Realistically, the private sector's approach to these issues is somewhat different. Very few corporations use the term *job classification* in the context of human resource management. Corporations need to make similar personnel decisions, but they divide these activities among several specialized groups. For wage and salary management, the term *job evaluation* is commonly used and refers to a decision process that looks at the relative value of each job. Jobs are not classified in the private sector, they are evaluated or "priced" relative to prevailing market pay levels. There are of course laws governing personnel management but not the same cultural concern with employee rights.

In the public sector, job classification is to work as accounting codes are to finance. Job classification systems comprise rules and codes. The rules govern how jobs are sorted by type of work (such as secretary, accountant, or prison guard) and level of work (such as trainee, journeyman, or expert). The codes label each type of work and level of work. Job classification is conceptually the same in every organization, although different systems have different sets of rules and codes.

With government wage and salary programs, classification decisions determine salary grade assignments. The classification system thereby governs individual salaries and influences the organization's payroll. With some classes the distinctions between job levels (such as between Accountant I and Accountant II) may be fuzzy and overlapping, which makes it difficult to make and defend classification decisions. The importance of these decisions to employees as well as to supervisors and managers makes them inevitably a cause for controversy and confrontation.

Until the early years of this century, government operations were relatively simple, and there was little need for sophisticated management methods. One generic title, government clerk, covered almost all civilian government jobs. The work of the great bulk of government jobs, especially at the national level, was regarded as simple and routine. It was assumed that most "fit" citizens could perform the work of government, and there was little reason to differentiate among them. As the national enterprise grew, however, so did the need for specialized work and knowledge and for better tools to manage them.

The first widespread use of job classification was borne on the wave of U.S. enthusiasm over scientific management in the 1890s. Modern job classification is characterized by a set of explicit rules that can be examined and challenged objectively. Scientific management of government was intended, among other things, to reform hiring and salary practices characterized by corruption and ineptitude. The work of government jobs would be defined, and the work of campaigning and soliciting campaign contributions would not be done on the public payroll. Only qualified citizens would be hired, and the qualifications required would be based on the work to be performed. By 1923, the U.S. government had passed the Classification Act, which established the foundation of classification processes and approaches still used in the federal and many other systems.

Many refinements have been made since this beginning, and there are several different job classification methodologies. Although the methodologies look different, they are all fundamentally similar, involving either a direct job-to-job comparison or an indirect comparison of jobs via standards. However approached, jobs of similar value (that is, requiring workers with similar duties and qualifications) are grouped to simplify personnel or human resource management administration.

WHAT PURPOSES DO JOB CLASSIFICATION SYSTEMS SERVE?

Job classification systems serve several important human resource purposes. Critics of classification systems often overlook these purposes and the implications for human resource management if the classification system is terminated.

Staffing and Selection

The concept of a *job* is essential to estimating staffing requirements. The job is the unit of analysis for work; it is the basis for determining how many of what kind of people to hire. The job exists before its incumbent; a person becomes an incumbent when officially assigned to the job.

Describing a job and classifying it by type and level of work is essential to the identification of qualified applicants in both internal and external labor markets. Required job qualifications are typically part of the information flowing from a classification decision. Job descriptions communicate the specific duties of a job in greater detail.

Work Flow and Strategic Planning

The distribution of work assignments is affected by job classification. At the unit level, job descriptions reflect the normal flow of work and the normal work of each employee. Supervisors assign and employees accept day-to-day work activities within this framework. At higher management levels, classification codes facilitate the assignment of additional or new work (for example, programs and projects) and serve to identify quickly the units with jobs that require qualifications relevant to the new work (plant biologists, for instance). Government employers can rely on this classification information to plan work flow and staffing requirements.

Wage and Salary Management

The concept of the job is central in most methods for managing pay. In an organizational context, pay levels can be evaluated only in relation to an assigned job. The classification process effectively determines a job's salary grade and range. Once the classification codes are established, this dictates the pay for all incumbents in a job regardless of the agency or, for most public employers, the location of the work site.

Evaluating Performance and Training Needs

To assess the performance of individual employees or to set standards for performance, it is necessary to establish a basis for understanding what the worker is to accomplish. The index to similar work provided by job classification is an important resource for supervisors in performance planning and management. If Jane is a secretary and Gina is an electrical engineer, the comparison of their work performance is like comparing apples with oranges. Although both Jane and Gina may get the same performance rating (for example, "acceptable"), deciding whether Jane has met acceptable work standards requires a comparison with work standards for secretaries. Further, by linking jobs with common performance standards, the job information flowing from the classification process provides a framework for identifying common training needs.

Comparing and Assessing Work Unit Productivity

To compare the productivity of organizational units, it is essential to have some notion of the types of work performed by the units and of the levels of resources available in them. If Unit A performs social casework and Unit B oversees environmental cleanup, comparison of their work performance is again an apples-to-oranges situation.

Although both units may achieve the same abstract rating ("meets plan," for example), assessing the productivity of Unit A requires comparison with other units that perform social casework. Further, comparing Unit A with another unit that performs casework (Unit AA) requires some consideration of the levels of resources available in each unit. It may be that Unit A operated with half of its case worker positions vacant while Unit AA had no vacancies. Perhaps Unit A had only one supervisor or senior worker for every eight caseworkers while Unit AA had three. Or maybe Unit A had 30 percent of its caseworker positions filled at the trainee level while Unit AA had no trainees. Job classification provides the codes necessary to identify similar units and, within units, to sort out types and levels of people resources required and available. Consequently, job classification information facilitates the comparative assessment of work unit performance.

Identifying Incumbent Rights, Obligations, and Entitlements

The classification of a job establishes the linkages to laws, regulations, and agency guidance and precedents that determine the eligibility of incumbents for, among other things, union membership, inclusion in a bargaining unit, eligibility for overtime, type of retirement (such as federal government or Social Security), level of security clearance required, and inclusion in management.

Classification is fundamental to management decisions governing the type of people to hire, how much to pay them, and their eligibility for union membership or their Fair Labor Standards Act (FLSA) status (whether exempt or nonexempt); the distribution of rewards; and how to report and explain staffing and pay to top management, regulators, and the courts. Although it is embedded in all these decisions, it is virtually invisible. Job classification is most often noticed in relation to managing pay.

JOB CLASSIFICATION: MANAGEMENT TOOL OR QUAGMIRE?

Job classification is essentially an information collection process that supports personnel decision making. As such, it functions as an element of an agency or government system for managing workers and controlling payroll and personnel actions. It frequently is a vehicle for micromanagement; there is deeply buried historical evidence that classification systems were conceived as control mechanisms rather than personnel or human resource systems. The earliest of job classification systems as we know them today were introduced around the turn of the century, prior to the creation of the field of modern personnel management. When classification is combined with step-in-grade salary administration, the reality is that the system provides for virtually no managerial discretion; it is very much a control system.

The amount of information made available to top management through job classification is seductive. The U.S. Congress, state legislatures and other governing bodies, chief executives, and budget analysts often cannot resist dictating how many jobs will be available to do work and how much each job can be paid. The information makes it possible for legislators, budget analysts, and chief executives to substitute their own detailed estimates of resource requirements for the estimates from the agencies that will carry out the work. This frequently becomes a difficult burden for managers and workers in an agency.

Managers typically do, however, retain the responsibility for assigning work, and assigned work is the basis for job classification. Work can be assigned in ways that either raise or lower the qualifications required for a job and its rate of pay. If, for example, Tom, Dick, and Mary are social service case workers, work can be assigned so that Tom decides all the most difficult cases, Dick processes cases of normal difficulty, and Mary specializes in rapid processing of the most routine cases. The classified level of Tom's job might be a pay rate of $30,000, Dick's $25,000, and Mary's $19,000. Alternatively, work can be assigned such that Tom, Dick, and Mary each handle the same types of cases. If each spends a substantial portion of time handling the most difficult cases (the percentage required varies per classification system) and must have the same qualifications, the classified levels of all three jobs would be the same, at a pay grade of $30,000.

In most public organizations, increases in pay grades caused by changes in classification of one or two positions are resisted only if those one or two positions have implications for other positions. It would be easier for the manager to live with three people paid $30,000 rather than to defend and explain why two are being paid less. The latter, to be sure, would involve a lower payroll, but the manager who is not accountable for the payroll may choose the easier but more costly path.

Senior agency executives see resources allocated to position classification that do not appear to lead to the accomplishment of goals or to improved performance. The classification process uses staff resources as well as the time and energy of middle- and lower-level managers who are reporting their own frustrations with classification back to the senior executives, which reinforces the skepticism. Managers often feel unduly restrained by what they perceive as the inflexibility of position classification. They believe classification restricts their ability to pay the salaries and hire the people necessary to accomplish their work. They often would rather be spending their time on their main mission-related work rather than on writing position descriptions and dealing with personnel specialists or classifiers to get what they need.

Attitudes toward position classification vary according to the kind of organization managed. Managers of rapidly changing organizations find it difficult to keep the classification system up-to-date. Organizations with interdisciplinary functions or work that depends on the unique talents of individuals, such as research organizations, are more likely to report difficulty with classification systems. Managers of organizations with very high-salaried employees such as medical doctors or certain kinds of lawyers report difficulties with pay that they attribute to the position classification system.

The frustrations have led to repeated attempts to improve or reform classification systems. One of the largest, the federal government's white-collar classification system that covers roughly a million employees, has not changed fundamentally since 1949 and retains basic features of the system set up in 1923. Yet it has been the object of repeated but unsuccessful reform efforts since 1968. In 1993, the National Performance Review (NPR) called for a major overhaul of the white-collar system, putting the Clinton administration solidly on the side of change. In a 1994 follow-up report[2] that refined and elaborated on the NPR recommendations, the National Partnership Council (NPC) stated the common frustrations with position classification.

The main white-collar classification system, according to the NPC, is not sufficiently flexible to support individual agency missions, structures, and cultures or to respond to ever-changing external conditions; lacks credibility with employees and managers and does not support the government's goal of flatter, less hierarchical organizations; is too complex; fragments accountability for classification among the Office of Personnel Management (the central personnel agency), agency personnel staff, and agency managers; and produces conflict among parties and prevents any one party from assuming responsibility for the consequences of classification decisions.

The NPC criticisms are typical of the complaints about the federal white-collar classification system in particular and position classification systems in general, but it is interesting to note that the report fails to address one of the overriding problems that has plagued the system for the past decade or more: an inadequate budget to keep the systems and its class standards current. That, as much as anything, has been responsible for the deterioration of the system's credibility.

In light of the public's concern with government performance and criticism of bureaucratic systems, the NPC conclusions are not surprising. Since the heyday of classification in the first half of the twentieth century, whole generations of managers have come on stage and then exited. Whole schools of management thought have come and gone. Since the classification concept was introduced, the world has been exposed to movements, revolutions, and wave after wave of new management theories: behavioral science schools, quality management movements, global competition, corporate and government reinvention, downsizing, rightsizing, and the computer revolution, to name a few.

HOW JOB CLASSIFICATION WORKS

The result of job classification is the identification of a job with the codes for the type and level of work assigned to it. Codes usually include a job title, designation of occupation, and classification level. Almost universally in civil service, the classification process determines the salary grade and range. The following are essential elements of the job classification process:

- Documentation of the work assigned in the form of a job description (usually controlled by the supervisor who may draft the description, although the incumbent usually is consulted or involved).
- Classification of the job—that is, matching the work of the job with previously defined classification standards and codes (usually done by a job classification specialist).

- Identification of appropriate clearances and personnel actions. If the job classification specialist finds that the job is the same type as another but that new duties warrant a higher classification level, the incumbent may be promoted or, if required, the job may be opened to competition.

- Identification of appropriate changes to documents. For example, even if the classification remains the same, because the job description is changed the performance standards may have to be updated.

Most managers and executives rely on personnel information and linkages provided by job classification decisions, but they often view classification as only a bureaucratic requirement limiting who can be hired and how much they can be paid. Classification specialists are the messengers who bring the bad news about constraints and limitations to managers struggling to meet their goals with inadequate resources. There is a natural tension between the mandates of job classification specialists and managers that sometimes generates an adversarial relationship.

Classification specialists, or classifiers, are expert in applying the rules of the job classification system used by their agency. In every agency, classification specialists are kept faithful to the rules of the system by knowing that any exceptions for one must become exceptions for all. In the federal system and several others, the job classification specialist is further restrained by the ethical implications of having the rules, or some part of the rules, written in law.

Gathering and understanding enough information about a particular job to classify it in the time available is an art, not a science. In every job classification system, classifying the work of jobs is largely a judgmental process. As with personality, the nuances make each job unique. Job classification specialists must reduce the job to factors that count in the agency's classification system and then select the best match for each factor with the classification standards for that factor. The subjective element means different job classification specialists may reach different conclusions about the same job.

Managers who do not understand how the job classification system works, and its limitations, can get caught up in the process and squander large amounts of time and influence to no avail. Managers who understand job classification often can influence and use it to stretch their resources.

Systems for job classification are designed to sort jobs into a planned hierarchy. The planned hierarchy becomes the criterion for the classification system. The critics of classification who question the "answer" for a specific job are actually questioning the ranking of the job in relation to the hierarchy.

The system design process focuses on the need to specify a set of clear and easily interpreted rules that, when applied, put jobs into the correct categories and levels. The combination of the rules and the job hierarchy is the job classification system. "Correctness" is a function of the criterion selected (such as the external labor market), the judgment of a committee of individuals expert in the occupations involved, or the judgments of legislators promulgated as law. All these criterion measurements reflect the values of the culture and of the world of work at the time the job classification system is developed.

After levels have been established in relation to the criterion, jobs are classified accordingly and a structure of jobs emerges. The incumbents of the jobs tend to establish a pecking order, or hierarchy within the organization based on differences in authority, wages, and the like expressed by the classification levels. It is very difficult to change relationships in the pecking order once it has been established. New systems generally encounter less resistance than changes to an old system, although there inevitably are some employees who feel that they lost because their job ended up lower in the hierarchy. As an example of resistance to change, salary relationships among federal white-collar jobs have been essentially static since the General Schedule was established in 1923.

THE JOB HIERARCHY AS LIGHTNING ROD FOR CRITICS

The public policy criticism of job classification is at a different level than the day-to-day criticism voiced by managers and employees, who are directly and often personally affected by the classification system and whose natural focus is the impact of a specific decision. The common claim is that an assigned salary grade is too low relative to the grades of other jobs or to prevailing market pay rates. The only realistic alternative is to argue that the classifier misinterpreted and misclassified the job.

If the classifier's assessment of the job is correct, the manager or job incumbent is in reality reacting to a perceived problem with the job hierarchy, perhaps that the job or job family is too low in the hierarchy or that the salaries paid at some or all levels of the hierarchy are too low. In many public systems, including the federal system, the hierarchy is locked into classification standards. Critics argue in these situations that the standard needs to be revised, but they are actually seeking higher salaries or higher rankings in the hierarchy.

Standards can get out of date over time as occupations change, however, which means that job classification results may not be credible in light of common understanding of the occupation. The cost to update standards is often an impediment. The federal government, which relies on a standards-based system, has many standards that have not been updated in decades. Yet a classification system is only as credible as its standards.

The reliance on standards or any set of static answers is a fundamental aspect of the problem. On the one hand, all job evaluation systems are designed to generate consistent answers. On the other hand, the dynamics of supply and demand economics influence labor market pay levels to shift slowly over time and to stabilize long-term job relationships. When a classification system is designed, it is locked into a set of job relationships or job hierarchy that is acceptable to all relevant groups. That hierarchy and the underlying factors that affect a job's ranking reflect shared and widely accepted values, and values are very slow to change. Level relationships within each occupation are remarkably stable over time. For example, individual education, training, and experience has for centuries been an important determinant of perceived job value in almost every society.

Relationships among occupations, however, are less stable. They are responsive to economic influences, especially in the short term. For example, rapidly changing technology may limit the supply of qualified people in an occupation and drive the pay for these individuals above the market value of jobs where there is an adequate supply. Organizations that hire in a tight labor market must make adjustments if they want to be able to hire and avoid losing qualified people. If the market changes are temporary, it may make sense to treat the salary adjustments as temporary (in the federal system, as special rates) rather than to change a job classification system. Nurses were for a number of years in short supply but currently the supply exceeds demand and pay increases are plateauing.

Some market changes, however, endure. For example, pay rates for occupations requiring college education have been going up more rapidly than blue-collar or office support occupations since the end of Work War II. This at some point dictates a change in the job hierarchy, and that logically means that classification standards need to be revised. Experience has shown, however, that increasing the assigned grades of selected occupations relative to others is difficult in a government environment, especially when the changes benefit higher-paid occupations. Corporations are largely able to avoid this problem because they typically have separate exempt (college education is a common requirement) and nonexempt (jobs that do not require college) salary structures and adjust the ranges differently each year.

Changes in the job hierarchy—that is to say, when one or more jobs are assigned to a new, higher, or lower grade—inevitably result in winners and losers. Some workers are better off, some are worse off. Inevitably the people whose jobs are to be reclassified to a lower grade are not happy campers and will take whatever actions are available to avoid this change. When the changes are based on market trends, there is at least a rationale that has a basis in reality. Too often in government the market is not directly relevant, so grade changes have to be attributed to changes in job content or job value decisions. The introduction of a new job evaluation system with new compensable factors will inevitably change the job hierarchy but without the demonstrated change in job content, which is particularly difficult to sell to adversely affected employees. These changes may require the strong support of an elected official. When the job hierarchy has been static for as long as the federal government's, history becomes a major impediment to overcome.

GETTING THE BEST FROM JOB CLASSIFICATION

Job classification is presented in many personnel manuals as an objective, even scientific, process for determining relative job worth. This is at best a partial truth. Job classification is in essence a systematic way to identify and document the relationships among jobs. However, the correctness of the relationships is based on custom and culture as reflected by the criteria used to develop the job classification system, such as the labor market or management or expert judgment. Correctness is not based on some physically verifiable fact or scientifically established theoretical model; it is based on judgments relative to job and organizational information. The only scientific component of job classification is the "science" of management. As with budgeting systems and the management of fiscal resources, job classification systems represent a tool for managers who need to manage their people. Managers must understand the process for classifying jobs and how to manage it in order to meet their needs.

As a manager, you should keep several points in mind when you request a job classification action, including all of the following.

Your Goal

Know what you want to achieve. Consider the hypothetical case of Mary, for example. She is a key part of your unit; she is competent herself and also helps all the prima donnas on the team get along with each other. In addition, she is the only woman on the team, and keeping her is essential to your diversity profile. She is building a good reputation, and other jobs at the next level are coming open in the agency. Creating a team leader position for Mary at a higher level would likely keep her on the team and free up more of your time.

Scope

Learn the full implications of getting what you want and find out what rules apply, including each of the following.

JOB CLASSIFICATION   Mary's team leader job may be classified at the same level as existing expert jobs, or creating a team leader job over other jobs on the team may cause other jobs to be classified at lower levels.

STAFFING   Mary may not meet the qualifications required for team leaders or may not be among the best qualified candidates. Or there may be other special considerations, such as giving hiring priority to a former employee who just won a lawsuit against the agency.

TRAINING   Team leader jobs may have mandatory training requirements that could take a significant amount of Mary's time and the unit's training money.

BUDGET   The money needed to cover unanticipated salary increases caused by Mary's escalation in your unit may be deducted from your division's merit pay pool.

ORGANIZATION   If team leader jobs are considered supervisory, creating Mary's team leader position could raise your ratio of supervisors to workers above the standard for a unit your size.

UNIONS   Creating Mary's team leader job may be considered a reorganization, and special clearances (including consultation with the union) may be required.

Players

Determine whose approval is needed for the classification and related personnel actions you want to achieve. Assess where you are likely to get good advice and information and tap those sources.

Classification Standards

After a job classification specialist has been assigned to review the proposed action, find out the specialist's views of what each of you should be doing and when. Ask the specialist which specific occupational classification standards may cover the types of work Mary performs. Request specific information on what differentiates between work at Mary's current level and at the higher level. Ask to see the organization charts of any similar units in your agency. Ask to see descriptions of other jobs at the higher level in situations similar to yours, and seek advice about what the impact on other jobs might be if Mary's job is moved to the higher level.

Job Description

Drafting a job description usually consumes considerable time and energy. There is no prize for original work; thus your best friend is a job description similar to what you are trying to specify for Mary that is already classified at the higher level. If you cannot find a similar job description, try to cut and paste from somewhat similar job descriptions, adding new material as necessary to describe the job. Seek advice about what, if anything, you need to do to the job description to make the classification (and the work of the job) match at the higher level.

Information

Information is a key to managing this process. Persist until you have all the information you need, as described in the previous paragraphs, and be sure you have it early on. Ensure that the classification specialist has received all the information relevant to classifying the job. It usually helps if you and the incumbent have reviewed the classification standards that will be used and have organized information about the job in the appropriate format. Show the classification specialist examples of work that match the higher level. Ask the specialist to discuss the work of the job before bringing fact-finding to a close. Some classifiers will discuss the classification decision before it is final. Others will not, due either to personal operating preferences or to human resource office policy.

The Job Classification Specialist

If you do not get the classification you want, ask why. Perhaps you do not have the higher-level work to assign or the authority to delegate. Although human resource directors can override classification specialists, they are restrained by the fact that exceptions for one manager eventually translate into exceptions for all. Misclassification links jobs to inappropriate qualifications requirements and performance standards, undermines justifications for external pay linkages, distorts internal pay relationships, and lessens accuracy of reports and statistics. If you believe the classification specialist cannot or will not consider relevant information or has misinterpreted the classification standard, you may request a second opinion or ask that someone review the specialist's work. As a manager, you shape your relationship with the job classification specialist as you shape other working relationships; all the same skills apply. Good or bad, your relationship with the classification specialist is likely to be long-term.

Paperwork

Request a list of all paperwork needed to finalize the action and negotiate a schedule with all of the players (such as the classification specialist or staffing specialist). Do your part on time; follow up on every deadline. Your diligence communicates the importance you attach to the action.

Other People

Most workers, especially good workers, see their work as centrally important. If a classification and pay level is increased in the unit, the unit manager must actively ensure that all other staff know the basis for the action and are convinced of its fairness. Even if no existing pay rates or prospects are affected, expect repercussions.

Your Boss and Your Boss's Boss

Public managers at every level are caught between too many missions and too few resources. Some managers make the mistake of assigning work to create a classification change without taking into account their boss and their boss's boss. Even job classification decisions that accurately reflect work will change internal pay relationships and, as a result, have repercussions. A manager may make a strategic decision not to coordinate change, but often changes are negative and unintended. An important part of management is managing the boss and the boss's boss, for whom all the same rules apply.

IS THERE A SOFTWARE SOLUTION?

Software solutions should be an obvious consideration. Job classification systems ride on the collection and analysis of information but can be effective only when the right information gets into the hands of decision makers. One of the important trends in the private sector for almost a decade has been the shift to computer-assisted job evaluation systems, and they have a track record that demonstrates their value. The explosion in information technology could open the door to a new generation of job classification systems.

Software is already available to classify jobs in many occupations; it produces related qualifications requirements and performance standards, and minimizes paperwork. The existing systems are generally occupation-specific. Managers can use the software from their own computer terminals. In this environment, job classification specialists are free to work on systems extension and development or to help managers make effective use of the software. Well-conceived software greatly reduces the frustration caused by job classification. It offers new possibilities for system design and provides enhanced management flexibility and, if desired, closer control.

The software developed to date for use by government agencies relies on database management architecture, which means the systems consist of large numbers of preclassified jobs or job duties. The systems are relatively inexpensive to develop but need to be updated periodically as jobs and the job environment evolve. They have trouble dealing with jobs that do follow not the pattern used to develop the system.

Expert systems represent an important but largely untested alternative. They rely on hundreds or even thousands of rules to classify jobs. The rules are those that would have been applied by experienced classifiers. Expert systems are elegant, accurate, and difficult to develop.

Automated systems in the private sector typically focus only on job evaluation and rely on statistical models that use job content data, supplied typically by an incumbent, to predict or estimate the appropriate salary grade. In contrast to traditional classification systems, they are not designed to collect data for other personnel or human resource applications; they are based on data from a sample of key jobs.

Regardless of the approach, the most important prospective difference for the future is in putting classification decisions into the hands of managers. A network or telecommunication system will be the manager's window to wide-ranging information and advice now controlled by personnel specialists. This could change the relationship between managers and classifiers forever. Personnel specialists will be able to focus on nonroutine matters and serve as consultants to managers considering possible personnel actions.

Automated systems have decided advantages. They are obviously faster—jobs can be classified in minutes—and they are more consistent; the same set of job facts always leads to the same answer. However, they cannot create better policies, procedures, or laws. They also cannot help managers avoid mistakes of judgment. By shifting the focus from personnel specialists to line managers, automation has the potential to make classification a management prerogative.

THE FUTURE OF JOB CLASSIFICATION

The National Performance Review recommendations, if followed, would effectively eliminate job classification in the federal government, although the recommendations do not specifically call for the end of the existing system. Clearly, this sentiment is shared by managers and undoubtedly elected officials in other public jurisdictions.

From a public policy perspective, however, this is not a feasible option. On some basis every employer needs some way to classify jobs. At a minimum there is a need to differentiate chemists from accountants or executive secretaries from clerk-typists. It may be that the private sector can live with less formal systems, but it too needs to document jobs and job requirements. When a job is classified, it leads to recruitment KSAs (knowledge, skills, and abilities) and performance criteria and provides a basis for assessing prevailing market pay levels. Classification information also makes it possible to audit personnel actions and address employment law issues. It also helps to define the employee's rights and entitlements. Classification on some level is essential to human resource management.

The logic of classification is basic to a number of other areas of management, such as accounting and inventory control, as well as to other professional fields, such as biology and library sciences. These are impersonal, more objective systems but the decision process is comparable. These fields could not exist without a classification system.

It is safe to assume that public employers do not need to recognize the hundreds of job series found in some government personnel systems. One of the problems since World War II has been the proliferation of new occupations and occupational specialties. Under the best of circumstances it would be a daunting challenge to stay up-to-date on all the information required to generate new classification standards for every new occupational specialty. An alternative is more generic definitions of jobs and occupations. For example, some employers have moved to adopt a generic classification standard covering clerical support jobs. The final list of occupations will always be somewhat arbitrary and therefore fail to satisfy everyone. Shortening the list means eliminating or combining job series and that can prompt resistance in people who do not want to see their identity lost or submerged with other job series.

The answer is not to throw in the towel and argue that classification is not necessary. An organization needs information about its jobs and its people. Some of the requirements are mandated by law; for example, employers need to classify jobs as exempt or nonexempt under the wage-hour laws and to be able to defend overtime pay practices. The legal requirements governing selection and recruiting create a need for job information and for documentation of applicant qualifications that are based on job classification. For many occupations, such as those in health care, there are certification and testing requirements that are uniquely defined for each occupation, which means the jobs have to be classified. For some occupations the qualification requirements change as an individual moves up the career ladder, so someone needs to determine the person's new level. In government, more so than the private sector, there has been a shared and deeply entrenched concern for fairness and consistency across agencies that requires some basis for comparing jobs and people. The need to classify jobs permeates the human resource field.

Does that mean existing classification systems should be locked in and remain sacrosanct? That is clearly not going to happen. At the federal level, the classification system has been under attack and allowed to deteriorate for more than twenty years. It has effectively lost credibility. This situation is similar to the experience in more than a few state and local jurisdictions.

There is a definite need for a new generation of systems. If the need was limited to job evaluation, there has been adequate developmental work done in the private sector and in a few public entities to develop new systems; government would not be starting from scratch (for more on this issue, see Chapter Six). However, if the federal experience is meaningful, it will be extremely difficult to gain the political support needed to fund the design and installation of new systems. Private sector systems cannot be transplanted into the public arena without some degree of modification. The value systems are not the same. If transplantation was feasible, it would have happened years ago.

In light of the multiple purposes served by a traditional job classification system, the first phase of any development initiative should be to specify the uses of job and incumbent information and then to consider possible alternatives to collect or generate this information. This means understanding and possibly reengineering the decision-making processes involved in the management of people. Involving managers and employees in the redesign initiative enhances the prospects for buy-in and acceptance—it has to become a management process.

Once there is agreement that the processes make sense, the focus shifts to the design of the support systems needed to ensure that decision makers, line managers as well as personnel or human resource specialists, have access to needed information. This is a basic systems analysis that results in system specifications. It may be that a multipurpose system is simply not a feasible alternative. However designed, the job classification system is then the engine for generating this information.

Job classification has been a centralized control system. The concept originated in an era when government had a more limited role, the work force was dramatically smaller, and work patterns were essentially static. The foundation of a centralized system is out of sync with emerging management thinking and with the reality of shrinking budgets. In the current environment, personnel decisions are clearly more complicated and sensitive and have broader implications for agency performance. Despite the importance of managing payroll costs, tight centralized control is not the key to better government.

Senior management has to agree on the goals for the new system and commit the resources needed for its development. If the goal is to develop a management system, the initiative has to start with senior management. This responsibility cannot be delegated to a task force or committee with limited time, inadequate resources, and no real power.

We can no longer afford to maintain classification systems that are strictly personnel systems. That is blatantly obvious in both the private and public sectors. In the private sector there is growing recognition that people are the only sustainable source of competitive advantage. That is to say, corporate success in the long run rides on its people. That makes people management and people management systems an important priority. It would be naive to suggest that traditional government classification systems are once again going to become important, but there is a definite need for better people management systems in government. The first problem is somehow gaining agreement that people and their performance are key to better government. That should serve to justify the investment in better systems for managing these resources.

Job classification has been the backbone of government's information system for managing jobs, people, and pay. The process supports the public need for executive control and accountability. It affects government's ability to manage its work force effectively and its ability to meet established legal requirements. The challenge presented by the need for a new generation of systems is daunting. However, the investment to develop new systems needs to be balanced against public policy and government's people management requirements. An important consideration is the readiness of managers and supervisors to make personnel action decisions. Government officials need to be confident that the support systems are in place to maintain this public trust.

Notes

1. Work assigned to one person is referred to by personnel specialists as a *position*. When several employees perform similar work, the positions are treated for classification purposes as a *job*. In common usage, *job* and *position* are often interchangeable.
2. National Partnership Council, *A Report to the President on Implementing Recommendations of the National Performance Review* (Washington, D.C.: U.S. Government Printing Office, Jan. 1994).

CHAPTER FIVE

Job Evaluation
The Search for
Internal Equity

Howard Risher
Lois R. Wise

T he widely understood purpose of job evaluation is the determination or measurement of job value. This has its origins in economic theory and has been cited in any number of internal policy statements and in the human resource literature for decades. But it is not accurate, and it establishes an unfortunate expectation for any new job evaluation system.

It is more realistic to view evaluation systems as simply an administrative mechanism for assigning jobs to a wage or salary grade or band. From this perspective the evaluation system is a component of a decision process that can help individuals be more consistent and objective, assuming those are important criteria. The system helps in making these decisions systematically and reliably—so that the same set of job facts will always result in the same decision—but does not guarantee such results. This is not unimportant, but it is a mistake to expect too much from any job evaluation system, regardless of how much time is invested in its design and implementation.

WHAT IS JOB VALUE?

There are no absolute measures of job value. That is an unequivocal statement. For things like temperature and weight, we can design instruments that generate measures that are both reliable and valid (which means any measurement instrument that has been properly designed and maintained will give us the same answer). Job value is at best a relative or comparative measure; we implicitly know and acknowledge that some jobs are more or less valuable than others. That means that the basis for evaluating jobs has to involve either a direct or indirect comparison of each job with other jobs. That comparison is the essence of job evaluation.

The basic problem in designing a job evaluation system is how to make the necessary comparisons. Jobs are complex; most organizations commit considerable resources to writing job descriptions, but everyone who gets involved in the process comes to appreciate that these documents do not capture all the information relevant to understanding a job's value. The nuances that make jobs different are one reason it is difficult to develop a solid consensus on a job's relative value. Several different job evaluation methods have been developed, although currently there are only two or three different methods in general use.

One of the inevitable problems is that the value of a job is in the eyes of the beholder. That is to say, our view of a job's value is based on our perception of the work involved and the skills needed for successful performance. Our view also depends on our, and in some respects society's, view of a job's importance. Human nature makes it all too easy for workers to believe their job is more valuable than its current salary grade indicates. Reasons for feeling undervalued and underpaid are both practical—"I want to earn more money"—and psychological-sociological—"I'm more valuable than you." Women have made the argument for over a decade that their jobs are underpaid. But if we modify the job evaluation system to placate a group of employees, it may change their perception in the short term but not their status in the long term. Meanwhile, it will shift concern with relative pay levels to other workers, because upgrading selected employees by revising the job hierarchy causes other employees to believe that their status is reduced.

Significantly, job value has only been superficially addressed under federal and state law. The interest in pay equity that emerged in the mid-1970s prompted some discussion and pressure for the adoption of universal job evaluation systems. This prompted increased interest in certain off-the-shelf systems that were already in use by prominent employers. The net result was an increase in the use of quantitative job evaluation systems, but the possibility of requiring the use of a specific system or one that met specified requirements never gained solid support in the United States. For the most part, relevant laws and judicial rulings have defined the standard for acceptable practice as the fair and consistent use of any professionally developed system. It is common, particularly in the public sector, to test a new system for its impact on protected classes; however, in the absence of absolute measures of job value the job hierarchy that is eventually accepted and the evaluation system's design are determined more by political and cost considerations than any theory or absolute criteria.

Virtually all of the widely used systems are premised on the need to identify a number of criteria that are intuitively related to job value. Jobs are in turn measured (actually, ranked is a better way to define this process) on these criteria. One of the basic job evaluation methods is referred to as *whole job ranking,* but it is less commonly used in the public sector than quantitative methods. (About one in four states reports using whole job ranking for some occupational groups.[1]) Ranking is a simple process to arbitrarily identify the most valuable job, the second most valuable, and so forth. It works well but is not completely reliable (it is not reasonable to expect to replicate the rankings if we involve different managers and supervisors). For reasons of system credibility the trend over time has been to adopt systems that base evaluation systems on a set of compensable factors that are the criteria used to assess a job's relative value.

Job value is also not expressed in dollars, although evaluation decisions clearly determine the range of base pay for each job. As organizations move to adopt incentive systems and, in the private sector, stock ownership plans, base salaries are shrinking as a percentage of an individual's total compensation. Moreover, wage and salary ranges vary over time as the labor market drives up (or in rare situations down) competitive pay levels. When we compare the value of jobs across organizations, dollars are the only basis for comparison. For example, government wage and salary ranges are often out of sync with ranges for superficially similar jobs in the private sector. Corporations may appear to value certain competencies differently than government employers, but there is no way to confirm that their jobs are truly comparable. Unfortunately it is all too easy to base job comparisons solely on relative pay levels.

From a practical perspective, organizations need a job evaluation system with at least face validity (that is to say, it is perceived as valid) to decide how much each job should be paid. Generally the relative value is expressed as a point total (the most widely used job evaluation method is referred to as *point factor*) that can be interpreted as an index that places a job in the organizational hierarchy. It is important to the organization that at least a majority of the managers and supervisors accept the hierarchy. But it is a mistake to describe the system-derived points as a measure of value, because doing so raises questions that the methodology was not designed to answer.

It is important to appreciate that most job evaluation systems were conceived and implemented at least a decade ago. This means that the compensable factors do not reflect the organizational changes of the past few years. One of the factors commonly used to evaluate managerial and supervisory jobs is the number of employees supervised; this may have made sense in a hierarchical organization, but it is clearly out of sync in a delayered or downsized structure. Factors that are contrary to the organization's needs can actually become an impediment to change. Older systems also do not reflect important recent trends such as the shift to teams, the increased emphasis on customer satisfaction, or the importance of continuous improvement. Job evaluation systems that ignore these trends do not reflect the way work roles are assessed in today's environment.

It is also important to appreciate that no two job evaluation systems will produce identical answers. When internal hierarchies are compared across organizations, individual jobs might be higher or lower in the internal hierarchy. The differences are attributable first to the choice of compensable factors. Although not as obvious, when the same factors are used but with different definitions or measurement scales, the results will differ. For example, systems covering hourly jobs commonly use physical effort as a compensable factor, accounting for perhaps 5 percent of the potential points. If we were to increase the weight for this factor to 50 percent or more, jobs that score high on it would be elevated in the job hierarchy.

If each job had an absolute value, it would be the same regardless of the evaluation system. These nuances reinforce the need to plan for acceptance of the system and its answers. The definitions and weights or relative importance of the factors have to fit the organization.

Ultimately, the system will establish a hierarchy of jobs that will be considered and assessed by everyone who sees it (at least in terms of its impact on the individual and coworkers). The factors and the way they are used are normally not important until the system begins to generate results, that is to say, until it is used to determine the relative value of jobs. If the resulting values are not credible and acceptable, the system could be scrapped. It is fundamentally important to consider the need for acceptance in designing and managing a job evaluation system. This is a lesson that has been repeatedly learned by stakeholders working to protect or enhance the interests of specific groups.

RECENT CRITICISM OF JOB EVALUATION SYSTEMS

The use of job evaluation as a management tool was more or less taken for granted until pay equity concerns were first voiced by feminists in the mid to late 1970s. This mounting criticism triggered considerable attention and the first innovative thinking about the topic in a quarter of a century. The computer-based systems that came into widespread use in the late 1980s were a direct outcome of the concerns expressed by the pay equity advocates.

More recently, critics have argued that job evaluation systems are out of sync with the way organizations now organize and manage work. One of the first of the prominent critics was Edward E. Lawler III, director of the Center for Effective Organizations, who discussed the advantages and disadvantages of job evaluation in his book *Strategic Pay*.[2] He argues that job evaluation causes or aggravates the following problems:

- *"Game playing" to gain additional job evaluation points.* The importance of job evaluation results prompts ongoing attempts to justify additional points by claiming changes in job content. It may also trigger an interest in empire building to justify higher pay.

- *Erosion of honesty and credibility.* The realization among supervisors and managers that job evaluation results can be "gamed" means that dishonesty is encouraged and may be rewarded. If inflated job descriptions result in higher grades, people look for excuses to rewrite descriptions.

- *Inflation of pay system operating costs due to need for additional administrative staff.* The conventional approach to job evaluation is based on close, centralized administration. If the evaluation process is managed properly, it necessitates an enlarged staff.

- *Overemphasis on grade changes and promotions as the basis for salary increases.* If the process is not closely managed, it becomes too easy to justify a grade increase or promotion. In some organizations, supervisors rely on reevaluation of jobs to trigger pay increases.

- *Inflation of payroll costs.* Job evaluation systems serve to increase the value of some jobs relative to prevailing market pay levels. If any jobs are paid more than market levels, it results in inflated payroll costs. This may of course be justified by strategic or political concerns.

- *Reinforcement of and increases in the importance of the job hierarchy.* The evaluation points effectively lock in and formalize the job hierarchy. In administering the evaluation system the focus is on the differences between steps in career ladders and thus on the job hierarchy.

- *Establishment of an impediment to organizational change and downsizing.* When job duties are reassigned, the relative value of affected jobs changes; some people win and others lose. Those who anticipate a reduced salary grade often resist the organizational change.

- *Promotion and perpetuation of bureaucratic management style.* The emphasis on writing job descriptions and the procedure for having a job reevaluated is distinctly bureaucratic. The conventional approach to system administration is not suited to rapid decision making.

- *Establishment of implicit limits on scope of job duties.* The focus on job duties as documented in a job description often prompts incumbents to think, "This is what I'm expected to do." This may make them reluctant to perform duties not on the description.

Lawler's criticisms may not be relevant to every organization, and it is certainly possible for the benefits of job evaluation to offset the problems. It is important to appreciate, however, that job evaluation is more than an administrative mechanism to establish pay levels. Each system affects the way workers interact with and think about their organization.

PAY EQUITY AS AN
ORGANIZATIONAL GOAL

The concern with pay equity became a public issue toward the end of the 1970s. Advocates then and for the next decade cited the gap between the average pay of men and women as evidence of pay discrimination. The data show that on average women currently earn 72 percent as much as men. Significantly, women earned less than 60 percent of the male average until the early 1980s. There has been a steady increase over the past decade.[3]

Under the Equal Pay Act, employers are required to pay employees performing essentially the same work on the same basis. Most court cases over the issue have involved people with the same job title or with similar duties. Under the law this is referred to as equal pay for equal work. Some states have gone beyond this for public employees with legislation requiring equal pay for work of equal value, which requires the use of an acceptable job evaluation process to determine each job's value. In North America, Ontario has the most extensive legislation covering all public and private employers alike.

Pay equity means different things to different groups, but the focus for salary management is on job evaluation systems that evidence gender neutrality. For pay equity advocates the goal is to close the gap between male and female pay levels. This, however, would require dramatic shifts in the occupations of men and women or for an organization to ignore the labor market pay levels for female-dominated jobs and arbitrarily adjust female pay levels to close the gap. The occupational distribution of males and females is, however, not pay discrimination but occupational segregation.

There are several basic and interrelated reasons for the gap; it is important to understand them as background for reconsidering job evaluation systems.

First, the critics of job evaluation systems argue that choosing compensable factors and assigning weight to (that is, specifying the relative importance of) the factors knowingly or unknowingly creates bias, so that greater value is assigned to traditional male jobs than traditional female jobs. This is a technical issue that can be tested and controlled prior to system implementation. Any changes will affect the relative pay levels of men and women by increasing the pay of female-dominated jobs, which could potentially be disruptive and costly. Still, these policy issues need to be addressed.

A second, related argument is that job evaluation systems are designed to perpetuate pay relationships in the labor market and that market-dictated pay levels reflect employer discrimination against women. There is undoubtedly some truth to this, and some government agencies have adopted policies to prevent or minimize the problem. One alternative is to base the system's design on market data limited to male-dominated jobs, which effectively ensures that any possible market bias affecting women will not be incorporated into the new system. This does, however, mean that payroll costs will be higher than if both male and female jobs were involved in designing the system.

The third and generally most significant argument in terms of dollar impact is that women have been channeled into traditionally low-paying jobs. The solution to this could involve a change in the pay system, but the change that would have the biggest impact is adopting new hiring and promotional criteria that change the composition of the workforce. There has been a gradual shift in female occupational choice over time that has only recently begun to affect the pay gap.

For several years in the mid-1980s, pay equity was an issue that triggered concern in the private sector human resource community, but it is probably accurate to say that this era has ended in the United States. This is in sharp contrast with Europe, where pay equity has gained ground in the 1990s. The push for pay equity coincided with the first meaningful use of computers in human resource management, and that prompted a high level of interest starting in 1985, when consulting firms first started marketing computer-assisted job evaluation systems. These systems are now routinely used in many corporations, although as support for job evaluation has waned in the corporate world the number of newly installed systems has dropped significantly. The advantage of the computer, in addition to enhanced response time, is that it provides at least a perceived increase in objectivity and in systematic, unbiased decisions.

Starting in this same era a number of government employers began to take steps to address pay equity concerns. In the most recent report by the National Committee on Pay Equity (NCPE),[4] forty-two states were reported to have conducted research or made an effort to study the issue in state government. In other states similar data was collected by women's organizations, unions, or others. They reported that the research in twenty-four states included a formal pay equity study that used a job evaluation system to identify comparable jobs. In twenty states the research resulted in salary adjustments to incumbents in female-dominated jobs to provide greater equity.

Pay equity has also been an issue at the county and municipality level. Only Minnesota has a state-mandated pay equity requirement covering all public entities. Among other states, only California, Massachusetts, New York, Washington, and Wisconsin have seen a high level of activity in local government. Almost without exception, pay equity activity has occurred in places where workers are organized for collective bargaining.

Among colleges and universities a high percentage have probably done some form of pay equity analysis comparing the salaries of female and male faculty members. This is true in both private and public institutions. The American Association of University Professors and similar faculty groups frequently took the lead in pushing for these studies and issued reports on how to conduct the analyses. With faculty, of course, job value is effectively displaced by rank-in-person arguments and the emphasis in analyses is on a comparison of individual salaries relative to personal demographic characteristics and professional credentials.

The federal government used its personnel data files to analyze the pay of female workers, but because these studies were done during the Reagan and Bush administrations they were not fully accepted as credible or valid. Not until 1989 did the Government Accounting Office contract with a consultant to undertake an independent pay equity study, but by that time support for pay equity had begun to wane, and the results were ignored.

Support for pay equity in the United States has effectively evaporated, partly because the results for women were so disappointing; NCPE-compiled data on activity in the public sector have been essentially unchanged since 1990. Occasionally a public employer still undertakes a pay equity analysis, but pay equity advocates have lost some of their political support, and government leaders have shifted their focus to other concerns. Interest in the subject by the corporate world has also evaporated, and in the absence of a legislated requirement that goes beyond the Equal Pay Act it seems unlikely that it will regain the importance it had in the mid-1980s. Although there is still an argument that female-dominated jobs are underpaid, it would be surprising in larger U.S. organizations, either public or private, to find females and males in equal jobs paid significantly different wages.

Several factors may account for diminished support of pay equity in the public sector. One obvious reason is that the states that were particularly receptive to the idea have already tried to put such plans into effect. The limited success in those jurisdictions may have discouraged other public employers. By the end of 1980s there was also a backlash that arguably may be associated with the increasingly conservative viewpoints of politicians elected to office. An issue in this opposition is the recognized cost to increase affected female salaries. The time is past when such legislation can slip by unopposed as it did in Minnesota. Finally, the criticism of job evaluation systems has recently triggered interest in newer, more flexible salary management models such as competency-based pay.

Perhaps the important long-term impact of the pay equity movement has been the heightened sensitivity to the impact of job evaluation systems on workers. There was very little interest in job evaluation in the first half of the 1970s. Pay equity prompted the first broad-based efforts in two decades to develop better systems, and these efforts led to the automated systems that are now widely used. Now when a new system is developed, a more or less standard step is to test its impact on female and minority workers. Public employers at all levels have introduced new systems in the past decade and in each case it is probably safe to assume that the new system was tested and, if necessary, modified before implementation. When a new system is installed and salary grades assigned, the salaries of affected workers are adjusted to fit the new range. The pay adjustments may not be referred to as equity adjustments but the effect is the same. Some pay equity advocates may disagree, but there has been considerable progress in addressing concerns about pay disparities in the two decades since pay equity first surfaced as a feminist concern.

Despite the lack of support for pay equity as a solution to the male-female wage gap in the United States, the developments in this country have had significant impacts in other countries. In Canada, for example, the pay equity movement in the provinces has been taken further than in the United States. The provinces are guided by the Canadian Human Rights Act, which requires federal workers (about

10 percent of the nation's workforce) to receive equal pay for work of equal value. Ten of the thirteen Canadian provinces have some form of pay equity legislation. The statute in Ontario requires public and private employers to take a proactive approach to eliminate any evidence of gender bias in salary management. Point factor systems are also gaining popularity in Europe, where rulings by the European Court have been interpreted to mean that proven approaches are a needed defense against charges of sex discrimination.

ALTERNATIVE JOB EVALUATION METHODS

Virtually all government employers use some form of job evaluation, which includes any method for systematically assigning jobs to wage or salary grades. The exceptions at the state level are Florida and Mississippi. Michigan has a job evaluation system, but does not use it to establish pay levels. Job evaluation systems are also widely used by public employers throughout the world. (Small private and public employers, however, often do not have or need job evaluation systems.)

For employers seeking a new job evaluation system, there are three realistic alternatives: a traditional classification system, a point factor system, or an automated version of one of the conventional systems. Evaluation systems adopted in the past decade or so have generally relied on the conventional logic, but using computers makes it possible to consider more job information in the evaluation process, enhance the system's perceived objectivity, and speed up the decision process.

Many corporations rely on what is referred to as market pricing, with salary grades determined by assigning jobs to ranges that provide for competitive pay opportunities. With this approach, internal equity is often not a consideration; the only goal is to maintain competitive salaries. Although no organization can completely ignore the labor market, the market-based philosophy may not be a viable alternative for government.

Outside of government, classification systems are essentially unknown. Salary administration specialists in the private sector have not had reasons to work with classification systems. Until the interest in computer-based systems started a few years ago, virtually every evaluation system introduced over the last couple of decades was a point factor system. The Hay system[5] was far and away the most widely used. Companies that chose to use another system or to develop their own almost always fell back on the point factor method. This has changed recently only in that employers now also want to consider systems that rely on computerized administration.

Point factor systems, which are used in about half of the states, are premised on the idea that relative job value depends on the importance of a set of compensable factors or criteria for assessing value. The generic factors—skill, effort, responsibility, and working conditions—are widely recognized as relevant to job value, and virtually every other factor can be categorized into one of these four. Factors such as problem-solving skills or exposure to hazardous conditions are typical of the long lists of factors found in evaluation systems. For each factor, there is a measurement or ranking scale with degree levels or steps defined by statements describing the level. The following list shows the compensable factors used in the federal Factor Evaluation System (FES), which may be the most widely used in the public sector.

Compensable Factors Used in the FES

- Knowledge required by the position (kinds of knowledge and skills required, how they are used)
- Supervisory controls (how work is assigned, employee responsibilities, how work is reviewed)
- Guidelines (nature of guidelines for performing work, judgment required)
- Complexity (nature of assignment, difficulty in determining what needs to be done, originality required)
- Scope and effect (purpose and impact of work)
- Personal contacts
- Purpose of contacts
- Physical demands
- Work environment

Jobs are evaluated by comparing them with the factor definitions deciding to assign them to one of the levels. Each job is ranked on this basis, factor by factor. This is the heart of conventional job evaluation. The process can be time consuming; in concept it takes considerable time to collect and interpret job information.[6] Regardless of how the evaluation decision is structured, it depends on someone's interpretation of a job description and the quality of the job information. Either a job evaluation committee or a job analyst (classifier) decides how to evaluate or score the job in question on each factor. These decisions require the evaluator to translate the job information into compensable factor terms. This is inherently a subjective process.

A key to the design of a point factor system is the process for determining the factor weights and for assigning points to each level. The final evaluation is the total of the points across factors, so the weighting system effectively controls how high or low in the final ranking each job falls. For example, if problem solving is a factor that accounts for 25 percent of the points, it would benefit a job that is scored high on this factor, such as systems analyst. If instead physical dexterity is a highly rated factor, jobs involving manual skills will be elevated in the job hierarchy.

Factor weights can be established arbitrarily (without the benefit of any underlying analyses) or based on statistical analyses. The arbitrary approach starts with someone allocating 100 percent of the points across factors (for example, the highest level of knowledge might be worth 400 points and the highest of physical demands worth 75 points) and then for each factor down the defined degree levels. The distribution of points is in concept based on the relative importance of the factors and need to be credible within the organization. The statistical approach involves multiple regression analysis, for which management needs to agree on the appropriate salary grades for selected benchmark positions. The regression analysis is planned to produce a statistical model that generates the planned grades. The weights for the federal Factor Evaluation System were defined with statistical analyses.

The selection and definition of factors and their relative weight or importance are organizational decisions. To be sure, it is possible to adopt a previously developed or off-the-shelf system. It would certainly be quicker to adopt FES, which was designed for government, or any other system, but that assumes the values reflected in the factors are the same across organizations. Furthermore, systems designed in the past reflect the organizational thinking of the past, and every existing system has critics who are convinced it is flawed. Relying on another organization's system may have made sense a few years ago, but new ideas have emerged, such as the importance of customer service and teams, that need to be built into a system to make it credible in today's organizational climate.

The possibilities for automating the evaluation process generally involve the development of a statistical model where information related to the compensable factors is used to estimate or predict the appropriate salary grade. The models are analogous to econometric models and are developed with multiple regression techniques. Typically, employees are asked to respond to structured questions[7] that provide information about their jobs. The responses are then reviewed and approved by at least one level of supervision before the data are used to evaluate the job.

The heart of automated systems of this type is sometimes referred to as the policy-capturing statistical model or equation. The model captures a planned policy in that it is developed to predict previously agreed-upon answers. That means, for example, that if accountants are to be assigned to grade 6, then the model is designed to use information relevant to these positions to predict the planned answers. Generally, with well-planned job evaluation models the predicted values are within plus or minus half a grade. This is a measure of a system's validity. The models are also reliable because the same data will always result in the same estimated value.

Automated systems facilitate the collection and analysis of job information, minimize the cost of data collection, and use structured-response questions that provide for an explicit comparison of data for multi-incumbent jobs and across people and jobs. They allow easy data collection that makes it practical to incorporate more data into the evaluation process, and the automated manipulation and analysis of the data reduce opportunities for evaluator bias. As automated systems that rely on policy capturing can be readily tested and modified to eliminate or minimize gender bias, it may be easier for them to gain organizational acceptance. But the disadvantages are that it costs more to design such systems and that reliance on multivariate analyses make the models difficult to explain and understand.

The questionnaires are designed to collect data relevant to an understanding of each compensable factor. From a different perspective, the questions serve to define the factor. For example, if the factor is technical knowledge, the questions might focus on the type of education required and the level of decision making. The questions tell respondents what is relevant to understanding each factor. Generally, two to five questions can provide adequate information to understand a factor. That means an evaluation system with ten compensable factors could be driven by a questionnaire with twenty to fifty specific questions.

Exhibit 5.1 shows the questions related to the factor *planning* as they would appear on a computer screen from a job evaluation system recently installed by a large public employer. With this system, employees respond interactively to questions related to compensable factors identified and defined by a task force. The advantage of an interactive system is that the answers to early questions can be used to control the screens an employee actually sees and thus reduce the number of questions he or she needs to answer. This means, for example, that managers and supervisors can be asked questions

---

PLANNING

Type the number of the ONE statement that describes for this job the employee's responsibility for planning his or her own work or the work of others. Use the Up and Down arrow keys to scroll through the choices.

HELP

1. Employee's work assignments are planned or determined by supervisor or others.   1

2. Employee plans and prioritizes own work.   1

3. Employee maintains calendars or schedules associated with projects or department operations.   1

4. Employee develops short-term (weekly or monthly) work schedules for projects or staff.   1

5. Employee develops complete detailed plans outlining resource requirements, timing, and cost.   1

6. Employee develops a detailed plan that reflects the integration of information or data from multiple sources. Plans typically have an impact on individuals or groups of individuals.   1

7. Employee assembles and consolidates multiple detailed plans into one comprehensive plan.   1

8. Employee manages the transformation of conceptual plans into detailed plans that can be used to allocate funds and resources. Plans require a thorough analysis of large quantities of data gathered from multiple sources.   1

9. Employee develops conceptual plans that outline major changes in services or operations within an agency.   1

Exhibit 5.1.   Analyst Question Text.

related to their responsibility for subordinates, and nonsupervisors can skip these screens and thereby reduce the time to complete the questionnaire.

The framework for the automated systems developed to date is an expanded version of the rationale for conventional point factor systems. The models are capable of handling more information; these systems are certainly faster, but they do not address any of the points voiced by critics other than the staff time required for administration. From a pay equity perspective the policy-capturing approach has the decided advantage that it makes it significantly easier to test for possible discrimination and also reduces possible user bias in system administration. If there is a policy decision to upgrade female-dominated positions, new factors or new factor weights can be introduced to accomplish this.

SELECTION OF COMPENSABLE FACTORS

The heart of a job evaluation system is its set of compensable factors. The choice and definition of factors is a fundamentally important policy consideration. Research has shown that from a technical perspective a system can function effectively with only three or four factors and suggests that adding more does not enhance validity or reliability. However, from a credibility and user acceptance perspective the factors have to take into account all relevant job characteristics. That often means new systems end up with anywhere from six to twelve factors. The FES factors are typical of the mix of job characteristics considered in point factor systems (although these factors reflect the thinking in 1970 when FES was being developed).

In designing an automated job evaluation system, almost any set of factors can be made to fit the policy-capturing objective. The analytical capacity in most statistical software makes it relatively easy to develop "what if" models and to test the impact of data for different factors (or questions). It may make sense to solicit input from interested stakeholders both to identify possible factors and to assess their acceptability. Comparable worth advocates have been particularly sensitive to factors that can be shown to be gender neutral. Statistical software makes it possible to test the impact of each factor on different occupations and also on protected groups.

If the existing salary program has a set of compensable factors, even if they are not formally integrated into a system (for example, some systems refer to job content issues considered in classifying jobs), they should be assessed for possible inclusion in the new system. People are always more comfortable with evolutionary rather than revolutionary changes. Moreover, employees have read or heard repeated references to the importance of the old factors. There should be a good reason for scrapping those factors in favor of new ones.

The factors finally selected should reflect the nature of the jobs covered under the system. If, for example, the system is to cover managers, the factors need to emphasize managerial issues such as fiscal responsibility. If the system is going to cover professional positions, technical knowledge and expertise should be prominent. It is advantageous to consider the choice of factors as a policy statement: "This is what makes your job valuable. This is what we are paying for." It also is useful to consider the message the factors send to covered employees. The factors communicate organizational priorities and values, and thus it is important to rely on factors that are consistent with the mission and goals.

From this perspective, public employers have different values than corporations oriented to the bottom line. The differences may be a matter of definition and nuance, but they are apparent when factors are discussed. In the same way, public school systems and colleges differ in their values. Group or consensus decision making, for example, is important in any educational institution and needs to be reflected in factors related to management and decision making.

Following are the factors incorporated in an automated system developed by the author for the Dade County (Florida) Public Schools. Each factor was defined by a series of questions and included in a questionnaire completed by all nonteaching staff.

1. Knowledge and skills
    Professional knowledge
    Communication skills
    Problem-solving skills
2. Effort
    Complexity
    Autonomy
3. Responsibility
    Instructional programs

Noninstructional programs and systems

Expenditures

Supervision

Contacts (internal and external)

Facilities and equipment

Information and records

The differences between organizations and the occupations to be covered by the system should be considered in system design. The tradition in the public sector has been to cover all employees under a single system. This practice overrides the obvious cultural and operational differences across agencies. If, for example, evaluation systems were designed independently for a transportation department and a public health department, there could well be significant differences. For similar reasons, evaluation systems limited to professional positions would intuitively be based on different factors than those that cover manual workers.

One design question is the level of coverage of a new job evaluation system. Traditionally, public employers have had omnibus systems that cover, or at least appear to cover, all employees. Police and fire workers, for example, have often been covered under classification systems but not included when there was a shift to point factor job evaluation systems. Similarly, managers have often been excluded. For reasons that have never been adequately documented, support personnel working for legislators and judges are often paid under separate salary programs. Public employers with quantitative job evaluation systems have often had different approaches or systems for different tiers or specialized subunits in the organization, driven in large part by the realization that one set of compensable factors may not fit the full spectrum of jobs.

That this has been a prevalent practice opens the door to the possibility of designing systems specific to an agency. Cultural differences alone could justify such a decision; a public health department probably needs a different system than a transportation department. Indeed, the federal government is moving in this direction, and North Carolina is also considering a change in its program that could allow it.

A system's accuracy and credibility does depend to a degree on the homogeneity of the occupations covered. If there were a need for a system that covers a single occupation and career ladder (for nurses, for example), the factors could be specific to the occupation and defined to include occupational jargon. A system covering diverse occupations, in contrast, has to rely on abstract concepts (such as knowledge) and nonspecific language. When covering diverse occupations, a system will be less accurate and more difficult to defend because it opens the door to arguments over the interpretation of nonspecific words and phrases. Such problems are the trade-off for a broadly applicable system.

Realistically, whenever a group of managers or employees is invited to discuss the selection of factors, group members will stumble somewhat at first; it is unlikely that they have ever been asked to think about the issue previously. They will need a period of education and ongoing guidance, but they can successfully reach conclusions that will have decided advantages over factor sets dictated by senior executives or found in off-the-shelf systems. Factors should be credible, and there is no better way to ensure it than by asking people who will be covered under the system to play a role in system development.

PLANNING THE ANSWERS

Assigned salary grades are the key to system acceptance. They must conform with the shared perception of the job hierarchy. If too many jobs end up higher or lower in the hierarchy than people anticipate, it could destroy the system's credibility and become a roadblock to implementation. If jobs had an absolute value this would not be an issue, but it is definitely possible to plan answers to salary grade questions so that they are critical to system design; as others have observed, a system that cannot be implemented is no system at all.

Job evaluation systems generate points or other measures of a job's relative value, which are in turn converted into salary grades. Grades trigger reactions from employees or supervisors; they effectively control salary levels and therefore drive payroll costs. If a new evaluation system raises the grades of jobs, it increases payroll costs; lowering grades reduces the payroll. The impact on the payroll needs to be estimated before the system design is finalized and the system implemented.

The answers can be planned in five different ways, and the choice among them is central to the way employees view a new system. New systems are actually planned around a limited number of benchmark jobs, not all jobs, and the focus is on the rationale for the salary grades for those jobs. The objective in planning a new system is to create one that results in the benchmark jobs being assigned to the planned grades. The system design phase involves analyses to determine the appropriate allocation of points across compensable factors and degree levels so that the point total for each benchmark job leads to the desired salary grade. This necessitates repeated system testing and refinement.

The least disruptive strategy (because employees inevitably react to salary grade changes) is to plan the new system to perpetuate existing salary grades. Existing grades may not represent completely acceptable answers, but employees usually have trouble accepting change. The first step in the design process is the selection of jobs that key people agree are currently in the appropriate grades.

A second alternative is to rely on an evaluation system developed and used in another organization. Then the answers will be consistent with those in the other organization. Using the federal FES, for example, will generate a job hierarchy similar to the federal government's. That may be appropriate if there are enough similarities across the organizations. If the system is sold as being universal, whatever that is, it may make it easier to gain acceptance. There may have been too much criticism of older systems, however, to make this feasible.

A third alternative, typical among corporations, is to design a new job evaluation system around grades and ranges aligned with competitive pay levels. If the market suggests that a secretary should be paid $18,000, for example, the competitive salary range has a midpoint at or close to that level. The job evaluation system is then designed to result in market-based grades. Each of the benchmark jobs is assigned to a competitive salary range and the point totals for each job are planned to lock the jobs into the grades. The planned grades are used to develop the evaluation system.

Another private sector strategy is to meet with managers throughout the organization and ask: "Based on your operational goals and organizational structure, which job will be the most important to the successful achievement of your goals? Which will be the second most important?"—and the third, fourth, and so on. If the manager has access to market data to help make the decisions, the jobs can be arrayed in a hierarchy that is designed to support the mission and contribute to the organization's operations. The strategy may result in above-market pay levels for some jobs where higher-caliber individuals are needed and other levels that are below market. This, however, is completely acceptable in a corporate environment if the differences support the business strategy.

The fifth strategy is to focus primarily on the relative weights of the factors (for example, under a policy edict that problem solving is to account for 15 percent of the total points) and to pay less attention to the resulting salary grades. This approach is often referred to in textbooks. The resulting weights should be consistent with the importance of the organization's value system. This may have an intuitive appeal but can result in unexpected situations where new salary grades are considered to be too high or too low, making it necessary to revise the initial weights to correct the salary grades.

Employees react to job evaluation results based on how their salary grade affects their salary and on how it compares with relevant others. That is to say, the system's credibility and final acceptance is decided employee by employee. This makes it important to plan the design and implementation process to enhance prospects for acceptance. It is often advantageous to start with focus groups to help understand the problems with the current system. Eventually, there has to be a general consensus that the system is fair and equitable. That depends on the final salary grades more than on any of the preceding work steps or underlying theories.

INVOLVING EMPLOYEES IN THE SYSTEM DESIGN PHASE

Traditionally, the design of job evaluation systems has been a "backroom" project with little or no involvement by employees except for their role in rewriting job descriptions. In many situations even managers and supervisors had little involvement in the system design process. That is changing in the private sector as well as in education and other not-for-profit employers. This is consistent with the increasing importance of empowerment and the involvement of workers in decisions that affect them.

Their role in the design process is normally limited to the selection of compensable factors and the definition of degree levels (or the wording of questions). This is an important role that ensures that the system reflects organizational values and is credible to employees. It is difficult for employees to criticize a new system if they have played a prominent role its design.

It is not as feasible to involve employees in the other side of the evaluation system, the planned answers. The final salary grades do of

course have significant implications for an organization and its operating costs. The planned answers will also affect an organization's ability to hire and retain adequately qualified employees. If employees are
asked to become involved in the system design process, they need to
understand the logic used to develop planned salary grades. They may
be asked to react to the grades for the benchmark positions, and they
may have useful suggestions. However, they need to understand why
the grades should remain a management prerogative. Workers are
adults, so it should not surprise them that management wants to
retain control over certain pay issues. If the organization has reasonable labor-management relations, the workers will appreciate an honest explanation and go on from there.

The typical employee task force is very serious about its involvement and agonizes over even unimportant decisions. Its members
want their coworkers to accept their decisions and want to reinforce
management's decision to open the door to an expanded role for
employees. They are at least as concerned with fairness and equity as
managers.

Realistically, there are some implications to involving employees in
the design process. Employers covered under federal labor-management
legislation may need to be aware of a recent case that came before the
National Labor Relations Board (NLRB), for example. It involved
a company, Electromation, that had employees serving on committees looking at bargainable issues; the NLRB decided that the committees had a status that effectively made them illegal company
unions. This may not be applicable to government employers, but the
issue raises questions about the appropriate role of employees in the
design of pay programs.

One of the realities in the private sector is that there is support for
changing the laws to fit the current environment. Most of the laws
governing labor-management relations were enacted in the 1930s,
including the Fair Labor Standards Act that defines the difference
between exempt and nonexempt jobs. The emerging paradigm and
redefined role of workers makes some of the legal requirements suspect. A number of leading corporations have formed the Labor Policy Association as a Washington-based lobby group to work for new
enabling legislation.

Aside from the legal constraints, employees generally relish their
expanded role in making these decisions. To be sure, the selection of
employees to serve on a system design task force has to be carefully
planned. They have to be seen by coworkers as credible representatives.

If there are important employee groups, defined by occupation or demographic characteristics, these should be represented. It also may be advantageous to involve the more vocal critics of management so that they have an opportunity to play a role in system design and therefore be co-opted.

As long as the ground rules for the task force reserve for management the decisions that affect payroll costs, the advantages of involving employees easily offset any disadvantages. The ground rules need to be defined—employees expect constraints—but there is actually little of substance to lose and a lot to gain. Trying to keep the plan design work as a back-room initiative may in fact become the reason for a new system's failure to gain acceptance.

TESTING THE SYSTEM
PRIOR TO IMPLEMENTATION

A new job evaluation system will always change the grades for some positions. That will trigger a reaction from both the workers in the affected jobs as well as from unaffected workers in other related work groups. The new system will formally change the hierarchy and, regardless of the validity of the new grade assignments, that will be difficult for some workers to accept.

The new system will inevitably produce winners and losers, and that needs to be considered in evaluating it. The employees who end up in higher grades are not going to be a problem, although a few will probably push for even higher grades. Every system that affects the status and income of employees effectively has stakeholders who will work as a group to protect their interests. The time to plan around the anticipated reactions is before the new system is rolled out.

The new grades will also affect the available range of salaries for workers moving into new grades. That will affect the payroll. It will also create the need for *red circle* and *green circle* pay rates. The former are salaries that are now above the maximum of the new salary range; the latter are salaries below the range minimums.[8] These changes need to be understood, assessed in terms of acceptability, and policy decisions made before the new system is announced and implemented.

If the answers are not fully acceptable, and it is unlikely that they will be at first, then the system needs to be revised and tested until it generates more acceptable answers. The answers can be controlled by modifying the factor (or question) weights, and the testing can be done relatively easily with appropriate software. This may take time, but it is manageable and necessary to ensure the success of the new system.

PLANNING FOR A NEW JOB EVALUATION SYSTEM

Job evaluation systems are not well understood. As they are more or less behind the scenes and relevant to employees only when there is reason to believe their salary grade should be reconsidered, most employees do not normally need to understand the system. Moreover, for reasons that go back to a different era, most organizations, private as well as public, do not do an effective job of communicating how their system works. If anything, employees have a distrust of the system that is attributable in part to the failure to communicate.

The failure to communicate is surprising in light of the importance of the job evaluation results. Existing systems are normally a focus of attention only when a specific job or group of jobs needs to be reevaluated. The introduction of a new system, in contrast, affects all covered employees and is one of the most potentially disruptive changes that an organization can undertake. All will be interested, if not anxious, about the impact on their wage or salary level. It is almost inevitable that there will be a level of dissatisfaction with the results. This makes it an important organizational change, and it is decidedly advantageous for workers to feel comfortable with both the goals and the intent in moving to a new system.

In today's environment there is much more concern with the opinions of people affected by changes in policies and practices. In an earlier era, when the development of new pay systems was handled in secrecy, the focus was on the ease of program installation and administration, not on system acceptance. The choice of a new system was based and sold to senior management on the use of the system in other organizations. Pay equity changed that; now the concern with how a new system will affect specific groups is at least equally important.

The introduction of a new job evaluation system also has consequences for the payroll that need to be carefully analyzed. A new system means some jobs will be upgraded; some will also be downgraded, but that rarely means individual salaries will be reduced. At a time when government budgets are under intense pressure, it is important to appreciate that the cost of a new evaluation system can be significant, but it is manageable. The concerns about equity that often trigger the interest in a new system need to be balanced with the implications for government operations.

Equity is an abstract concept and dependent on individual perception; it cannot be defined or measured except with reference to the perceptions of individuals. Thus equity is a relative term that involves comparison of pay levels across the organization. The point of comparison, all too often although not surprisingly, is to a group of highly paid jobs, and the argument is that the people expressing the equity argument should be paid more. It would be very unusual to find higher-paid workers contending that they are paid too much relative to lower-paid workers. An understanding of equity concerns is important to the design of a new system.

The older, traditional systems have been heavily criticized by pay equity advocates. The critics have argued that traditional systems overstate the importance of job characteristics that are important to male-dominated jobs (such as physical strength) and understate those important to female-dominated jobs (such as communication, manual dexterity, and customer or client service). This criticism affected the credibility and effectively destroyed the utility of some previously popular systems. Many of the older systems were modified in response to the critics, but the changes are sometimes viewed as Band-Aids and the systems are still viewed as part of the problem.

The process orientation that has emerged over the past few years has reinforced the value of buy-in and ownership. Experience has also proven that it is relatively easy to design a job evaluation system that is credible and acceptable to covered workers. The phrase *process orientation* refers to the strategy and the role of employees in the work plan used to design and implement a new system. At one extreme, covered employees can be completely excluded from this process. At the other extreme, they can be responsible for the entire project. There are, to be sure, a range of possibilities between the extremes but the redefined role for employees is an important philosophical and strategic consideration.

There have been more changes in job evaluation practices in the past ten years than in all the years from the end of World War II through the mid-1980s. The computer is primarily responsible for the new ideas. Not only do computers facilitate statistical analyses but they also make it possible to respond rapidly and effectively to concerns about salary grades. Virtually all of the automated systems are still based on the traditional decision-making logic, but the use of computers provides a dramatic leap forward. As organizations move toward local and wide-area computer networks, the next generation of job evaluation systems will make it possible to delegate day-to-day responsibility to line managers. That could effectively take the administrative control out of the hands of personnel specialists. The impediments to this change are cultural, not technical.

When organizations make the decision to move to a new job evaluation system, the technical considerations are now relatively easy to address. This opens the door to an increased concern for internal political considerations and for the employee relations strategy. One of the initial planning sessions should focus on the organizational goals in moving to a new system. The more specific the goals, the easier it is to determine if the new system is successful. A related consideration is the value of fully understanding why a new system is necessary and planning the new system to fully meet organizational needs.

One of the basic questions relates to the role of managers and supervisors in the administration of the new system. It has been easy in most organizations to blame unpopular decisions on the personnel department. As organizations shift more to management accountability, this can be defined to include accountability for people management, including the management of subordinate compensation. This possibility needs to be balanced with the traditional personnel overview responsibility for workforce management issues.

Another basic issue is the expected nature of the changes in the organization over the next few years. If the foreseeable future is as dynamic as the past decade, organizations will be very different by the end of the century. In the past, job evaluation systems were installed without any thought about their future obsolescence. That is unrealistic in today's environment, and if acceptability is an important criterion then it is essential to do a little crystal-ball gazing to try to anticipate future organizational changes that will affect the system. As difficult as that may be, it would be shortsighted to introduce a system today that may have to be replaced in a year or two.

A future orientation prompts a question about the role of job evaluation in tomorrow's organizations. The high level of interest in new ideas like broad banding suggests that traditional job evaluation systems will be less important in the future. Although it is premature to contend that job evaluation will be discontinued, if one were to extrapolate from the shift in organizational thinking in the past year or two, clearly organizations are placing less emphasis on the more precise or exact measures of job value. There is a trade-off between the time and resources needed to maintain a job evaluation system and the organizational benefits derived from the system. In the future it may be harder to justify this use of increasingly limited resources. There will always, however, be a need for some type of management system to control payroll costs.

Public employers more than private companies need to be able to demonstrate that salaries are being effectively managed and that the system treats people fairly. This makes some form of system almost mandatory. Employees have to be assigned to a salary range or band, and this has to be done systematically. There are several stakeholders who have to at least accept the decision process. In light of the conflicting needs and agendas, that is not an easy standard to satisfy.

Notes

1. Unless otherwise noted, data related to state practices are based on a 1995 survey conducted by Lois Wise.
2. Edward E. Lawler III, *Strategic Pay: Aligning Organizational Strategies and Pay Systems* (San Francisco: Jossey-Bass, 1990).
3. U.S. Census Bureau, *Current Population Reports,* Series P–60 (Washington, D.C.: U.S. Government Printing Office, 1995).
4. National Committee on Pay Equity, Newsletter, Sept. 12, 1993.
5. The Hay system was developed and introduced after World War II. Marketed by the consulting firm Hay Associates, it relies on three broad compensable factors: know-how, problem solving, and accountability.
6. The process on paper is time consuming, but realistically an experienced job evaluation specialist can assess a job by skimming a job description and tentatively assigning it to a salary grade in a few minutes. That preliminary evaluation may be off by a grade or possibly two. The time is spent developing the rationale and in drafting an explanation for the files. This is decidedly different than the picture painted by the typical personnel function.
7. Structured questions generally involve checking off a box or filling in a blank to answer questions expressed in a quantitative format related to job content. These data are treated as independent variables in the analysis.
8. Workers in red circle jobs are commonly not eligible for salary increases until range increases over time are enough to catch up to and encompass their salary. Workers in green circle jobs are generally granted salary increases to bring their salary to their new range minimum.

CHAPTER SIX

Rewarding Skills in the Public Sector

Nina Gupta

As we approach the twenty-first century, more and more segments of society are adopting the maxim that smaller is better. In the private sector many businesses are downsizing (or, euphemistically, rightsizing); in the public sector Congress continues to debate reducing "big government" and elaborate bureaucratic structures. The challenge is to reduce waste and efficiency and at the same time improve productivity and economic well-being. Simple cuts in bureaucratic structures may lower costs, but they are apt to reduce revenues or services concomitantly. So we must reduce the number of people and also ensure that those who remain give us their best. This is indeed a daunting task. It cannot be accomplished by just telling people they must do more "or else." A punitive approach may work in the short term, but in the long run it is quite likely to be self-defeating. As scholars of bureaucratic structures, it is incumbent upon us to come

I would like to thank G. Douglas Jenkins Jr. for his many helpful comments on a previous draft of this chapter.

up with solutions to the challenge that accomplish both society's short-term and long-term interests. A basic look back at what makes people tick may be useful as a starting point.

Inherent in this chapter (and indeed in this book) is the assumption that one of the most critical things that makes people tick, at least in the workplace, is money. To set up reasonable administrative systems, we must use money (that is, people's pay) in the best way possible.

WHY DO PEOPLE DO WHAT THEY DO?

Perhaps it would be nice for people to do things just for the good of the organization. Unfortunately, for the most part this is not what happens. Most people first do what they think is good for themselves. As organizational decision makers, our task is to create systems where people do what is good for themselves, and in doing so also do what is good for the organization. This highlights three essential issues that must be addressed for effective use of human resources:

- *What behaviors do we want people to exhibit?* The first challenge is to identify carefully what it is we want people to do. Do we want large quantities of work, or do we want good quality of work? Do we want good client relationships, or are we willing to sacrifice some quality to gain speed of service delivery? Do we want specialization, or do we want versatility? The answers may seem self-evident, but in this less-than-ideal world we must make trade-offs and choose only a few of all possible desired outcomes. For the most part, organizations do not conduct a thorough and comprehensive analysis of this issue before setting up their bureaucratic systems.
- *What do people want from work?* Obviously, there are many things people can and do get out of work, but it would be a mistake to assume that money is not important. If it were not for pay, all our organizations would be volunteer organizations. How many people would work in these volunteer organizations day in and day out for the sheer joy of it? Probably not many. Although it is necessary to look at the different things people may get from work, it would be fatal to underestimate the critical role that compensation plays in organizational functioning. In answer to the question, people want many things from work, but primary among them is money.

- *How can people get what they want from doing what the organization wants them to do?* This is the rub. Many organizational structures are set up so that what the organization wants people to do is completely independent of (and sometimes antithetical to) what people must do to get rewarded, and specifically to get money.[1] Absent a close connection between desired behaviors (from the organizational perspective) and desired rewards (from the employee's perspective), it is not surprising that inefficiencies, waste, and abuse prevail.

In short, if an organization is to be effective, its compensation system must be structured in such a way that people get what they want (money) for doing what the organization wants them to do (provide high productivity, give good service, be versatile, or whatever). Any pay system is not good or bad in and of itself, but only to the extent that it achieves (or fails to achieve) this link.

With this as background, we can look at the circumstances under which skill-based pay can be effective. But before that, it is useful to have a shared understanding of exactly what skill-based pay is all about.

FUNDAMENTALS OF SKILL-BASED PAY

Skill-based pay is an industry-driven compensation system, not one derived by academics based on rigorous theoretical and scientific analyses. Each skill-based pay plan is unique, with many variations across plan components, implementations, and successes. Nevertheless there are some commonalities.

In a typical skill-based pay plan, employees start out at an entry rate and learn a specified skill unit. Once the skill unit is certified as mastered (that is, once the employee has acquired a competency), the pay rate is increased. Employees perform that skill unit for a (sometimes specified) period of time and are then eligible to learn and master another skill unit. As more and more skill units are acquired, pay continues to increase until some predefined maximum is reached: that is, when employees top out (they can acquire and retain proficiency in only a finite number of skill units).

At its core, skill-based pay is a person- rather than job-based compensation system. Traditional compensation textbooks and experts (with an eye to internal equity) emphasize that pay and pay rates should be based on the job, not on the person doing it. Skill-based pay defies this perspective, basing pay on what an employee can do for the organization rather than on what the employee happens to be doing at any particular point in time. This philosophical premise emphasizes that employees are valuable human resources who should be treated as individuals, not as extensions of machines. The specific elements that distinguish skill-based pay from traditional compensation systems can be summarized as follows:[2]

• *Skill units as the basis of pay.* Traditional compensation systems use the job as the compensable unit, with knowledge or skill used as one of the factors that determines the relative worth of the job. In skill-based pay plans, however, skill units, which may be components of a job or may cut across jobs, are the basis of pay determination. Employees are paid for the number of skill units they can do, rather than the job title they have.

• *Focus on repertoire of skills.* A fundamental assumption behind skill-based pay plans is that it is organizationally valuable for employees to be multiskilled, that is, each able to perform several different functions. Pay rates are therefore tied to the number of different functions or skill units that an individual can perform. The more different and diverse functions an individual can fulfill, the higher the pay rate.

• *Competency certification.* Traditional compensation systems typically assume that individuals have the skills to perform the job (presumably ensured in the selection process); tests and certifications of job mastery are neither required nor form the basis for compensation. By contrast, most skill-based pay plans incorporate formal processes to assess and certify competency in a skill unit before compensating for it.

• *Job changes and pay changes.* In traditional compensation systems, it is assumed that pay changes accompany job changes. It is rare for employees to change jobs without a concurrent change in pay. In skill-based pay plans, however, pay changes are tied to mastery of skill units. Employees may move from job to job without pay changes; employees could remain in the same job but change pay because of the acquisition of a new skill unit. Thus, pay changes are tied to mastery of skill units and to broadening the repertoire of functions that an employee can perform.

• *Role of seniority.* As noted, skill-based pay systems tie pay increases to the number of skills an employee has mastered. Seniority is relevant only tangentially in that it takes time to master skill units. But seniority usually plays a central role in traditional compensation systems, particularly those in the public sector. Movement through the pay grade (and therefore pay raises) is most often tied to time in rank. In other words, seniority occupies a much more central role in traditional than in skill-based compensation systems.

• *Advancement opportunities.* Within traditional compensation systems, particularly those used in the public sector, employees are often stuck in a pay grade for many years. Within skill-based pay plans, however, the acquisition of additional skill units is formally encouraged and recognized. Employees who can perform many functions are particularly valued by the organization. Thus there tend to be greater opportunities for pay advancement in skill-based than in traditional compensation systems.

Most scholars studying skill-based pay argue that it can be very useful but only under the right conditions and with the right objectives. Before discussing some of these conditions and constraints, it is prudent to examine the context of compensation systems in the public sector and the dynamics within which they operate.

PUBLIC SECTOR COMPENSATION DYNAMICS

Although compensation systems in the public and private sectors bear some resemblance to each other, there are also substantial differences. These differences are critical not only for how the system is structured but for its relative dynamics and effectiveness.

Locus of Decision Making

Compensation systems in the private sector are typically planned and managed internally, that is, by organizational managers and executives who determine how much and on what basis people will be paid. In the public sector, by contrast, these decisions are usually made externally. Federal, state, or county legislators determine budget allocations, voters approve or disapprove particular funding or spending programs, and distinct organizations (such as the U.S. Office of Personnel Management) may be able to influence the compensation system but not control it. In the private sector the locus of decision making is primarily internal, whereas in the public sector it is primarily external.

Accountability

Corporate officials are typically accountable to a small constituency (stockholders), but public administrators are accountable to a variety of constituencies representing different opinions, values, and priorities. Compensation systems in the public sector come under much greater public scrutiny than those prevailing in the private sector. Whereas private sector compensation systems need make sense only to a small, relatively homogeneous group of individuals, public sector systems must appease many diverse groups.

Traditions and Expectations

There are many traditions and expectations with respect to public sector compensation. For instance, the federal civil service is expected to guarantee lifetime employment, public servants are expected to receive annual raises, public school teachers are expected to receive salary increases for additional educational accomplishments, pay raises are generally associated with increased seniority, and the like. Private sector compensation systems are more idiosyncratic and are mired in fewer traditions. It is easier to experiment and innovate in a new organization than in an existing one. Likewise, it is easier to experiment and innovate when there are fewer, less entrenched traditions and expectations.

Secrecy Versus Openness

Individual pay levels are often considered confidential information in the private sector. But individual salaries of public servants are typically a matter of public record. Again this fundamental difference in the approach to compensation creates differences in accountability, need for justification, and willingness to attempt basic changes in the compensation structure.

Desired Outcomes

The desired ultimate outcome in the private sector is usually profit; the desired ultimate outcome in the public sector is somewhat elusive.

What is it that we want from our public bureaucracies? What do we want our public servants to do? What is a "good" public agency? One that can work its way to superfluousness? One that increases dependence on it? There is clear consensus on what private organizations are in the business of doing; there are significant philosophical and political differences about the desired outcomes for public agencies.

Role of Competency or Merit

Merit, at least espoused merit, plays a major role in compensation systems in the private sector. Almost all private organizations make the claim that merit is incorporated as an intrinsic component of compensation for most jobs. A debate about whether this is actually the case is beyond the scope of this chapter, but the point is that private organizations claim to give great deference to merit considerations in their compensation systems and go to some length to assess merit. The situation is somewhat different in the public sector, with pay raises usually tied to seniority.

Furthermore, within the private sector, it is often possible to assess performance objectively at some level—be it corporate profits, department sales, or something else. Public sector work, by contrast, is focused on services, with inherent difficulties in obtaining clear measures of merit. These two factors—the greater espousal of merit and the easier assessment of merit in the private sector as compared to the public sector—entail critical differences in the philosophies and dynamics of compensation structures.

In short, there are many major differences between the context and environment of compensation systems of the public and private sectors. These differences have a significant impact on the viability and effectiveness of any compensation technique. They must be addressed when examining the value of skill-based pay as a compensation technique in the public sector.

CAN SKILL-BASED PAY BE USED IN THE PUBLIC SECTOR?

Many strategic and tactical issues are involved in the decision to use skill-based pay in the public sector (just as there are in the private sector[3]). As noted above, skill-based pay is not a panacea. As a compensation system and as a philosophy, it makes sense only under a limited number of conditions. The strategic and tactical issues must be carefully considered and a deliberate decision made that skill-based pay is right for the situation before such a pay plan can be used effectively. Following are some of the major issues to be considered.

Institutional Constraints

In the previous section, differences in parameters when designing compensation systems for the public and private sectors were outlined. These differences can have a substantial impact on compensation effectiveness. They must be incorporated into examinations of the potential success of any compensation system, particularly those that challenge tradition and conventional wisdom.

The first issue is the extent to which stakeholders (lawmakers, constituents, employees, and others) would accept the notion of skill-based pay. Entrenched thinking is disturbed by people's being paid not for the specific job they are doing at a specific time but rather for the number of different jobs they are able to do. A major philosophical shift is necessary for decision makers to understand and appreciate the value of skill-based pay in specific situations. Without such acceptance a decision to use skill-based pay would be futile.

The second potential institutional constraint is whether decision-makers have the flexibility to make drastic changes in the compensation system. Such a shift is often not possible. Federal bureaucracies may preclude the use of person-based pay (with the exception, of course, of annual seniority adjustments, which are person based); city government structures may do likewise. There may be only a small number of public sector decision makers who actually have the freedom to make drastic compensation changes in their agencies. With increased focus on reinventing government, that number may grow.

Other issues to consider are those listed in the previous section: who has the authority to make the decision to change the compensation system, to whom the decision maker is accountable, what traditions skill-based pay may violate, whether the pay system can withstand public scrutiny, and the role of competency (the last issue will be discussed further later). Skill-based pay should be explored seriously as a compensation alternative only when these concerns can be addressed successfully.

Managerial Philosophies and Styles

Skill-based pay is typically found in flat (rather than tall) organizations with, on average, only two tiers separating the lowest-level employee from the top manager. There is usually a team-based approach to management, and employees are empowered in many ways. It is common to use survey feedback, job enrichment, self-managing work groups, and similar nontraditional programs in conjunction with skill-based pay plans. In addition skill-based pay users typically provide their employees with information about operating results, business plans and goals, technologies, and competitors' performance, a rarity in organizations using traditional compensation systems. Hierarchical and authoritarian management styles and philosophies are not conducive to successful skill-based pay use.

Bureaucracies and hierarchies still prevail in the public sector. At the same time the recent push for downsizing may loosen this constraint. As government agencies downsize, the rigid hierarchical structures of the past may erode. Conditions may then be ripe for innovations such as skill-based pay, which thrive in flatter, more participative organizational environments.

Organizational Context

It is often argued that skill-based pay should be used only in small, new, nonunionized plants located in manufacturing industries. Skill-based pay plans are indeed more likely to be found in these settings, but the evidence also indicates that on most contextual dimensions, skill-based pay users are similar to non-skill-based pay users. Effective skill-based pay plans are found in a variety of industries, in new and old plants, in unionized and nonunionized settings, and in a variety of employee groups (although most common with direct labor and skilled trades employees). Employee demographics in skill-based pay plans resemble workforce demographics in general. In short, contextual characteristics do not place a barrier to the use of skill-based pay.

Within the public sector, there are many organizational contexts requiring direct labor and skilled trade jobs (for instance, highway maintenance and warehousing operations). These types of jobs have been shown to be reasonably responsive to skill-based pay as the compensation structure. Furthermore, many private sector companies are now experimenting with skill-based pay in white-collar jobs, such as tellers, loan officers, insurance agents, and others. In short, organizational context in the public sector per se should not be a barrier to the use of skill-based pay. To the contrary, it could provide fertile ground for innovative compensation practices.

Commitment

As noted, the use of skill-based pay requires fundamental changes in the way organizations are managed. Effective implementation necessitates that top management be committed to these changes. Employees also play somewhat different roles within a skill-based pay plan. They tend to participate in day-to-day operational decisions; they may be called upon to make selection, performance appraisal, and termination decisions. Without employee commitment to these different roles, skill-based pay plans fail to realize their potential.

Traditional compensation systems, by definition, have enjoyed long usage and thus experience few logistical and administrative difficulties; they are more prone to philosophical and outcome-related difficulties. But skill-based pay systems are relatively new. Most organizations installing them experience unanticipated problems during implementation. It is essential that those in the managerial echelons, as well as the employees themselves, be committed to the plan and willing to work through these difficulties. Absent such commitment, the organization will most likely regress to a more familiar, that is a traditional, compensation philosophy. This is more damaging in the long run than if skill-based pay were never tried in the first place.

In short, skill-based pay plans require immense commitment at all levels of the organization. It is not strategically prudent to proceed with the implementation of skill-based pay without such commitment at every level. This caution is applicable regardless of whether the organization in question is in the private or the public sector. The issue redoubles in significance given that, in the public sector, commitment is needed not only from organizational decision makers but from external constituencies as well.

Temporal Perspective

The decision to use skill-based pay entails short-term difficulties and costs. People must learn multiple jobs or skills, increasing training time. Employees perform suboptimally during training; in the short run organizational effectiveness may be impaired. But when a skill-based pay plan is mature and has been in place for a period of time, anticipated benefits such as higher productivity, satisfaction, quality, morale, and flexibility are likely to ensue.

Organizations seeking short-term success will be disappointed in the payoffs of skill-based pay; in contrast, organizations with a longer-term focus may benefit greatly. In this context it should be remembered that multiple constituencies must be satisfied in the public sector. Are voters (and therefore elected officials) able to accept the long-term view? Will people accept short-term costs for future flexibility and future gains? Can the public be educated? (The handling of the national deficit suggests that people rarely take the long-term perspective.) At the same time, without such education and acceptance, not only skill-based pay but compensation systems in general (and other managerial systems as well) are doomed to failure given the economic outlook in the years to come.

Desired Outcomes

Organizations use skill-based pay to promote a variety of outcomes. Some of these outcomes are linked to success; others are not. Effective skill-based pay users pursue outcomes such as employee flexibility, satisfaction, quality of work life, employee growth and development, and better quantity and quality of production. These outcomes are consistent with the overall focus on employee empowerment as the route to effectiveness. Unsuccessful skill-based pay plans are often installed as ways to avoid unionization, to lock in employees by compensating them for skills that are not externally marketable, or as a current fad or quick fix for immediate problems. A careful evaluation of the desired outcomes, and the consistency of these outcomes with skill-based pay dynamics, is essential.

In the public sector a new compensation system is unlikely to be adopted for union avoidance or to make alternative employment opportunities look less attractive. A quick fix may sometimes be attractive, but even that as a reason for compensation system adoption is doubtful in view of the somewhat slower decision-making process of most organizations in this sector. Slowness is an advantage in this sense, as it allows time for a deliberate consideration and weighing of alternatives.

Paramount among the financial reasons for skill-based pay adoption is the desire to have leaner staffing, a multiskilled workforce, and workforce flexibility. These outcomes are uniquely desirable in times of downsizing and smaller bureaucracies. As budgets for agencies at federal, state, and municipal levels are slashed, decision makers must develop ways of providing high-quality services with fewer employees. The multiskilled workforce that skill-based pay promotes may be ideal for addressing this contingency if conditions are right.

Consistency

The compensation system is one of the strongest communication channels for conveying organizational philosophies and processes. Thus it must be consistent with other managerial policies, procedures, and practices. Organizational structure, managerial philosophies, work design, compensation, and the like must all mesh into a unified whole to promote effective organizational functioning. Skill-based pay must be embedded within a comprehensive approach to organizational dynamics.

In this sense, organizations in the public sector are no different from those in the private sector. They have wide variations in organizational structure, managerial philosophy, desired outcome, and in other ways. As in the private sector, it is imperative that skill-based pay be consistent with the overall approach to human resource management, not just something that is implemented in isolation.

Operational Myths

Operational myths about skill-based pay abound. For example, its use supposedly increases the potential for discrimination lawsuits, as men and women doing the same job may be paid differently based on the number of skills they have. The experiences of skill-based pay users show this myth to be unfounded; no increases in litigation are reported. In addition there is usually a much more careful consideration of the bases of gender differences in skill-based pay plans; a potential lawsuit can thus be countered more easily.

Another myth is that skill-based pay cannot work in unionized settings. But when labor-management relationships are collaborative, unionized organizations report effective skill-based pay use. Public agencies considering the use of skill-based pay should consult and involve relevant unions or professional associations from the start. The probability of successful implementation will then be greater.

It is argued that skill-based pay will create resentment among those employees not covered under the skill-based pay plan. This concern has validity, and organizations must address this issue carefully before and during the implementation of skill-based pay. In the public sector as in the private sector an entire organization would probably not be converted to a skill-based compensation structure (top management, at least, is usually excluded). The importance of addressing the concerns of noncovered employees should never be downplayed.

Skill-based pay is sometimes charged with being prohibitively expensive to implement. The use of skill-based pay does increase administrative costs, training costs, and average hourly wage rates. But these costs are counterbalanced by improvements in product or service quality and quantity; by employee tenure, flexibility, commitment, and loyalty; and by the leaner staffing that skill-based pay permits. Specific costs may be higher, but overall costs are generally lower. In fact, skill-based pay is probably cost-effective and more attractive in leaner economic times when downsizing is the norm rather than the exception.

Skill-based pay is also alleged to be simply the product of compensation technocrats gone berserk. This charge may apply to those who sell a compensation plan as a cure-all; thoughtful investigators of skill-based pay are cautious about the circumstances under which its use is advisable. The charge is equally valid for those who advocate job-based pay under all circumstances as for those who advocate skill-based or person-based pay under all circumstances. The folly is the myth of universal applicability; as noted, many issues limit the circumstances under which any compensation system can be successful.

In short, the difficulties and problems often claimed to occur with skill-based pay use are either anecdotal and unsubstantiated by empirical data, or they are issues that can be preempted by careful planning and analysis.

In an era of budget cutting, downsizing, and organizational restructuring, public agencies must break away from traditional ways of thinking to examine different ways of working smarter and better. Skill-based pay results in multiskilled employees. It can align what organizations want (flexible employees who can do many different jobs) with what employees want (more money). It can be a useful alternative to traditional compensation practice. To maximize its potential, it must be adopted with prudence and care and only after a comprehensive determination of its appropriateness for the specific organizational environment, context, and constraints.

APPLYING SKILL-BASED PAY IN THE PUBLIC SECTOR

In public agencies as in private agencies, once a decision to use skill-based pay is made, many operational issues must be addressed to ensure that the plan specifics are tailored to the unique demands of the organizational context. These include answering the following questions:

• *What other changes will accompany the use of skill-based pay?* As noted, skill-based pay is usually embedded in a network of changes. It is often accompanied by employee empowerment programs and team-based structures. These innovations must mesh to produce the desired outcome of an effective leaner, more flexible, and multiskilled workforce.

• *Will skill-based pay be used agencywide?* In most circumstances, the answer to this question is no; managerial employees, at least, are often excluded. Even if an entire agency (or a large proportion of it) is to be included, provisions for phased implementation may be needed.

• *Which employee groups should be covered?* This question may already have been answered in the earlier decision to use skill-based pay. Nonetheless, it is useful to consider the subgroups of employees included and excluded from the plan and to address the potential of resentment and hostility among excluded subgroups.

• *How broadly will skill units be defined?* In the private sector, some plans have microdefinitions of skill units, with as many as two thousand skill units. More common, however, is to define skill units as specific job functions, much like the different jobs people do on a team, and to have six to ten skill units in the plan.

• *How will skill units be defined?* Generally, this is done through some variation of job analysis techniques. As in traditional job analysis, a cross-section of subject matter experts is usually assembled to define skill units.

• *How will skill units be priced?* Traditional market surveys are mostly irrelevant in pricing skill units, that is, in determining how much of a pay bump should accompany the mastery of each skill unit.

This is because comparison agencies in the market are unlikely to have similar skill units. An approach commonly used for pricing skill units is to tie them to training time. Skill units with longer training times are presumably more complex and are therefore associated with greater pay increases.

• *How will skills be certified?* This question has two aspects: development of certification standards (usually done through some variation of job analysis procedures) and determination of certifiers (usually done with input from a combination of coworkers and supervisors).

• *How long is the payback period?* It would not be organizationally functional for people to be learning new skills continually, to always be in a training mode and displaying suboptimal performance. Usually skill-based plans build in a payback period, where an employee certified as having mastered a skill unit must perform that skill unit for a designated period of time before becoming eligible to learn another skill unit.

• *How will skill retention be ensured?* It is unreasonable to pay employees for skills they have forgotten or in which they are no longer proficient. Organizations handle this concern in different ways, through periodic rotation of employees through the different skill units in their repertoire, periodic recertification of skill unit proficiency, or the like. Nonetheless, how compensation is handled for employees whose skills have atrophied should be a critical consideration.

• *How will skill obsolescence be handled?* Technological and structural changes sometimes render a compensable skill obsolete. Employees should, of course, no longer be paid for this skill. But because employees have little say in the adoption of new technology or changes in structural configurations, pay decreases are not advisable; they lead to resentment, hostility, and counterproductive behaviors. Employees could even be red-circled (frozen at their current pay rate) until a replacement skill unit has been mastered.

• *How will bottlenecks be handled?* It is not unusual for people to be held up—that is, to demonstrate proficiency in a skill unit, perform it for a while, and be ready to learn another skill unit when there are no openings for them to move to. This is an administrative holdup, and companies sometimes address it by having special holdup rates.

• *What provisions are made for topping out?* Depending on the number of skill units in a plan, it is possible that some employees will top out—become proficient in the maximum number of skill units possible. Provisions for this contingency are important because traditional annual pay raises for topped-out employees (presumably the most valuable, because they are the most flexible given their large skill repertoire) are probably motivationally dysfunctional. One approach is to include these employees in some sort of organizationwide bonus plan.

These and similar operational issues must be addressed before the implementation of a skill-based pay plan. Absent such consideration the plan may be doomed; even if it is considered, kinks and problems will undoubtedly arise as the plan becomes operational and plays itself out. It is critical in these circumstances that the managerial echelons retain their commitment to the utility of the plan and to their willingness to work through problems.

REINFORCING THE VALUE OF COMPETENCY WITH SKILL-BASED PAY

The issue of rewarding public employees is often accompanied by a concern for rewarding competency through competency-based pay. It was noted earlier that, at least in theory, merit seldom plays as central a role in public sector pay as it does in private sector pay. Indeed, many of the troubles ailing public agencies are blamed directly or indirectly on lack of accountability or lack of the need for competency among public agency employees. War stories of frustrating encounters with public bureaucracies are the order of the day. Clearly, if our public agencies are to increase efficiency and the quality of services, it is imperative that competent behaviors be rewarded and incompetent behaviors punished. So how does competency-based pay dovetail with skill-based pay? In two words: quite well!

Definition of Competency in Skill-Based Pay

In an earlier description, we noted that skill certification is an integral element of most skill-based pay plans. As the plan is designed, designers focus not only on compensable skill units but also on criteria that determine whether an individual has attained proficiency in a skill unit. In a traditional compensation system, job analysis is supposed to provide information about job duties and responsibilities as well as performance standards, but many analysts develop only the former.

In contrast most skill-based pay plans in use today include some sort of performance assessment before certifying an individual as proficient. Skill proficiency is synonymous with competency.

In addition skill retention is of major concern in designing skill-based pay plans. Most plans include provisions to ensure that employees retain the skills for which they are being paid. There is ongoing assessment of the extent to which employees continue to be competent in the skills that constitute their skill repertoire. This is the role that annual performance assessments are designed to fulfill in traditional compensation systems. As the evidence abundantly shows, however, performance appraisals are seriously deficient on this count. Skill-based pay plans, perhaps because they are still novel and therefore better thought-through, take this role more seriously.

Another major concern is that of skill obsolescence, that is, the plan of action to be followed with respect to compensable skill units that are no longer valued by the organization. Most skill-based pay plans include provisions for adjustment of employees' pay and work when compensable skill units are rendered obsolete through technological innovations, organizational restructuring, and the like. This too ensures that competency is maintained in valued skill units and that adequate attention is devoted to revisions in the structure of the compensation system through time.

Competency Assessors

In a traditional compensation system the immediate supervisor is generally the sole assessor of competency, with inherent potential for bias and distortion in the performance appraisals. But in skill-based pay plans, performance is usually assessed through the joint efforts of team members and the team leader. The assessment is less prone to either contamination (that is, irrelevant behaviors being assessed) or deficiency (that is, relevant behaviors being ignored). Competency assessment is typically more valid under these conditions.

Timing of Competency Assessment

Performance is typically assessed annually in traditional compensation systems. Skill-based pay plans assess competency before an individual is certified as proficient in a skill unit, and as needed thereafter to ensure skill retention. Assessment as needed, rather than following a rigid (and often irrelevant) bureaucratically mandated schedule, is preferable from the standpoint of efficient management. Skill-based pay plans usually do so.

Competency is an ongoing theme in skill-based pay plans. Moreover, the importance of acquiring new skills reinforces the importance of competency. Most skill-based pay plans incorporate procedures to ensure that proficiency is attained, displayed, and retained. These provisions are not antithetical to traditional compensation systems, but they prevail with much greater frequency in skill-based pay plans.

RECOMMENDATIONS AND CONCLUSIONS

The use of skill-based pay in the private sector provides many lessons for public agencies considering its potential. These cautions, caveats, and considerations must be kept in mind in assessing the value of skill-based pay for a public agency. Skill-based pay succeeds only when the right kinds of outcomes are sought:

- Skill-based pay must be tailored to prevailing managerial philosophies and styles.
- Skill-based pay must be consistent with and embedded in a network of organizational processes that form a coherent managerial approach.
- There must be substantial commitment to skill-based pay in all echelons of the organizational hierarchy.
- Skill-based pay must be used with a view to long-term, not short-term, success.
- Skill-based pay can be used effectively within many different organizational contexts, but the managerial culture should be one of participation and employee empowerment.
- Detailed planning and analysis prior to the installation of skill-based pay is essential.
- Most skill-based pay plans encounter unanticipated problems and kinks that must be carefully addressed.
- In unionized organizations, cooperative relationships between labor and management are conducive to skill-based pay success.

- The special concerns of employees not covered under the skill-based pay plan, as well as of those who are covered, must be addressed.

- The use of skill-based pay can raise administrative and training costs and the average wage rates for employees, although overall labor costs tend to be smaller due to leaner and more flexible staffing.

- Skill-based pay plans must be tailored to the unique characteristics of each organization; a boiler-plate or one-size-fits-all approach is destined to fail.

- The success of individual skill-based pay plans has not been investigated systematically or evaluated comprehensively. Without such evaluation, definitive implementation and design prescriptions are fruitless.

In conclusion, skill-based pay will not work in all public agencies. Rather, it has the potential for considerable success when used for the right reasons in the right circumstances. As a quick fix or faddish adoption, skill-based pay can be disastrous. Traditional compensation systems are well suited to bureaucratic tall hierarchical organizations. But as budgets are slashed, cost-cutting is emphasized, and agencies are flattened and downsized, a multiskilled, flexible workforce may prove invaluable in achieving the agencies' objectives: higher and better performance with fewer costs.

Notes

1. For excellent discussions of the problems reward systems can create, see S. Kerr, "On the Folly of Rewarding A, While Hoping for B," *Academy of Management Journal*, 1975, *18*, 769–783; and E. E. Lawler III and J. G. Rhode, *Information and Control in Organizations* (Santa Monica, Calif.: Goodyear, 1976).

2. For more detailed descriptions of skill-based pay plans, see N. Gupta, G. D. Jenkins Jr., and W. P. Curington, "Paying for Knowledge: Myths and Realities," *National Productivity Review*, 1986, *5*(2), 107–123; G. D. Jenkins Jr. and N. Gupta, "The Payoffs of Paying for Knowledge," *National Productivity Review*, 1992, *4*(2), 121–130; E. E. Lawler III and G. E. Ledford Jr., "Skill-Based Pay: A Concept That's Catching On," *Personnel*, 1985, *62*(9), 30–37;

and H. Tosi and L. Tosi, "What Managers Need to Know About Knowledge-Based Pay," *Organizational Dynamics,* 1986, *14*(3), 52–94.

3. For a discussion of these issues in the private sector, see N. Gupta and G. D. Jenkins Jr., "Strategic Considerations in Skill-Based Pay," *Compensation News,* 1993, *1*(1), 6–9; and G. D. Jenkins Jr., G. E. Ledford Jr., N. Gupta, and D. H. Doty, *Skill-Based Pay: Practices, Payoffs, Pitfalls, and Prescriptions* (Scottsdale, Ariz.: American Compensation Association, 1992). (The annotated bibliography contained in this last monograph can be particularly useful.)

CHAPTER SEVEN

Competency-Based Pay
The Next Model for
Salary Management

Howard Risher

T he field of salary management is moving away from the traditional focus on job value and experimenting with concepts that consider the value of the individual. The trend was prompted by the shift away from the more or less static organizational concepts toward the more flexible and frequently redefined approaches to organizing and managing work that are rapidly becoming the norm. The traditional salary program is increasingly viewed as an impediment to organizational change. The criticism of job evaluation systems discussed in Chapter Six has come together with W. Edwards Deming's criticism of merit pay practices. As these have been the cornerstone of traditional programs, criticism of them has triggered a high level of interest in alternative concepts.

If the subjects discussed in professional journals or at conferences indicate a trend, interest in alternatives is extremely high. It has been rare for two or three years to find articles or presentations focusing on ideas to improve traditional methods. The professional focus is now on radically different ideas that have yet to be fully developed or tested.

The interest in moving away from the traditional focus on jobs has caused a shift to program concepts that consider the value of individuals' capabilities. Skill-based pay is one of these concepts; it has been in use for over twenty years and has established a solid niche in the compensation field. The applications, however, have been largely limited to occupations involving manual skills. Experience with skill-based pay has also been mixed. At least one major corporation, Motorola, has announced termination of a number of skill-based systems.

THE NEW ALTERNATIVE: COMPETENCY-BASED PAY

A new alternative, competency-based pay, has become hot within the past year or two. Competencies are generally understood to be similar to skills, but a broader connotation makes the concept relevant to every occupation. In contrast to the common reference to predominantly manual jobs in discussions of skills, competence is a concept applicable to every job and every employee. It is reasonable to define competencies for physicians as well as for housekeepers. Moreover, reference to a worker as competent suggests solid performance. A competent worker is by common understanding a good performer.

It is important to point out that the concept is so new that few corporations and even fewer public employers have developed applications for more than small groups of workers, and it is probably safe to state that no organization has developed a competency system covering all its employees. Where the concept has been rolled out, it is too early to understand the strengths and weaknesses or to conclude that one methodology has definite advantages over others.

The intent in developing a competency-based system is to define what successful workers are expected to be able to do at each level on their career ladder. In contrast to the traditional focus on minimal qualifications, the focus shifts to competencies that better, full-performance workers are expected to demonstrate. Manual skills might be included among the competencies.

Some organizations differentiate between professional competencies that are specific to a narrowly defined occupation (such as classifier) and the generic competencies needed to function effectively within an organization or externally with customers, suppliers, and others (such as being good at teamwork). Professional competencies normally require formal education, training, and relevant work experience, which can be taught through in-house training programs or transferred from one occupation to another. The differences, although real, are important only if the distinction facilitates program understanding and acceptance.

An important program design issue is the level of specificity reflected in the competencies. Compensation analysts, for example, need to be able to use a calculator—a skill—to analyze salary survey data, but they also must be able to interpret the results and make recommendations related to the information. Expected competencies can be defined for workers on a narrow career ladder, such as compensation analysts, or the program can focus on groups of jobs in broader job families, such as human resource analysts, or even broader families, such as administrative analysts. The competency for the broadest group might be defined as "the ability to analyze and interpret data relevant to professional field."

One of the advantages of the competency orientation is its focus on successful workers and what workers need to be able to do to be successful. Experience has shown that there is generally a high level of agreement about who the best workers are and about the competencies needed to be successful. This emphasis on identifying and rewarding the better workers is an important message that is consistent with the beliefs and values of many organizational leaders.

Interest in competencies is not limited to salary management. It is rapidly being adapted for use by specialists in staffing, training and development, performance management, and career management; the concept is becoming the common thread that ties together each of these human resource systems. Underlying each of these areas is the recognition that employee competency is a central concern that drives organizational performance.

In the corporate world, it has a logical linkage to another hot-button issue, core competencies. In strategic planning terms, core competencies are the capabilities and technical expertise essential to the organization's success. The role of the human resource function is then to take the lead in ensuring that the organization's capabilities are sustained at the levels needed to support the business goals. The generic competencies such as teamwork or customer focus are often categorized as core. This for the first time provides a solid linkage between the business strategy and the human resource function.

There are at this point still differences in how competencies are operationally defined. In the broadest definitions, competencies encompass employee knowledge, skills, attitudes, traits, motives, and values. Defining competencies broadly necessitates a complex methodology that is capable of assessing and interpreting a large block of information for each job (or role, to use the emerging jargon). In the narrow understanding of the concept, competencies are focused on a limited number of capabilities required to perform the job. For a typical job or role this might involve six to ten competencies.

The broader definition was introduced by psychometricians who normally focus on the requirements for a specific job. Their purpose is to understand the employee characteristics common to successful performers. This is directly relevant to staffing and selection. In evaluating job applicants, knowledge, skills, and abilities as well as traits and motives are normally important to the decision-making process. Each job is generally studied independently and conclusions are specific to the job in question.

Salary management, in contrast, involves the comparison of jobs and people. Traditionally, comparisons across job families have been a central consideration in assessing internal equity. Though this consideration is decidedly less important now than it was even in the early 1990s, it is still important in many organizations and should be considered in planning a new program. The focus may shift from jobs to people, but pay systems still need to reflect differences in relative value. At a minimum there is a need to develop a method for comparing people relative to expectations at each rung or step on a career ladder.

The underlying philosophy of a competency-based pay system reflects belief that employees' value depends on what they can do, based on individual competencies. The more an employee can do, the more the organization can expect and the greater the individual's value. The purpose in considering the differences between jobs or people is to assess the relative value of the jobs or roles, which is used in determining appropriate salary grades (or bands).

The comparison across jobs and people is also important to career planning, training needs analysis, and human resource planning. Each requires data relevant to the similarities and differences across jobs. The applications involve a comparison of people and job requirements or a comparison of jobs. For example, with competency profiles for each job and an assessment of each individual's competencies, career planning can be used to place people in jobs requiring demonstrated competencies or in those where competencies can be developed. The methodology therefore has to develop comparative data that can be used for making these decisions.

Competency-based pay is consistent with organizational values and with societal values in a meritocracy. The intent of the pay system is to make sure the most competent employee on a career ladder has the highest salary, the second most competent employee has the next highest salary, and so forth. Moreover, future salary increases depend on enhanced competency. Employees who do not continue to grow and improve their capabilities will be passed over for salary increases as well as promotions.

This is not a totally new concept in salary planning; it is similar to the rationale underlying the merit matrix concept. With a merit matrix, employees paid low in the range are eligible for larger increases than those in the upper half of the range. The assumption is that individual performance and value follows a learning curve. A year of experience for new employees should enhance their value more than the same year for those who have years of experience in the job. Long-service employees are not eligible for an increase (except for a possible "range adjustment" increase) unless they demonstrate improved performance.

The competency concept is also compatible with the logic underlying credentials-based pay systems and longevity-based systems. The assumption underlying pay systems for teachers, for example, is that additional graduate degrees will help them to perform better in the classroom.

Traditional job evaluation systems have never been fully accepted for use with occupations where steps in a career ladder are somewhat arbitrary, such as nursing, accounting, engineering, and the sciences. The issue with these job families and others is that incumbents at the top of the career ladders perform many of the same duties as people at the bottom. The performance expectations are higher for employees who have moved to the top of a ladder—they are expected to handle the more difficult problems and to assume greater responsibility—but there is considerable overlap in actual job content, in terms of tasks performed, from step to step on the ladder.

The competency concept is also compatible with government classification systems. The federal classification system is typical with its four-hundred-plus occupational series. The purpose of the system is to establish a rationale for defining the steps of each occupational ladder. The goal is to explain how, for example, a Clerk III differs from a Clerk II. At each step there is typically a statement of minimal qualifications, including relevant knowledge and skills. The differences between levels could be readily restated and defined in terms of competencies.

The shift to the competency orientation was in part triggered by the problems associated with traditional systems. It specifically avoids the widely recognized problems associated with job descriptions. It also is a response to the criticism of merit pay in that last year's performance is not directly linked to this year's wage or salary increase.

Competency orientation sends important messages to workers. First, it gives a new emphasis to the importance of being a competent worker. This is particularly important now that most organizations, private as well as public, are trying to "raise the bar" and improve performance. Second, the discussions related to identifying and defining competencies help everyone to understand what it takes to become a successful worker. This process and the involvement of individuals in the career ladder are important to the credibility and acceptance of the results. The third and perhaps most important message is the profile that emerges in defining the competencies expected of workers at each level.

The profile for what workers need to be able to do to be successful is important because it is available to every worker. With traditional performance appraisals, supervisors are expected to help their people understand their strengths and weaknesses. It is widely recognized, however, that these are often not meaningful discussions; the supervisor is rarely comfortable delivering an honest message, and the subordinate has reasons to be defensive.

After the competency profile is defined, workers can assess their own strengths and weaknesses. In their heart of hearts people usually know where they have weaknesses. The role of the supervisor shifts to helping the employee develop plans to improve. That is a decidedly better and more productive conversation. The profile makes it possible for employees to manage their own career prospects. It gives them a basis for planning personal development actions or developing career alternatives.

PLANNING A
COMPETENCY-BASED SYSTEM

Planning decisions in effect establish the framework for the system. The planning process needs to consider human resource applications or uses, the time available to develop and roll out the new system, and budget constraints. The basic question is the occupational focus in defining competencies.

The job-by-job orientation and in-depth analyses that flow out of the methodologies used for employee selection represent one end of a spectrum. With this approach, each job is analyzed separately, resulting in large, complex databases that are difficult to compare across jobs and job families. The other end of the spectrum is the logic that has been used to develop job evaluation systems. The intent with this approach is to identify a set of compensable factors—competencies— that apply to all the jobs to be covered under the new system. The problem is that in relying on generic, universal competencies, the results may not be credible for any single job. If, for example, "inter-personal skills" has to be defined in nonspecific terms for job evalua-tion, it will be a hurdle in developing a definition for a competency system.

One of the initial decisions relates to the breadth of the system in terms of covered occupations or job series. It may make sense to develop a system based on competencies uniquely defined for each job series. That would be consistent with the logic of classification systems, which may make it more readily accepted. A related alternative is to group series based on common job characteristics. For example, a set of competencies could be defined for all clerical support jobs. Other broad occupational groups such as the administrative series, allied health series, or scientific series could be created for this purpose. It might make sense to develop separate competencies for a single unique series such as physician but to group others into a broad related job family. It also may make sense to develop different competencies for different agencies. For example, health care specialists working in a prison system need different competencies than those working in a medical research facility.

Planned applications are another important project planning issue. Each of the possible applications—selection and staffing, career man-agement, training needs analysis, performance management, and salary management—has somewhat different information require-ments. For example, decisions related to the appropriate grade or band (previously referred to as classification or job evaluation decisions) require comparative grade-by-grade competencies. If the information is to be used for multiple applications, the information requirements need to be specified and reflected in the data collection process.

For each application, it is useful to define the data requirements and to document how the data will be used in decision making. The applications require somewhat different information, and it may be difficult in the future to justify the cost to collect additional data. One of the decided advantages of the competency focus is the possibility of developing a multiple purpose database, but this requires adequate planning.

If managers are expected to use the information in making decisions related to their people, their roles need to be defined and the information structured in a way that facilitates their decisions. They effectively become the customers and their needs should be a key issue in planning. They need to be involved at each step in the project.

It also will be important to agree on the schedule for studying job families and to develop a cost estimate for the overall project. The process for understanding competencies is similar to that commonly used to develop class standards. It involves an in-depth understanding of the jobs in question, and has to be done one series (or group of series) at a time. Budget constraints need to be considered in light of the number of groups and the planned methodology.

The identification and definition of competencies is labor-intensive regardless of the approach employed. The approach that requires the most time is based on behavioral event interviews (BEIs), in which job incumbents are interviewed to identify incidents of high performance and the competencies—defined in the broadest sense as knowledge, skills, attitudes, traits, motives, and values—required to perform at this level. As the interviews must necessarily involve an adequate cross-section of incumbents, it can require considerable time to understand the competencies for even a single job title.

The alternative is to rely on selected high performers or supervisors to serve on a panel of subject matter experts (SMEs). The goal of panel discussions is to focus on the key competencies that are expected of successful full performers in each job. Experience shows that in most situations the panels will be comfortable with six to twelve competencies. Because the competencies are generated by coworkers, this normally facilitates acceptance. It is natural, of course, for workers to define competencies with language that is meaningful within the organization.

Behavioral event interviews generate the most valid data but require considerably more time, which of course translates into a significantly higher cost. Steps to increase the validity of the competency information drive up the cost rapidly.

Compensation management does not require completely valid information. Though it is essential that the information have face validity, which is the same as saying that people believe it is valid, there is no legal or practical reason for the information to meet the higher standard. The competencies have to be credible and reasonable, but the courts have not required evidence of validity in job evaluation systems and there is no reason to expect a different standard for competency-based systems.

There are, of course, legal reasons to develop valid data for selection purposes; that standard is well established. Even for this, however, it is useful to assess the importance of valid data in light of the cost to generate it. Realistically, none of the applications other than staffing needs valid information. Even staffing decisions can and often are based on information that has not been validated. From a practical perspective, if employees and managers accept the data, it is valid enough.

FOCUSING ON CAREER LADDERS

One common practice in planning competency systems is to use a career ladder as the framework. Research has shown that most successful workers go through four stages in their careers. Individuals who are not seen as solid performers for various reasons get stymied at one of the stages. By defining the competencies expected at each stage, workers can begin to assess their prospects for continued success. One of the advantages of using the career ladder concept as the framework is that it helps to assure workers who are at the same point in their careers that expectations will be essentially the same across job families. The four stages and examples of work that demonstrate their fulfillment are as follows.

- *The learning stage.* Here, assignments are normally an element of a larger project, typically detailed but routine in nature and completed under close supervision. Typically individuals at this stage work with a mentor who helps them to develop or enhance their competency. As they learn, they are given increasing responsibility.

  Possible competency: Complete assigned tasks involving detailed work that meets the expectations of a supervisor or mentor.

- *The independent contributor stage.* Here, individuals have their own projects or areas of responsibility. They are now expected to work on their own and to be accountable for results. They are also expected to manage their own time. They typically develop specialized competency in a specific area that becomes the base for career direction.

Possible competency: Develop recognized ability to plan and carry out a project independently with little direction from supervisor or mentor.

• *The mentor stage.* Here, individuals' technical expertise is recognized by the organization and they are expected to originate ideas and work through others who do the detail work. At this stage, individuals may be appointed as managers or supervisors. They begin to play a role in a professional network with peers in other business units and other organizations. Their recognized expertise enables them to influence projects outside their immediate area of responsibility.

Possible competency: Provide the conceptual thinking and leadership needed to plan, develop support for, and complete a project involving subordinate personnel.

• *The visionary stage.* Here, the individual leads the organization into new areas or ways of operating. Individuals who reach this stage typically work as internal entrepreneur, organizational leader, or recognized expert in a professional field. They often have established a reputation recognized in their profession. They are expected to represent the organization in external professional meetings and may serve as a leader in professional groups.

Possible competency: Be recognized as a world-class professional in the field.

Organizations commonly recognize at least three of the four stages. For nonprofessional occupations the fourth stage may not exist, but there are always people at the other three levels. Competencies may also focus on different bodies of knowledge and different tasks, but many of the behavioral roles will be similar. Not every occupation defines its career ladders this way, but the stages have an intuitive logic that fits the way people think about their careers and the way most organizations manage people.

Career stages provide a framework for an organization's managers, job incumbents, and human resource or personnel specialists to discuss careers. The framework facilitates the identification and definition of competencies. These in turn provide a framework that can be used for staffing and human resource planning, career planning and management, and developmental planning. When the stages are aligned with grades or bands, it facilitates salary management in terms of both classification decisions and merit increase decisions.

COMPENSABLE FACTORS VERSUS COMPETENCIES

With conventional salary programs based on a job evaluation system, the framework for decision making is the set of compensable factors. There are generally between six and twelve factors with measurement scales to guide decision making. Significantly, employee knowledge, skills, and abilities (defined to include such factors as education, know-how, specific skills, and the like) typically account for 50 percent or more of the evaluation points. This could make the transition to competency-based pay a logical and acceptable alternative.

The logic of job evaluation can be carried over directly to a competency system and could involve the development of measurement scales and a weighting system for assigning points. It may make sense to carry over knowledge factors with minimal change if they can be reinterpreted as competencies. This would reduce the acceptance problems often triggered by the introduction of a new system. It also would obviate some criticisms of the new system, as it simply shifts understanding of value from the job to the individual. At the same time, of course, this may not be an acceptable alternative if the job evaluation system is viewed as part of the problem.

One of the reasons for starting with this alternative is the need to develop a system that fits the understanding of managers and employees. Their acceptance is a key to the success of any new system. The system effectively defines the value of work in the organization, so management needs to decide how much change it wants to introduce. Perpetuating the knowledge and skill factors in the job evaluation system should or could minimize changes in the relative value or hierarchy of jobs.

One of the more fundamental policy issues is the traditional concern with internal equity. With the shift away from a job-based program, equity is a much more difficult concept to manage. If the new program is based on the banding concept, the assignment of jobs to bands can be loosely based on internal equity. However, if the organization continues with a traditional salary grade structure and its relatively small distinctions between grades, there will still be a need for an administrative mechanism to make these decisions. It would be possible to design a competency-based system that emulates a traditional job evaluation system, but to date organizations have not elected to take this route.

Despite this, it still may make sense to design the competency system to resemble a job evaluation system. At each grade or band the competencies expected are defined to create a profile for full performers. The career stages could provide a convenient framework for defining profiles; the profiles then can be used to assign jobs (or roles) to grades. These decisions cannot be as scientific as those based on a point factor system because they are inherently subjective. Moreover, jobs are compared with the overall profile and assigned to the grade with the best match. This is a simple but credible alternative to a conventional job evaluation system.

This approach is understandable and, based on early experience, acceptable. People need enough substance to feel that the decision-making process is logical and defensible. It can be a problem if the decisions are overly simplistic (for example, managerial positions evaluated on the basis of staff size). The decisions are not as clean or precise as those based on a job evaluation system, but of course such systems have never been fully accepted.

The profile for each grade also serves as a framework for assessing an employee's competency. The expected competencies are integrated into the performance appraisal process and used to determine annual salary increases. The individual's assessed strengths and weaknesses are also considered in career management and in determining common training needs across employees. Thus the competency concept serves to integrate these human resource applications.

STRATEGIES FOR LINKING COMPETENCIES TO PAY

The switch to a competency-based system represents a significant organizational change. It introduces a new value system that affects both job value and individual value. This makes it important to evaluate the anticipated impact on the organization and to develop an implementation strategy that minimizes possible resistance.

The simplest use of the competency profiles is as a basis for annual performance appraisals. This involves minimal change, as developmental needs are commonly discussed in these sessions. In this context the competency assessment replaces or supplements the traditional merit pay policy. It may make sense to have supervisors and their people discuss and develop preliminary competency definitions in the appraisal meetings. The results will not meet validity tests, if that is deemed to be important, but it is a way to introduce the competency concept and to prompt discussions of competencies between supervisors and the members of their staff.

The logic for assigning jobs to salary grades depends on competencies that are defined differently at each level in the organization. Core or generic competencies (such as customer focus) that are expected of everyone are not useful for this purpose. Competencies have to intuitively increase at progressively higher salary grades, and that needs to be reflected in the design of the system. That is an essential point in using competencies for salary management.

Organizations that elect to maintain a traditional salary structure with overlapping grades and ranges still need an administrative mechanism to determine salary grade assignments. One possibility is the development of a job evaluation system predicated on competencies. That would require generic competencies used for all covered jobs. This is analogous to relying on compensable factors.

A more likely alternative is to rely on profiles for jobs or roles at each level. Job evaluation systems generate comparable profiles of compensable factor scores (although the profiles are not used for system administration). Job profiles are then compared with the standard profiles assigned to each grade. This is effectively the same logic as classification where class standards are used as the basis for grade decisions. The use of profiles in this manner appears to be the most widely accepted approach in the corporate world.

The third alternative is based on the career ladder concept. The framework depends on defining competencies at each stage in the career ladder for each job family. Individual competencies are then assessed and the individual compared with the four basic stages in the career ladder. With this framework, individuals can progress up the ladder as quickly as their competency justifies. Those who are contributing at a stage three level should logically be paid at that level, regardless of title or years of experience. The individual's value depends on the contribution level or stage in the planned career ladder; everyone performing and contributing at the same stage, regardless of any other considerations, should be paid within the same grade or band. This is a very aggressive compensation philosophy and certainly more acceptable in a corporate environment.

It is important to note one of the primary differences between skill-based pay and competency-based pay. Skill-based pay has traditionally been introduced for jobs with predominantly manual duties. Typical skill-based programs were designed around narrow, easily defined skills, with incumbents paid a cents-per-hour increase for each skill acquired. The amounts can be as small as ten or fifteen cents per hour. As a control mechanism, the program typically requires the employee to pass a paper-and-pencil or work sample test. That means everyone who demonstrates the skill automatically qualifies for the pay increase, regardless of the employer's need for the skill. The added skills result in an increase in payroll costs even if the skills are not regularly used.

Competency-based pay, in contrast, is normally based on subjective assessments, not tests, and salaries are adjusted at year's end if warranted. The increases are rarely automatic. Promotional increases are awarded only when openings occur and then to the best-qualified worker. In this respect competency systems are administered in essentially the same manner as merit systems.

The interest in competencies is not limited to the specialists responsible for classification and compensation. In fact, the number of potential applications is a primary reason why there is such a high level of interest. This means, however, that it will be fundamentally important to consider each application and its information requirements. Compensation management has very specific needs and the competencies need to be structured in a way that supports this application. It may prove infeasible to rely on information collected for other applications. That question should be the focus for planning if the decision is made to shift to competency-based human resource systems.

CHAPTER EIGHT

Executive Salary Management

The Clash of Political
and Labor Market Realities

Howard Risher

———

E xecutive salary management is not simply an extension of salary management for lower-level employees. The policies and administrative procedures may be the same, but the salaries are high and decisions are made in the goldfish bowl of public scrutiny. For senior positions below the elected official and political appointee level, the importance of functional expertise and managerial skills means the pay determination process is governed by the labor market. Above this level, however, pay is a political land mine and subject to heated debate. In most jurisdictions the salaries of elected officials represent an impermeable ceiling that constrains pay for all lower-level managers.

Government executive positions are not interchangeable with those in the private sector; the duties listed in job descriptions may be the same but the competencies and the management styles required to be successful are different. The two sectors represent separate labor markets, as there is little crossover from one to the other. A few corporate executives have accepted government appointments but they have seldom achieved comparable success in their public roles. The periodic reports focusing on the public-to-private comparison generally highlight the gap in pay but stop short of explicit job-to-job comparisons.

Fortunately, there are well-qualified people willing to run for public office and to accept political appointments despite reduced compensation. The reality is that there are only a relative handful of positions in any jurisdiction where the political process governs job opportunities. The balance of the public executives and managers who work their way up civil service career ladders do not have these options. Their salaries are constrained by the public's perception of government and of acceptable pay levels for civil servants.

One of the prominent differences in the way corporate executives are compensated is the prevalence of cash incentives. Executive incentive plans are virtually universal across American industry. There is a widely shared belief that well-designed incentives can be instrumental in achieving key organizational goals. The trend is to extend participation in incentive programs to include lower-level employees. If, as the adage argues, you get what you pay for, it may be that incentives could play a similar role in improving government performance.

COMPARABILITY AT
THE EXECUTIVE LEVEL

The principle of comparability is solidly entrenched in the public sector. It has been the statutory basis for adjusting the federal General Schedule since 1970 and reconfirmed with the passage of pay reform legislation in 1990, when it was adopted as the basis for the new locality pay program. It also serves as the basis for the Federal Wage System as well as numerous public pay programs at the state and local level.

The policy is based on the assumption that selected benchmark jobs in the public and private sectors are comparable and that public employees deserve to be paid the same salaries as their counterparts in the private sector. The job-to-job comparisons are based on an analysis of job duties. This comparison process is used in virtually every wage and salary survey.

For executive jobs in the private sector, the comparison is complicated by the assumption that industry breakdowns and company-size measures, typically sales revenues, need to be considered to ensure apples-to-apples comparisons. Executives in a cross-section of companies might be responsible for the same basic duties, but a common assumption is that incumbents in large companies deserve to be paid more than those in smaller companies. The job is arguably "bigger" in the large company, and this justifies higher pay. Statistical analyses, primarily regression techniques, are used to analyze company data. The purpose is to determine or estimate the competitive pay level for the benchmark positions in a specific company, based on its size and industry.

There are significant differences between government and corporate jobs. These have to do with the basic objectives of management, the application of industry and functional expertise, and the management styles that are effective. Some successful executives in one sector might be able to move directly into a similar position in the other sector and be equally successful, but experience shows that not many are able to make the transition.

There are also differences in the career paths and education. Many government executives did not start their careers with a plan to become an executive; at some point in their careers they shifted to a managerial role often because that was the only route to a higher salary. Corporate leaders are more likely to have majored in business at the undergraduate and increasingly at the graduate level. The differences do not necessarily make the corporate executives better at their jobs, but they do provide a different career orientation and open the door to different career opportunities.

This makes any comparison of private and public sector executive jobs suspect. There are a few staff functions where there is a direct equivalence of professional expertise, such as information technology, engineering, and human resources. But the senior executive positions and line functions in the private sector, such as marketing, manufacturing, and finance, have no government counterparts.

The federal government overcomes this problem for its senior executive service positions by using the salary survey data compiled for lower level positions (GS–1 to GS–15), calculating a policy line to align the lower grades with the survey results, and extrapolating the line to the executive level grades. (This methodology is not used, however, for political appointee positions.) The assumption is that the survey results represent a reasonable basis for adjusting the executive grades, even though no survey data is collected. The problem with this is the absence of hard data that proves the need to adjust public sector salaries, although this has only infrequently affected the pay-setting process.

For cabinet-level positions as well as executive-level grades, the federal government has relied on comparative analyses and conclusions reached every four years by the Commission on Executive, Legislative and Judicial Salaries (the Quadrennial Commission, or Quad Com). The first commission was created by legislation in 1967, with a new group formed every four years prior to presidential elections. The commission was responsible for assessing the need for salary adjustments for members of Congress, judges serving on federal courts, and certain high-ranking government executives. Commissions over the years relied primarily on analyses of income opportunities outside of government. In 1989 the authority to make salary increase recommendations was shifted to a new group, the Citizens' Commission on Public Service and Compensation, under the Ethics Reform Act. For political reasons, however, the new commission that should have been formed in 1993 has yet to meet. There is little likelihood that the issues will be studied again in the current political climate.

Recent history is not a denial of the comparability principle; it should be an integral annual step in managing every wage and salary program. It is a feasible step for every public employer and is relevant to a broad array of public executive positions. At the state and local level, most departments and functions have counterpart positions in other comparable jurisdictions. A limited amount of salary information is available in various publications (for example, the Council of State Governments compiles an annual summary), and some states and local government employers conduct their own surveys. But the surveys that are conducted often focus on lower-level jobs; perhaps it would be wise to commission periodic executive salary surveys.

There are direct counterparts for executive positions in public education, public safety, public transportation, and public health. It is also possible to compare executive positions and conduct surveys in places like zoos, airports, and museums. Many of these organizations have professional associations that already collect and publish salary survey data. As the executives who run these organizations have specialized expertise, they get involved in searches to fill job openings in other areas; the best ones move across the country to take higher-paying jobs in the same manner as corporate executives. Generally the salaries paid to the top executives in these independent agencies are not subject to the same constraints on pay as elected officials, so they are often higher paid. Some of these annual salaries are now approaching $200,000.

The pay-setting process for executive positions in these organizations is handled in essentially the same way as in corporations. Someone has to identify a group of peer organizations, which could take into consideration size, location, and the perceived excellence of management. The data from the peer group are then analyzed to determine competitive pay levels. In all respects these labor markets function in the same manner as those for corporate executives. The executive search firms are as active here as they are in corporations.

In fact, as privatization grows in importance, there will be a need to collect and analyze data for both private and public organizations. Trash collection, for example, involves the same management skills in both the private and public sectors. Generally private entities offer higher salaries now so that this trend will over time raise the salaries for their counterparts in comparable public organizations. Now, as an example, the executives in private colleges and universities are paid more than their counterparts in public institutions.

One of the problems that needs to be addressed in analyzing and interpreting salary survey data is the difference in prevailing pay levels across the country. Though the private sector would rarely if ever consider cost-of-living increases in setting executive salaries, pay levels in some costly urban areas, particularly in New York and California, are correlated with living costs. The zoos in Los Angeles and Indianapolis, for example, have a lot in common but the directors are paid differently. On the same point the salaries in nonurban areas are typically below national averages. The variations across the country in reliable surveys show differences of 20 to 30 percent between high-pay and low-pay areas.

THE QUESTION OF ADEQUACY

One overriding issue is the adequacy of executive and elective official salaries. In concept government pay levels should be adequate to attract and retain high-quality people but not so high as to entice individuals solely for the income. In the current antigovernment climate it may be that any salary is too high. From the perspective of the average worker, executive salaries in any sector look egregious but, for reasons that are deeply ingrained in our culture, it is easier to accept a Madonna or Michael Jordan making $50 million than a government official making $100,000.

The media have made corporate executive compensation levels a hot-button issue over the past few years. Every year it seems an increasing number of executives earn more than $1 million; a few, when they exercise their stock options, earn $10 million or more. In part because of this media scrutiny, corporate board members have begun to assume control of their executive programs and establish much closer ties between company performance and executive pay levels. Despite this, the articles that begin to appear in the spring (after proxy statements disclosing executive compensation information are mailed to stockholders) reinforce the public's perception that corporate executives are overpaid.

Below the executive level, new MBA graduates often start at salaries of $50,000 or more, and the best legal graduates can command salaries of $75,000 or more. When new graduates start at these levels, there is little room in the public sector for future salary increases.

The reality is that million-dollar compensation packages receive all the attention, but in more than a few corporations hundreds of managers and professionals (in some major corporations as many as a thousand) earn more than state governors. In larger corporations, middle management starts at base salaries of $100,000 plus eligibility for cash incentives and stock options.

Despite the prevalence of high pay levels in the private sector, the public's view of the salaries paid to government officials is best illustrated by the comment made by a nationally prominent Democratic senator in a brief conversation with the author a month after congressional salaries were increased in 1990. He commented that his father, who had never made more than $30,000 in any year of his life, "can't figure out why I'm paid more than $100,000." The same senator was at that time sending two children to college and claimed to have taken out a second mortgage to pay for it. He went on to say that it would be instructive to check the family status and children's ages of U.S. senators, implying that only the independently wealthy could afford to be in Congress when their children are of or approaching college age.

At least elected officials volunteer for the job and know they usually will only be in office for a few years. Career civil servants, in contrast, find it difficult to move to the private sector. There was a time when federal and more recently state and local government careers were exciting and attractive to the best and the brightest. Over time, as these individuals worked their way up the career ladder, they lost almost all prospects for securing a new, better-paying private sector job. For all practical purposes they are locked into government careers. With the reduced status and respect accorded to government careers, today's outstanding college graduates are increasingly unwilling to consider government jobs.[1]

Pay levels are adequate when government is able to attract adequately qualified candidates who are interested in public service. There is certainly nothing wrong with independently wealthy public servants, but clearly the pool of qualified candidates should not be limited to those who can afford to accept poor pay. The public may not hold its public servants in high regard, but many executive jobs in government are extremely demanding and require highly capable individuals. Even with all the downsizing and cost cutting, government officials are still often responsible for multimillion-dollar budgets. That makes the qualifications of the incumbent an important public policy issue.

ELECTED OFFICIAL SALARIES

The salaries of elected officials and political appointees bear little relationship to job difficulty or responsibility level. The bigger jobs—that is to say, the positions in larger public entities—are generally paid higher salaries, although this is not consistently true. The prevailing practice is, however, to pay all officials with the same status (such as all agency heads) the same salary, regardless of job difficulty or impact on government operations. Elected officials in the larger states and cities tend to be paid more, but the pattern is not consistent across the country.

Fortunately, our country has many people who are anxious to run for elected office, regardless of the base salary. The base salaries are well above the average income of citizens, but not high enough to be attractive to successful executives or professionals in our society. It would be unfortunate if only wealthy people were willing and able to afford to run for elected office.

Realistically, many elected officials could earn more money in other occupations. The typical (or median) governor earned $86,100 in 1994; thirteen earned more than $100,000 and twelve earned less than $75,000. The highest paid governor was New York's George Pataki. Lieutenant governors earn significantly less.[2] The salaries for other appointed officials generally, although not universally, are below the salaries of the elected officeholders.

At the federal level, members of Congress were historically paid the same as senior agency executives (specifically, congressional salaries were equal to executive level II salaries) and circuit court judges. That linkage and the political difficulty of justifying pay increases for elected officials occasionally made it difficult to gain agreement on executive salary increases, which resulted several times in our history in pay compression affecting multiple levels of management in federal agencies. On the one hand, congressional members wanted to take advantage of the pay increases needed to maintain comparability with the private sector, which made it attractive to perpetuate the linkage; on the other hand, there was insufficient political support for recurring pay increases for senators and representatives. The result was a stalemate that affected the federal salary program for several decades.

That problem was alleviated with the passage of the Ethics Reform Act of 1989. This law severed the linkage and introduced pay increases indexed to changes in the Employment Cost Index that is generated by the U.S. Bureau of Labor Statistics. (The Employment Cost Index is a measure of increases in wage and benefit plan costs in our economy.) That statute provided for catch-up increases for proposed but previously denied increases in 1988, 1989, and 1990. With subsequent increases, the salaries of senators and representatives were raised effective January 1, 1993, to $133,600. The Speaker of the House of Representatives and the vice president (president of the Senate) are paid $166,200 per year.[3] In addition, these elected officials are paid allowances for living expenses in Washington, office space in their home state, travel to and from Washington, and the cost of mailings in conducting of congressional business.

FEDERAL SENIOR EXECUTIVE COMPENSATION

The Senior Executive Service (SES) was established in 1979 as a separate personnel system for senior executives. The SES covers mostly managerial and supervisory positions. There are no grades; salaries and career status are primarily based on the individual, not job content. The federal system is often cited as a model for other government employers at the state and local level. The goals of the SES system follow.

- Provide greater authority to agencies to manage executive personnel.

- Enhance the recruitment and retention of competent executives.

- Have the flexibility to assign executives where they can contribute to an agency's performance.

- Hold executives accountable for individual and executive performance.

- Provide for a flexible, merit-based system.

- Provide for the development of executives, reward outstanding performers, and provide the discretion to remove poor performers.

The SES levels begin above GS–15 and include all executive and managerial personnel except presidential appointments. There are six pay levels, ranging in 1994 from ES–1 at $95,771 to ES–6 at $119,275. The lowest rate must equal at least 120 percent of the first step of GS–15. Beginning with the 1994 salary increases, the locality-pay legislation was extended to SES positions so that there are now slight salary differentials across the country.

The merit staffing system requires open competition for first-time career appointment to SES. An agency establishes the qualifications required for its SES positions. There is generally some type of technical or program content expertise (for example, computer science) along with a set of competencies based on the Leadership Effectiveness Framework. In addition, many SES positions require substantial professional or program experience.

The salary rates are negotiated between prospective job applicants and the hiring agency based on such considerations as qualifications, prior experience, and current salary. Salaries can be set at any of the six authorized ES salary levels.

Agencies can pay recruitment bonuses as well as relocation bonuses to entice qualified applicants to accept hard-to-fill vacancies. The law also provides for the payment of a retention allowance to retain highly qualified executives. The bonus payments can be up to 25 percent of base pay.

In addition, each executive must have an annual performance assessment. By law, the appraisal process must provide for at least three rating levels: unsatisfactory, minimally successful, and fully successful. Agencies can provide up to two rating levels above fully successful. SES executives whose annual performance is fully successful or better may receive a performance award or bonus that can vary between 5 and 20 percent of base pay. The total of such awards in most agencies is limited to 3 percent of the agency's SES payroll.

Executives rated as exceptional for at least three years may be nominated by their agency for one of two presidential ranks or ratings,

Distinguished Executive or Meritorious Executive. The former is limited to 1 percent of the career SES cadre and provides for an award of $20,000, normally presented by the president in a special ceremony. In 1993, Distinguished Executive awards were made to only sixty-two federal executives. Meritorious Executive designations can be made to 5 percent of the SES staff and include a $10,000 award.

MANAGING EXECUTIVE SALARY INCREASES

The most difficult ongoing hurdle has been gaining agreement on salary increases for elected and appointed officials and for government executives. The sensitivity of these decisions has made it politically difficult to go forward with recommended increases. That in turn has led many jurisdictions to exclude elected and appointed officials from the annual round of pay increases. Consequently, their salaries often fail to increase at rates consistent with those of lower-level employees.

After a few years there is a realization that the executives are falling behind, their jobs have become less attractive, their lifestyles could realistically be affected, and their salaries need to be increased to alleviate the situation. That triggers a political problem. Voters are never happy to see elected officials receive big pay increases, and everyone ends up a loser in trying to justify the increases. This is a real catch-22 that occurs regularly across the country.

When executives fail to receive their salary increase, it causes compression for the next levels of management. Compression is loosely defined in the compensation field as too little difference in salary between organizational tiers or levels. It is perceived as a problem, but it has never been shown to have any implications for the organization other than informal complaining. The perception is based on prior experience and salary differentials before the situation changed. But when compression exists for any period of time, it becomes the norm and people learn to live with the situation.

In the private sector, executive salary increases are universally based on merit, although there is less reliance on formal performance appraisal systems. Executive salary increases tend to be larger (as a percentage of salary) than those granted to lower-level employees. This pattern has been consistent for years and in fact can be traced back to the period just after World War II. In effect it confirms the relative balance of supply and demand for labor in each group. The comparison

Occupational Group	1994 Planned (percent)	1993 Budget (percent)	1992 Budget (percent)	1991 Budget (percent)	1990 Budget (percent)	1994–1984 Total (percent)
Executives	4.4	4.4	4.8	5.1	5.8	+69.6
Exempt personnel	4.3	4.3	4.7	5.0	5.5	+65.8
Nonexempt personnel	4.2	4.2	4.6	5.0	5.4	+63.8
Consumer Price Index (CPI)	+2.7	+3.0	+3.0	+4.2	+5.4	+37.8

Table 8.1.   Private Sector Trends in Merit Increase Budgets.

Note: Budgeted increases are smaller than the actual average increase.
Source: American Compensation Association and Bureau of Labor Statistics.

of government and corporate increase rates is confounded by the prevalence of step increases combined with range adjustments in government. The private sector trends reflect merit increase budgets only. The data in Table 8.1 show the recent private sector trends.

It may be difficult to gain acceptance for a merit pay policy for government executives. There is simply no basis for generating valid performance ratings unless customers are asked to assess the level of service provided.

This of course does not negate the need to develop an annual increase policy. Private sector practice is based solidly on labor market analyses and recognition of increases in competitive pay levels; salary ranges are adjusted to keep pace with prevailing market levels. Corporate salary ranges may not be adjusted every year, but the textbooks say they should be.

As an alternative, government employers have relied on either increases in the Consumer Price Index (CPI) or in the Employment Cost Index (ECI). The latter is an index series compiled by the U.S. Bureau of Labor Statistics. Neither is directly relevant to executive salary management.

On one hand the CPI is designed to track living costs for a family earning less than $50,000. It effectively overstates the cost increases for families at higher income levels. (That is to say, increases in living costs are not proportionately the same at all income levels.) Moreover, there has been recent technical criticism of the CPI because it does not reflect increases in quality or changes in spending patterns as prices increase. In the late 1970s and into the 1980s, when inflation was running in double digits, there was broad-based acceptance of a "keep them whole" philosophy. Union contracts often included cost of living allowance (COLA) clauses and living cost trends were an important issue in salary planning at all levels. However, over the past decade or so, COLA clauses have virtually disappeared, and salary planning in the private sector is now focused on market analyses. At the executive level, increases in the CPI have never been an important factor.

On the other hand the ECI is designed to track increases in total payroll costs, including paid time off and benefit costs. It also is designed around lower-level workers, who account for a high percentage of payroll costs. The ECI is sometimes confused with CPI, although one tracks living costs and the other labor costs.

When the federal government planned its pay reform legislation in 1990, the choice between CPI and ECI was debated, with the ECI adopted for future range adjustments in years when labor market surveys are not conducted. Significantly, if increases had been based on the CPI over the past decade, government salaries would have fallen progressively behind those in the private sector. When the differences are compounded, they are significant (up 69.6 percent for executive salaries versus 37.8 percent for living costs). The ECI is at least in concept the appropriate measure to maintain alignment with private sector pay increases.

THE FUTURE ROLE OF CASH INCENTIVES

Cash incentive plans have both supporters and critics in our society. The cultural history of the country has numerous rags-to-riches stories of individuals whose accomplishments resulted in financial rewards; an important element of our heritage is the expectation that hard work and diligence will enable people to move up in society. These expectations and dreams ride on financial success. At the same time we are appalled by greed and offended by individuals who seem to make the acquisition of wealth too important in their lives.

From a different perspective, incentive plans are almost universal in corporate America. Virtually every corporation has an incentive plan in place for at least the senior executives. Moreover, in the past decade employers in the not-for-profit sector have added incentives to their executive programs. This is true in health care, associations, and quasi-public institutions such as Fannie Mae and the FDIC. There is also an important trend in the corporate world to extend eligibility for incentives to lower organizational levels. It is important in this context to appreciate that corporations use other types of incentives such as stock options, so that many have both annual and longer-term incentives overlaid on base salaries. In the larger publicly traded corporations the base salary may account for as little as 50 percent of an executive's total compensation.

Experience with incentives shows that plan participants may not work harder—the old motivation argument—but the plans do help to focus the individual's efforts. When a group or team is tied to the same performance measures, prospective incentives help to create and reinforce a sense of team work and heighten the belief that "we're all in this together." Research shows that organizations that use incentives perform better over time.

In the corporate world, incentives are an integral component of the compensation package, not a special occasional add-on as in the federal government. The focus in planning the program is generally on cash compensation, which is the total of base salary and annual incentive payments. In the planning process the cash package is divided between base salary and incentives, using a target or guideline award concept to define the incentive opportunity.

Target awards are normally expressed as a percentage of salary. At the $100,000 salary level the typical target award might be 20 to 25 percent of salary. If salary surveys show, for example, that the competitive pay level for a job is $125,000 and the target award is 20 percent, the total is divided by 1.20, resulting in a base salary of $100,000 and a target award of $25,000. The target award percentage is a policy decision and rides on the risk-reward philosophy that flows from the business strategy. If the company expects the executive to assume greater risk, the target is increased and the base salary is reduced.

Target award levels are specified for each executive position. At the CEO level, awards of 50 or 60 percent of salary are common. Reduced award levels then cascade down the management ranks, typically in increments of 5 percent, although not every company follows this practice. At the lowest plan participant levels, where salaries might range up or down $50,000, target awards could be as low as 10 or 15 percent of salary.

The target award amount is what an executive can, in concept, expect to earn in an average or typical year. If the company has an outstanding year, actual awards will be above the target amount; conversely, when performance is poor, awards are reduced and the executive's take-home pay for the year falls below the competitive level. This simple logic serves as the foundation for hundreds of corporate incentive plans, making it possible to manage executive cash compensation levels relative to market levels even though actual earnings fluctuate each year.

It is important to point out that the extremely high levels of compensation reported in the press are almost always attributable to stock ownership opportunities. Moreover, as that form of income rides on stock appreciation, reported income levels may fall with a stock price decline before the individual actually acquires the shares and receives the income.

Actual cash incentive payouts depend on how well the company performs and in most cases on the achievement of departmental or individual performance goals. Although there is wide variation in practice, it is common for each plan participant to establish three to five performance goals, with weights to indicate their relative importance, and then to have year-end incentive payments ride on actual performance against the goals. This linkage to the business planning process works better in some companies than in others, but the practice is widely used.

The concept makes sense in government. It is important to appreciate that the underlying logic makes the incentive payouts an integral component of the pay package, not icing on the cake. By design, when performance is below planned levels, the individual's take-home pay is below the competitive level. Awards may look high to the public, but the individual's income is presumably planned to be in line with pay levels in other companies. This subtlety may sometimes be difficult to sell to the public, but it is an effective basis for managing executive compensation.

As an example, for an executive paid a base salary of $80,000, a target of 10 percent or $8,000 might be appropriate. For truly outstanding performance, we might establish a maximum of $10,000. The actual incentive award could then fluctuate between zero and $10,000.

If necessary, it could be structured so that a percentage of the individual's salary is lost if the objectives are not achieved. That could help overcome some of the objections to extra payments for doing what the individual would be expected to accomplish anyway. The school superintendent in Philadelphia, as an example, is currently eligible for a 10 percent award, but if the school system fails to meet certain objectives, he not only does not earn an award but he can also lose up to 5 percent of his salary. Experience shows, however, that plans that make participants feel like winners are more effective than those where individuals can only lose.

The concept depends, of course, on being able to establish realistic performance objectives. In a corporation this is normally not difficult. The basic question is "What do we have to accomplish to be successful?" There is no reason to think government agencies would be unable to develop answers to this question. Chapter Nine, on performance planning and measurement, should provide some insight on defining missions and on setting objectives.

A key to planning and gaining acceptance for incentives is this linkage to performance. If an agency can define its mission and translate it into a few important goals, this should provide justification for rewarding the responsible officials for achieving those goals. The private sector focuses on "stretch" goals—achievements that represent solid accomplishments—and that concept is certainly meaningful in government. If we are to have accountable government leaders, then linking their pay to their accomplishments is a tested way to reinforce the public's expectations.

There may be a need for a board of directors or community oversight body to review proposed goals and to assess year-end performance. That works in the private sector. On this point corporate boards are being pressured to do a better job of establishing performance goals and evaluating executive performance. The trend toward having some group not directly involved in day-to-day management oversee executive plans and play a role in planning and goal setting is pervasive in every sector but government. For reasons that may have been lost in history, we have rarely held government executives accountable for their performance or for setting and working to achieve realistic but difficult goals.

Where we can define what we want a group to accomplish and agree on ways to measure their performance, there is a basis for introducing an incentive system. Experience in every other sector confirms that organizations operating in this manner tend to achieve higher levels of performance. That has been confirmed in health care as well as other not-for-profit organizations. The high level of interest in improved government performance suggests the time has come to try incentives in government.

SELLING CHANGES IN
EXECUTIVE PAY LEVELS

Changes in the pay of elected officials and public sector executives may not be front-page news, but the plans for them are news. It may be inevitable that voters will be interested in proposed changes and more often than not oppose them; this may be the reason needed changes are delayed until the incumbents' standard of living is affected. Then it becomes necessary to recommend and work to obtain approval for a significant and politically sensitive increase.

Pay adjustments would be considerably smaller and probably less sensitive if they were granted annually. However, in a political climate where some voters are experiencing layoffs and others receiving no salary increase, any system that provides for more or less automatic increases is not going to win broad support. Congress has already experienced the backlash from its modest increase system based on the Employment Cost Index.

In reality the cost of maintaining adequate executive salaries is not the issue. In the private sector there is a rule of thumb that the executive team represents only 1 percent of an organization's workforce. With 10,000 workers that means only 100 could be categorized as executives. In government the percentage of people in politically sensitive positions is even smaller. Their salaries in the aggregate may represent 3 or 4 percent of the total, and planned increases at any point are at most 5 percent of that small amount, based on current practice. To translate this into dollars, with a $50 million payroll executive salaries would be $2 million and possible salary increases $100,000, or 0.2 percent of the total. Out of a total government budget, the increase in executive salaries could almost get lost in rounding!

The economics of planned increases are of course never addressed in media coverage; the increases are a symbolic lightning rod that would attract criticism regardless of the cost. This suggests that someone has to develop a strategy to market and sell the importance of the increases to local decision makers. At some level the voters may follow and express concern about planned salary increases, but it would be unusual for this to become a cause of concern unless a few key people start beating the political drums.

When the Bush administration wanted to sell federal pay reform, the focus of the selling campaign was on a select group of senators and congressmen who served on key committees. A few years ago when the state of New York wanted to sell salary increases for senior state executives, the focus was on local chambers of commerce across the state along with the people responsible for editorials in key newspapers. Every jurisdiction has a few key community leaders who have the clout locally to ensure enactment of proposed increases—as long as there is an acceptable rationale to justify the change.

It would certainly be useful to have data available to justify the increases. The information should probably include pay data from other similar jurisdictions along with survey data relevant to trends in living costs and in executive salary increases in the private sector. There has to be solid justification under any circumstances. However, data alone are probably not going to convince enough people to win support; that strategy has seldom proven adequate.

Significantly, the experience with the federal Quadrennial Commission and later with the indexed pay increases for members of Congress may be a useful illustration of the problem. The logic of Quad Com's public testimony and objective analyses sounded good at the time of its enactment but rarely resulted in a report that was accepted. In those years when increases were actually adopted following the report, the recommendations were effectively nothing more than the starting point for political maneuvering. With more or less automatic increases based on the Employment Cost Index, the process ran into a shift in the public sentiment after less than five years, coinciding with the majority change from Democrats to Republicans in Congress. The change in the public's perceived view of government prompted the White House to deny funding for the new Citizens' Commission that had been scheduled in 1993, so it never got off the ground.

This experience suggests that it is unlikely that any automatic increase system will be acceptable over an extended period of time. There are simply too many unforeseeable changes in the political climate to expect any answer to remain untarnished. This effectively shifts the focus to deal making and the need to generate support among local decision makers. That makes it difficult to expect annual increases; the political quid pro quo cost to work out a new deal every year is too high. Thus it is unlikely that any jurisdiction can find an acceptable long-term solution to this problem.

SUMMARY

Contrary to the rhetoric, elected officials and government executives are not overpaid relative to individuals in other occupations in our society. There are examples of individuals in all aspects of life that make less of a contribution and are paid substantially more than the leaders of our public institutions. To be sure, the pay for high-level public leaders is well above that of the average voter; that can never be ignored. However, if society wants to raise the performance standards for public administrators and hold them accountable for improved performance, it must also agree to commensurate increases in pay.

The adage that says you get what you pay for does have relevance to compensation planning. Every talented individual has career options; the pull of alternatives outside of government is increasingly difficult to ignore as the gap gets wider. This is particularly relevant to midcareer people with families who will be asked to live with a diminished lifestyle if they work in government. The expectation that the best and the brightest will be interested in working in government at any point in their careers has declined over the years.

Perhaps one reason for the public's disdain for government is the virtual absence of any performance expectations. It seems at times to the public that government goes on without goals or agreement on how performance will be measured. When there is no agreement on what a person is to accomplish, there can be no reasoned conclusion that performance is good or bad. It is obvious from the public debate over government that the public needs to be convinced that government is contributing to the quality of life. That requires agreement at some level on the goals and the standards for assessing performance.

An important issue in this debate is the image of government and the increased willingness at all levels in the past decade or so to have disdain for government. Career choice is affected by the public's regard for career alternatives. Relative pay levels can offset the public's image to some degree, but it is completely unreasonable to expect talented people to choose a career where compensation opportunities are falling along with the perceived status of the occupation.

When compared with salaries for government executives throughout the world, U.S. pay levels are behind those in several leading countries, including Japan, England, Canada, and Germany.[4] Although these comparisons are complicated by prevailing local practices, exchange rate fluctuations, and different structures for government entities, the facts suggest that government officials in U.S. civil service are paid roughly 35 percent less than the senior positions in Japan. Comparison with other countries also emphasizes the difference in the way elected officials are compensated relative to career employees.

In the United Kingdom, for example, members of Parliament are paid less than half as much as permanent secretaries (cabinet-level executives).

In some occupations society can afford to have the work performed by less-talented people. Even with a downsized government, however, budgets are still going to be very large by most standards, and the job of accomplishing more with less is going to demand more-talented rather than less-talented people. That makes executive pay a central issue regardless of one's view of government. The role of government may be radically redefined, but the remaining operations, often with budgets still running into the millions, need to be led by talented individuals.

There unfortunately are no completely rational or factual ways to establish appropriate pay levels, though there are many sources of at least peripherally relevant information. In most other sectors there is general agreement on how jobs and pay levels will be compared and pay adjusted. Those methods are used to monitor and adjust pay for lower-level public jobs, but there is little evidence that they are used meaningfully at the executive level. Any information is generally better than none when decisions have to be made, so it would be worthwhile to try some of these methods.

Within this context cash incentives could be an alternative that fits the arguments of both sides of this debate. Incentive opportunities represent a way for executives to increase and to some degree control their income. Incentives also provide a rationale to send the message that society is willing to pay more only if performance meets agreed-upon expectations. This is going to be a difficult hurdle to get over because many people still view incentives as a giveaway or special treatment for a privileged few. That perception may be warranted in some cases, but it certainly should not be a blanket condemnation of incentives.

The reward system for public sector executives is an important societal issue. If the demands for improved government service continue to escalate, the need for improved management systems will continue to be a central question. Well-designed compensation systems can play a role in helping workers at all levels focus on key performance issues. To this point the public sector has elected to ignore the potential value of compensation as a management tool. The symbolism of escalating pay might be offset by the realization that it is contributing to improved performance.

Notes

1. See National Commission on the Public Service, *Leadership for America: Rebuilding the Public Service* (Washington, D.C.: U.S. Government Printing Office, 1989).
2. *The World Almanac and Book of Facts: 1995,* Microsoft Bookshelf '95 (Redmond, Wash.: Microsoft, 1995), CD-ROM.
3. Congressional Research Service, *CRS Report for Congress* (May 19, 1995).
4. Based on 1990 rates, from data maintained by the Senior Executive Association (Washington, D.C.).

PART TWO

Linking Pay
to Performance

Undoubtedly the most important trend in compensation management is the movement away from policies and practices that contribute to an entitlement culture and higher fixed payroll costs. Corporations are now placing more emphasis on merit pay and rapidly introducing group incentive plans. Many of these organizations are in a trial-and-error mode, trying new ideas and working to strengthen existing plans.

Merit pay has always been important in the corporate world, but it is important to appreciate that merit pay policies are acknowledged to be less than completely effective. W. Edwards Deming was an outspoken critic of traditional performance appraisal and merit pay practices; in his opinion they are counterproductive. He contended that, among other problems, they place too much emphasis on individual performance. Despite his criticism, however, merit pay has become more, not less, prevalent over the past decade or so.

Deming's argument against performance appraisals and merit pay suffers from his failure to provide a viable alternative. Salary adjustments are always needed, as is a rationale for them. If merit pay is not acceptable, the fallback is a tenure-based policy (for example, a step increase system) or across-the-board increases. But when corporate leaders are working to control cost increases, these are not acceptable options.

Corporate leaders are also strongly opposed to an entitlement culture as being contrary to the work ethic and the reward philosophies that permeate corporate values. The cultural history of the United States includes numerous rags-to-riches stories, and working hard to get ahead is part of the American dream. The entitlement problem has its origins in the period of rapid inflation and wage controls, when inflation and pay increases were in double digits; no one wants to return to that era.

One of the reasons government human resource policies are viewed with disdain is the perceived entitlement culture and minimal performance standards. Although most voters or for that matter corporate leaders do not have direct knowledge of government practices, the public perception is that pay increases are essentially automatic and workers can get by with minimal effort. Political leaders have obviously contributed to this perception, and trying to introduce the facts at this point is not going to alter it.

The interest in the pay-for-performance concept in the corporate world also reflects the realities of global competition. Companies are searching for any source of competitive advantage. Pay levels in the United States are comparatively high, triggering a need to bring down costs to survive and spurring interest in reengineering and downsizing. The pressure to control, if not reduce, labor costs has become almost an obsession in many companies. Executives as well as workers in the private sector have to live with this every day. This reality contributes to the pressure to reinvent government workforce management practices.

From a more positive perspective there is considerable evidence that pay-for-performance arrangements do in fact contribute to improved performance. That is to say, they influence employee behavior. Research sponsored by the American Compensation Association over the past several years shows clearly that organizations that introduce performance management systems aligned with financial rewards realize improved performance. The public sector has too little experience with financial incentives to conduct similar research, but there is no inherent reason to expect contrary results.

It is also important to acknowledge that experience with financial incentives has not been wholly positive. Many individuals are philosophically opposed to the idea. Some would argue that it may be a viable concept in the corporate world but inappropriate in government.

The counterargument is that the problems are largely attributable to poor plan design. If the rewards are linked to the wrong behaviors or the wrong results, it should not be surprising when the system is ineffective. For example, so-called piece-rate incentive systems that reward employees for the volume of output but ignore its quality probably are out of sync with today's workforce management thinking.

Actually, some of the negative view of cash incentives is probably related to the experience with piece-rate systems in the post–World War II period when they were prevalent in factory operations. Until recently the focus of pay-for-performance systems was on incentives linked to individual output. These originated in the scientific management era and were clearly designed as a control mechanism to maximize production. But they triggered a lot of ill feeling between management and labor; industry has effectively abandoned piece-rate systems.

The new work management paradigm is based on different principles and on understanding employee motivation. The emphasis now is on group or team performance, not individual performance. The new systems are commonly referred to as *gainsharing plans,* a label first used in the 1930s. The original gainsharing plans were narrowly based on sharing savings in labor costs with employees, but in current usage the phrase encompasses almost any group incentive arrangement. Increasingly, phrases such as *success sharing* and *goal sharing* are used to refer to these plans. There is also mushrooming interest in team-based reward systems where there may be a small number of participants.

The latter phrases and plan concepts reflect the new philosophy recognizing that employees can make a major contribution to a firm's success and will make a more concerted effort and be more willing to contribute their ideas if they can expect to benefit when their organization is successful. This is far different from the carrot-on-a-stick control orientation of the old piece-rate systems. The new thinking is based solidly on the belief that we are all in this enterprise together.

Perhaps surprisingly, given government's experience, research shows that employees would prefer to be rewarded for their performance if, and it is a big if, they can trust their supervisor to do a competent job of appraising that performance. Realistically, a supervisor's ability to handle this aspect of the job depends on training, and that means more than an hour's exposure to a new appraisal form. Employees would also like to contribute to their employer's success and to know that management recognizes their contribution. That requires effective, ongoing communication. Finally, they would like to know that when their organization is successful, they stand to benefit too. To make that so, organizational success has to trigger desirable rewards for individuals; the rewards do not have to be limited to cash, but the perceived value has to be commensurate with the employee effort and degree of success.

In a government environment it should be possible to pay cash incentive awards. Payouts in the range that is typical of gainsharing plans—perhaps 4 to 8 percent of base pay—are not prohibitively costly, particularly as the payouts come about only through improved performance. Moreover, the payouts are not going to be made in succeeding years unless improvement continues. When employees see and accept the linkage between their individual efforts and the success of their work unit, they should react very much the same as individuals working in the private sector. Certainly there will be skeptics among the employees—the private sector has its share—but that is one of the beauties of group or team incentives: coworkers can often get people to overcome their reluctance to make the effort. With time their reluctance should diminish.

Industry has learned that performance can be improved with a well-conceived and carried out strategy. This should include the reconsideration of the overall work system. Quality management and reengineering are really only the tip of this iceberg. Anecdotal stories abound of dramatic performance improvements, such as productivity increases of 50 percent or more, when organizations redefine the way work is organized and managed.

Within this context the pay-for-performance system should be seen as a potentially valuable tool. Financial rewards, or any rewards for that matter, cannot be effective in a vacuum. Complementary policies and practices, such as a performance management system, must also be in place along with solid top management support, a meaningful and ongoing system to measure performance, and a communications campaign to make sure everyone knows how well the organization is doing relative to its goals. The public sector has barely opened this door.

People like to work for successful organizations. In the right environment they will make an incredible commitment to the organization's goals and enjoy the experience. Skeptics need only watch the movie *Apollo 13* to see how people in one public agency were committed to realizing their mission. That may be a unique story, but the public sector has a lot of people who started with a strong motivation to contribute to the solution of a problem affecting society. Bureaucracies have a way of dampening that excitement. When one talks with people who started a federal career in the 1960s, it is obvious that they bought into the shared commitment of that era only to become disillusioned and frustrated by their more recent experience.

The pay-for-performance concept is certainly not a panacea to overcome the bashing of government employees by politicians and in some cases by the media. It can, however, be an effective tool to align the interests of workers and increase their commitment to organizational goals. There is no reason to think that government workers are much different from those working in industry. No one is going to work hard in an environment where worker efforts are ignored or where workers are alienated from their managers. In the right environment a well-designed reward system can be an important tool in improving performance.

CHAPTER NINE

Managing and Assessing Employee Performance

Doris Hausser
Charles H. Fay

Most private sector organizations view employee performance as the key to organizational success. The best strategy, the most detailed business plan, and the cleverest marketing approach are worth little if implementation relies on employees who perform poorly. Information and production technology may circumvent some problems, but if employees cannot or will not perform, investments in technology are largely wasted. Close supervision may reduce some performance problems, but competitors whose employees perform well on their own will provide better products at lower cost. This is particularly true in the service sector, where a corporation's success frequently relies on high performance by those lower-level employees who deal with customers, suppliers, and other critical outsiders.

As the largest provider of services, the public sector is particularly dependent on the performance of its employees. Most complaints about government come from people who have had to deal with individual government employees who, rather than providing service, appeared dedicated to frustrating their needs. This is not to say that most or even many public sector employees are incompetent or malevolent; the fault frequently lies in the system designed to serve the public, and in the management and performance systems used to plan and implement those services.

Performance management is a particularly important part of reengineering service processes. In "reinventing government," reforming the performance management system is critical to refocusing the efforts of employees and reinforcing high performance when it occurs. The efforts of the federal government (in particular the Office of Personnel Management [OPM]) to reform this system provide a useful case study of a change effort that might be usefully emulated by other public sector organizations.

FEDERAL PERFORMANCE MANAGEMENT PROGRAMS

The performance of any government agency, division, work team, or the like comes down to the performance contributions of individual employees. As with its other physical, financial, informational, and temporal resources, an organization creates processes, however formal or informal, effective or ineffective, to manage (that is, plan, lead, and control) employee performance.

The traditional core processes in managing the performance of the federal workforce are the formal assessment elements: planning and measurement. The most visible assessment aspect is usually the formal appraisal apparatus—the performance elements (measures on which performance is judged) and standards (the level on a measure equating to a given level of performance), the rating methods, and the summary rating of record. These performance appraisal components are what most people, in and out of federal government, automatically think of (and often condemn) when the term *performance management* is used.

Performance management processes and their results can be applied with multiple objectives in mind. When private sector companies were asked to rank fifteen possible uses of performance assessment information in order of importance,[1] the top five were the following.

1. Improving work performance

2. Administering pay based on merit

3. Advising employees of work expectations

4. Making promotion decisions

5. Counseling employees

Using performance management and assessment to serve multiple purposes is a long-standing tradition. In the federal government a key objective of the Civil Service Reform Act (CSRA) of 1978 was to make performance management the centerpiece of human resource management. To do this, emphasis was placed on the two formal assessment elements of planning and measurement. Specifically, management would establish job elements and standards for employees (plan) and then, at least once a year, appraise (measure) the employees against those standards. This summary appraisal would be firmly tied to rewards, training, promotion, retention, and the like, all of which should motivate employees to perform better. The whole system was oriented around establishing and maintaining individual accountability. Taxpayers could be assured that federal employees who fail to meet performance standards could be removed from their jobs.

After an initial period of experimentation immediately following CSRA, the federal government adopted a highly standardized approach to appraisal and performance management. (More recently, policy changes—described at the close of this chapter—have been introduced that give federal organizations an opportunity to apply the lessons and best practices to be discussed here.)

For the past dozen years federal policies have reflected the theories and practice of the late 1970s. The logic and promise of creating a summary rating that could serve multiple purposes was compelling. Under this centralized vision of performance management the expectations for it typically rest on the technical and "scientific" validity of the appraisal apparatus itself—the forms, scales, events, requirements—to produce the desired effects. But insufficient attention was paid to the fact that payoffs result from the way such apparatus is used; instead, faith was placed in the experts' ability to design the "best" system.

As in many other areas of public policy, however, using one approach or technique to serve multiple policy goals can be problematic. In the years since CSRA, practitioners have come to realize that achieving multiple purposes within a rigidly designed, centrally controlled performance management system can lead to serious conflicts for organizations and employees.

Broadly stated, there are two basic purposes for performance management: allocating rewards and sanctions and providing feedback and developing performance capacity. Unless an organization ignores performance (that is, treats all employees the same regardless of performance), achieving these purposes under even the best of conditions is challenging, creates tension, and requires difficult decisions.

In the federal government, failure to achieve different objectives had been virtually guaranteed by an excessive reliance on technically correct, centrally directed planning of measurement systems that attempted to meet too many objectives. In many agencies the performance management system functioned principally as a command-and-control mechanism owned and operated by the personnel office. The system came to be viewed as a set of demoralizing, sterile, and burdensome rituals that add no value and whose results (inflated ratings) were driven inexorably by consequent personnel actions linked mechanically to summary appraisal ratings. Table 9.1 illustrates the linkages that exist in the federal system and that clearly serve the purpose of allocating rewards and sanctions.

Committee on Performance Appraisal for Merit Pay

The merit pay system Congress put in place for the government's midlevel managers was one key reason the federal performance management system was highly centralized in the mid-1980s. That system, the Performance Management and Recognition System (PMRS), was the subject of constant controversy. As part of an effort to develop sound legislative proposals for reforming that system, OPM requested that the National Academy of Sciences establish a National Research Council study committee to analyze contemporary research on performance appraisal. In its 1991 report,[2] the Committee on Performance Appraisal for Merit Pay provided a comprehensive review of research and practice on performance assessment and performance-based pay systems. Given its charter to examine appraisal-based pay decisions, the committee focused primarily on the "allocate rewards" purpose of performance management, but its review covered the uses of measurement to support performance development as well.

The committee's review points out appraisal's roots in a psychometric tradition that emphasizes the measurement properties of any appraisal system. An applied tradition places greater importance on

Table 9.1. Linkages Between Federal Performance Appraisal Levels and Employee Rewards and Sanctions.

Centralized Federal Performance Appraisal System (Summary Rating Levels)		Percent with Rating (1994)	Pay Administration (Requirement for Within-Grade Step Increase)		Monetary Recognition		RIF Retention Credit	Adverse Action
SES	Non-SES		General Schedule	Prevailing Rate	Rating-Based Award	Quality Step Increase		
Other levels of fully successful	Outstanding	34.00	Acceptable level of competence	Rating of satisfactory or better	XX percent	Eligible	20 years	
	Exceeds fully successful	42.60			X percent	Ineligible	16 years	
Fully successful	Fully successful	23.03			x percent Eligible		12 years	
Minimally successful	Minimally satisfactory	0.26			Ineligible		0 years	
Un-satisfactory	Un-acceptable	0.11						Demotion/ removal

Note: XX is largest; X is smaller; x is smaller still.

Source: National Academy of Science's NRC Committee on Performance Appraisal for Merit Pay.

the utility of the measures, particularly for affecting organization-level outcomes. One of the most telling findings for OPM's purposes was the study's conclusion (p. 151) that "the goal of a performance appraisal system should be to support and encourage informed managerial judgment and not to aspire to a degree of standardization, precision, and empirical support that would be required of, for example, selection tests."

In addition, the committee took pains to note the importance of context for the success or failure of an appraisal- or performance-based pay approach. It outlined three categories for that context: the nature of an organization's work, its structure and culture, and external factors such as economic climate and stakeholder pressures. The clear lesson from research and experience is that an appraisal approach must fit its context.

Given the vast diversity of the federal government and its component organizations, the committee recommended that policies be adopted to decentralize the design and implementation of appraisal- and performance-based pay systems. Allowing such design to be approached as an integral part of each organization's overall strategy would require a good deal of flexibility for design features and choices. Such decentralization and flexibility could occur within a framework of policy guidelines that would maintain some essential government-wide equity. OPM's immediate application of these recommendations was to support the extension of PMRS with some additional flexibilities while the issue of performance appraisal for rank-and-file employees was considered further.

National Performance Review

As one of his first actions in office, President Clinton directed Vice President Gore to undertake the National Performance Review (NPR) to identify ways to create a government that works better and costs less. In its initial report, *From Red Tape to Results*,[3] the NPR recommended a decentralized approach to performance management: "Agencies should be allowed to develop their own performance management and reward systems, with the objective of improving the performance of individuals and organizations" (p. 25).

The NPR encouraged employee involvement in system design as a means of creating ownership and commitment to the performance management process. It also made a point that the government's centralized system had been intended to serve multiple purposes but ended up serving none of them particularly well. Instead, systems should focus on improving individual and organizational performance, which would emphasize the "develop performance capacity" purpose.

At the same time, however, the NPR wanted individual accountability maintained. So the "allocate sanctions" purpose still got attention as proposals were made to improve the system for dealing with poor performers, always a political priority for public policymakers.

In its more detailed accompanying report, *Reinventing Human Resource Management,*[4] the NPR made more specific proposals for how the performance management system should be reformed. It recommended that flexible, decentralized systems be developed by managers and employees and their representatives and that policies be revised to support an overall change in organizational strategy such that organizations are structured around teams rather than bureaucratic hierarchies.

In addition the NPR proposed that performance be appraised and summarized in as few as two ways: meets or does not meet expectations (standards). This directly responded to the many calls for "pass-fail" appraisals; despite quality guru W. Edwards Deming's fierce denouncements of such systems, proponents have long argued that if it is politically necessary to maintain a system of individual accountability, at least unhealthy individual competition for high ratings could be removed by using pass-fail appraisal.

Summary of Problems

These review groups, OPM, and other researchers studying the centralized federal appraisal system concluded that it suffers from many of the ills characterizing traditional appraisal systems in the private sector. Because of the size of the federal government, problems that might be marginal barriers to managing performance in many private organizations assume critical importance in improving performance in the public sector. These problems include the following.

SINGLE SYSTEM FOR ALL AGENCIES   Various federal government units have widely disparate goals, strategies, cultures, work systems, and employee types. The probability is low that any single management system could be appropriate for a research unit staffed by Ph.D. scientists and engineers, a social services unit staffed by outreach staff, and an administrative unit staffed by clerical and supervisory staff.

OVERCENTRALIZATION Centralizing design and overview functions of the process for managing performance in a single support agency increases the likelihood that the system will not be sensitive to unit needs. Even though OPM has performance management and appraisal expertise, its resource and staff reductions make it unlikely that it can respond to the needs of all the government units using the system.

OWNERSHIP BY PERSONNEL OFFICE, NOT LINE MANAGERS Line managers are the users of the system and need to feel ownership of it if they are to use it. Many of them have come to see performance management and appraisal as just one more thing foisted off on them by OPM and their own units' personnel departments.

TOP-DOWN MANAGEMENT The centralized governmentwide system focuses on management-subordinate interaction, with most of the initiative for the process left to management. There is little room for peer, client, or subordinate input into the definition, measurement, or appraisal of performance. As more work systems are built around teams, this top-down approach becomes less appropriate.

USE AS COMMAND-AND-CONTROL MECHANISM The focus has been on the appraisal part of the system rather than the performance planning portions. Similarly, the centralized system seems more concerned with providing consequences for previous performance levels and allocating rewards and sanctions than with developing employee performance.

NONINTEGRATION The centralized appraisal system tends to stand alone rather than being integrated with other human resource and performance planning programs. Because performance rating distributions are so skewed (see Table 9.1), data generated by the system are not very useful for planning future human resource strategies or for promotion and other staffing decisions. Similarly, they are of only limited use for decisions concerning needed training. As noted earlier, there is little emphasis on performance development.

EXCESSIVE TECHNICAL CONCERNS   Because the emphasis in the centralized system is on performance appraisal rather than management of performance, the focus tends to be on finding the perfect appraisal form—a goal that has eluded the efforts of hundreds of industrial psychologists for fifty years and that is now largely recognized to be futile. Evidence suggests that efforts to improve the performance management process provide much larger paybacks than investment in better rating forms.

LIMITED CREDIBILITY   Perhaps the greatest cost of the severe rating inflation that occurred over the years was the lost credibility of the foundation of the whole performance management system: its measures. Although by law the measurement system had to be criterion-referenced and forced ratings distributions were illegal, the notion that three out of four federal employees could exceed their "fully successful" performance standards simply lost credibility with both external and internal observers. Too often the measures look solely at the individual process inputs that employees could be held accountable for. A summary rating came to represent coming to work and fulfilling the position description, rather than achieving particular outcomes or results. Worse yet, the centralized system ties cash awards to these less-than-credible performance ratings. In some cases the awards became virtual entitlements spread very wide and very thin, although public criticism of them did lead to some curtailments.

FOCUS ON POOREST PERFORMERS   The performance system came to emphasize its role in dealing with poor performers, requiring specific due process procedures and the right to a third-party review by the Merit Systems Protection Board (MSPB), by an arbitrator, or (for protected groups) by the Equal Employment Opportunity Commission. These requirements in turn led to volumes of case law interpreting and embellishing the system.

The complicated procedural requirements of pursuing performance-based actions have created a perception that managers must rely on the personnelist's expertise to pilot them through these shoals. This reinforces the personnelists' belief that ownership of the negative side of performance management is thrust upon them and that they are accountable for making it work. The net result has contributed to managers' denying responsibility for dealing with poor performers.

A particularly unfortunate outcome of the government's approach to dealing with poor performers is the counterproductive effect it has on the organization's performance assessment efforts. Scrutinizing and revising performance standards to ensure that they are "MSPB-proof" and able to support adverse action shifts ownership of the standards from the line organization to the personnel shop. This undermines their use as a meaningful management tool for the 95 percent or more of employees who are not problem performers. As a result, the utility of assessment in providing feedback to and developing performance capacity for the vast majority of employees was sacrificed to the uncertain quest of ousting poor performers. Although it may be possible to streamline some of the bureaucracy in the performance-based action arena, long-standing public policies with respect to due process, employee rights, nondiscrimination, and the like limit the scope of this option.

LESSONS FROM THE PRIVATE SECTOR AND RESEARCH

Because of global economic pressure, and especially because they must increasingly compete with overseas organizations with much lower hourly labor costs, private sector organizations in the United States have focused on increases in individual and group productivity. Research in performance measurement, management, and appraisal has resulted in great changes for them in both the manufacturing and service sectors. It seems likely that many of these practices could also be applied in the public sector. But if performance-based pay, for example, is to come to the public sector, a new role for performance measurement and management will have to be adopted, particularly if the performance appraisal is to drive it.

Indeed, one conclusion of the Committee on Performance Appraisal for Merit Pay was that the Civil Service System's emphasis on egalitarianism and freedom from partisan manipulation in its performance appraisal system may make private sector experience irrelevant to federal performance-based pay plans. Subsequent changes suggest that such constraints may be lessening. Also, the experience of state and local governments indicates that private sector approaches to performance measurement and management can indeed be successfully transferred to the public sector.

Performance Management Versus Performance Appraisal

Perhaps the most important development in private sector performance is the shift toward emphasizing performance management rather than performance appraisal. Performance appraisal focuses on after-the-fact measurement of how well an individual has performed; performance management focuses on the entire performance process, relegating appraisal to a minor role. There are variations, but a typical performance management system consists of three stages.

STAGE ONE: PERFORMANCE PLANNING   In the first stage, performance must be defined and performance goals set. Most programs focus on joint development of performance definition by manager and employee, but in an authoritarian culture it still may be possible to run a successful system with definitions of performance drawn solely by management. Performance definitions typically start with individual outcomes that are thought to support organizational objectives. Because such outcomes do not typically cover all relevant aspects of performance, they are likely to be supplemented with definitions of expected employee behaviors.

Given a set of outcomes and behaviors thought to define performance, the manager (again, with the collaboration of the employee where that matches the organizational culture) sets standards of performance. A typical system might specify five levels of performance:

- Greatly exceeds standards
- Exceeds standards
- Meets standards fully
- Meets standards marginally
- Fails to meet standards (unsatisfactory)

Note that the levels of performance refer to the standards rather than the "goodness" of the employee. The purpose is to make the system more objective and make it more likely that performance feedback (see the next step) can be given and accepted.

The final part of performance planning is getting the employee ready to perform. This is typically done through goal-setting techniques.[5] The purpose is to get the employee to commit to stretch performance goals; research suggests that such commitment results in higher performance than would otherwise be achieved. The resulting commitment is sometimes referred to as the performance contract. However, if conditions change during the performance period the contract is subject to renegotiation; for this reason, some organizations avoid the term as implying a fixed, unalterable agreement between manager and employee.

It should be noted that the performance goal is not the same as the performance standard. Ideally, the goal should be to exceed or greatly exceed the standard. One reason most management by objective programs (whether in the public or private sector) have failed has been confusion about goals and standards. Goal setting promises higher performance, not necessarily goal achievement; if employees really commit to stretch goals, they are likely to perform above standard but frequently will still not achieve the stretch goal. If they are punished for this, they will attempt to set easily achievable goals, particularly if they see other employees rewarded for goal achievement against easy goals.

STAGE TWO: THE PERFORMANCE PERIOD   A variety of activities take place during the performance period (the time between the finalization of the performance plan and the formal appraisal of performance). These are the management part of the performance management system. Most consist of positive or corrective feedback, as appropriate. When the employee performs at a high level as defined by the performance standards, it is incumbent on the manager to note it, and to do so in terms of the standards. (That is, the manager notes to the employee that the performance has been recognized, refers to the relevant section of the performance plan and to the standards, and praises the employee for the performance achieved.)

When poor performance is observed, the manager provides corrective feedback. The performance is noted and compared to the relevant section of the performance plan and to the standards. Managers are much more willing to deal with poor performance and employees are much more willing to accept corrective feedback when it is stated in terms of the performance plan and standards, rather than of shortcomings of character. The emphasis is on correction rather than punishment; a critical part of corrective feedback is to determine how the situation can be corrected and performance put back on track.

The typical performance management system prescribes frequent feedback. Employees should understand how they are doing at any given time against the performance plan. Having the plan contributes in itself to this understanding, as some performance measures (particularly outcome measures) will be self-evident. Some organizations specify quarterly or bimonthly formal feedback sessions to make sure this understanding exists.

STAGE THREE: THE PERFORMANCE APPRAISAL AND REVIEW   It should be fairly obvious that if stages one and two are done well, stage three becomes somewhat anticlimactic. The appraisal itself is a summary of performance against the plan standards. The performance review process becomes oriented more toward planning for the next performance period than toward listing achievements and deficits in the previous period.

Decisions or Development?

One of the difficulties noted with the centralized federal system of performance appraisal is the use of results for two different purposes: for decisions about rewards, sanctions, and staffing, and for development of employee performance. Although the private sector has not solved the problems accompanying this dual use of performance management systems, it does appear that organizational commitment to the performance management system described earlier reduces the problems that occur when the summary appraisal is the focus of the system. When the emphasis is on managing performance, frequent feedback to participants allows for correction of performance deficiencies before the summary appraisal is made.

Linkages to Strategy and Organizational Goals

Another critical change in the management of performance in the private sector is recognizing that good performance can be defined only within the specific organizational context, particularly the context of organizational goals and the strategy developed to attain them. This change recognizes that off-the-shelf approaches (such as "borrowing" an appraisal form from another organization) are not likely to provide a system that will support the enhancement of organizational performance.

Instead, private sector organizations begin the development of a performance management system by articulating both organizational goals and the strategy for achieving them. Business units define their own performance goals in light of organizational goals and each organizational sublevel proceeds to define its own goals in a series of goal cascades. For the manager of a small unit, the question becomes "What must my unit do to help achieve the goals of the next larger unit of which we are a part?"

At the level of the individual employee the question is similar: "How does my performance help the unit I work in achieve its goals?" This may be difficult to answer if the line of sight between the individual's activities and the organization's achievements is nebulous. Part of management's role is to help employees understand organizational strategy and the importance of individual efforts in achieving organizational goals.

Teams and Performance Management

The nature of work in many organizations has changed radically over the last two decades. In the industrial engineering tradition, work was defined as a stable series of tasks performed by an individual and the unit of analysis was the job.[6] In many organizations that definition is no longer appropriate, at least for much of the work done; in such cases work may instead be defined as the changeable process used by a group to achieve specific outcomes. If performance management is to form the basis of rewarding employees who work in teams, the system must be adapted to meet the new work context.

Fortunately, the performance management system described earlier is readily adapted to team contexts. Several adaptations may occur:

1. A team leader might replace a manager. If the team is an autonomous work group, performance planning, feedback, appraisal, and review become team activities.

2. Performance definitions could change in two ways. First, definition of team performance might focus primarily on outcomes measured at the group level and on the success of team processes (such as conflict resolution, work sharing, and the like). Concern over how well specific tasks are done is likely to diminish; rapid

change in ways of doing things seems to be inherent in team-based work. Second, definition of individual performance might focus primarily on how well the individual employee supports team efforts. At the very least, team support becomes a critical performance dimension for every individual.

3. Feedback for individual performance, both positive and corrective, is likely to become embedded in group processes—to become part of "the way we do things." Feedback on team performance will come from outside the group, but self-appraisal is likely to be the focus of regular team meetings.

Performance Measurement

Approaches to performance measurement have increased in variation in the private sector. This is because organizations that recognize how critical performance improvement is to survival in the global economy become willing to invest in measurement systems. The quality control movement has supported this trend.

The generic categories of performance measurement include traits, behaviors, competencies, and outcomes. The initial measures used by most systems were of traits, such as creativity, initiative, dependability, and cooperativeness. But the bias inherent in trait ratings pushed organizations to focus on output measures, and then on behavioral measures.

Carl Thor has developed a broader perspective on performance measurement[7] that sidesteps categorical arguments. Among his points are the following:

• Measurement areas are a function of what the customer considers important.

• Customer priorities translate into strategic priorities; what to measure then becomes obvious.

• The performance of any organization, organizational unit, or work group can only be described and analyzed by a family of measures.

• Every key process, every group, every organizational level needs its own family of measures.

• Measures must be understandable to users; precision is less valuable than utility.

- Participative development results in better measures, but the culture must support this approach.

- Both group and individual measures are necessary; the mix will depend on the situation and the organizational culture.

- Cross-sectional performance measures are not enough; performance trend measures are also necessary.

To Thor, the important aspect of measurements is the process used to derive them. Most performance measures will focus on productivity, quality, or innovation.

Technical Issues

The most interesting reality of research and organizational practice is that the technical aspects of performance appraisal (such as scale points and levels of performance) are not the crucial issues in system development. Instead of focusing on rating formats, the emphasis is on the performance management process and on ensuring that managers and their direct reports understand how performance is defined, how it will be measured, what the consequences of various performance levels will be, and how performance can be enhanced.

Choice of Raters

In traditional performance appraisal systems, managers were usually responsible for observing performance, appraising performance, and making decisions based on appraisal results. Not that the role of other sources of performance ratings has gone unrecognized; the armed forces have long used peer ratings for the officer cadre,[8] and private sector organizations have experimented with peer and subordinate ratings since the late 1970s.[9] A few federal organizations began including peer appraisal input even under the centralized performance management system.

Particularly as organizations have moved toward team-based work systems, making customer service and employee empowerment familiar mantras, the trend toward use of multiple rating sources has increased. The culmination of this emphasis on multiple sources of rating is the 360-degree rating, which synthesizes ratings from peers, subordinates, supervisors, customers, and even vendors.[10]

THE NEW FEDERAL PERFORMANCE MANAGEMENT SYSTEM

In August 1995, OPM released rules for a new approach to performance management in the federal government. The individual accountability features of the law had to be served, and as a result a considerable amount of regulatory material had to be retained to ensure that the system could still be used effectively for that purpose. Nonetheless, nearly every recommendation that OPM had fielded over previous years was implemented. The key principles of decentralization and flexibility have been adopted, including the following.

Agency Specificity

Each agency must develop its own approach to performance management. No longer is there one governmentwide approach to performance management or appraisal. An agency may be as internally centralized or decentralized as it chooses.

Broad Choice of Rating Technologies

With respect to planning and assessment, the widest possible range of approaches and techniques is permitted. Once the minimum requirements for establishing individual accountability are met, organizations are free to adopt and apply all kinds of performance information to performance management processes. Everything from traditional supervisory assessment of individual behavior and outcomes to 360-degree assessment to statistical process control information could be used as appropriate within a particular context. The new system offers flexibility to rebuild the credibility of performance measurement. For internal credibility, context should be considered. For external credibility, performance outcomes and results should be included in the measurement system, as well as the process inputs on which individual accountability rests.

Broad Choice of Performance Management Processes

Having opened up the performance measures that can be used, the new system clears the way for tailoring the fundamental management processes of planning, providing ongoing feedback and development, and periodically recording a formal review. The system leaves particular design choices and emphases up to agencies. For organizations that have developed effective work planning and measurement techniques that they wish to keep separate from human resource management systems, employee performance management can be relatively perfunctory, using a minimalist approach to simply ensure that individual employees continue to meet basic expectations. Other organizations can design performance management programs that integrate elements such as individual, team, and organizational performance goal setting, measurement, feedback, and rewards.

Ability to Focus on Teams or Groups as Well as Individuals

The regulations that establish the new system carefully avoid terms that denote traditional hierarchical organizations of first-line supervisors and direct reports. Performance is almost never given an individual connotation and can be planned, measured, monitored, and summarized almost entirely at the group or team level. The exception, of course, is the legal requirement to maintain individual accountability by establishing at least one performance element and standard at the individual level. That individual element, however, can be a minor facet of the organization's overall performance planning, assessment, feedback, and development that otherwise focuses substantially on group or team goals and standards.

Encouragement of Participation by Managers and Individuals

Employee involvement is strongly supported, especially through interest-based labor-management cooperative approaches, but it must proceed within the limits of the law, particularly the Federal Service Labor-Management Relations Statute. Although case law and rulings by the Federal Labor Relations Authority are needed to determine the extent, it is expected that the removal of governmentwide regulation in many areas will result in wider collective bargaining of performance management procedures.

Performance Redefinition
Allowing Program Integration

The definition of performance was broadened beyond position-based orientation to encourage the use of employee performance management and assessment with other work restructuring and reengineering approaches that may be more process oriented. In particular, employee performance management programs can be integrated with other performance-based management approaches such as those being implemented under the Government Performance and Results Act (GPRA) of 1993. For example, agencies have been directed to establish customer service standards, which tend to be more like goals than job-retention standards. Including these service targets in employee performance plans and providing ongoing feedback could give them far more meaning for employees than simply posting them in the lobby. At agency option, meeting (or not meeting) those customer service standards could even affect employee performance ratings to some degree. (The regulations would not permit most measures of customer service to be used as grounds for removing an employee, however.)

Focus on Good,
Not Poor, Performers

Encouraging the use of performance measures other than those that could support a removal action is one of the greatest changes that the new system brings. The old centralized system, operated out of the personnel office with its roots in individual accountability, saw little benefit from spending energy on performance assessments that could serve no purpose for fundamental personnel administration. If a performance element and standard could not be taken to MSPB, why bother with it? The fact that the organization's performance might actually be managed more effectively out on the line (such as by using group results measures or emphasizing goals over retention standards) did not serve the objectives that were being emphasized for the old system. Clearly, the new system leaves a place for identifying and dealing with poor performers, but it allows a significant shift in emphasis from the rare poor performer to the legions of average and good performers in agencies everywhere.

Greater Flexibility on Rewards and Incentives

The new system's flexibility for performance planning and measurement is matched by more flexibility for designing reward and incentive schemes. In the past the regulations called for agencies to make maximum use of their authority to grant cash awards on the basis of summary performance ratings. Such exhortations have been removed and agencies are free to use or not use the various authorities available. The new possibilities for introducing more credible measures of organizational accomplishment lead very naturally to creating new links between such measures and recognition and rewards. As measures are refined and their credibility grows, they can form the basis of a wide variety of incentive and reward approaches, including the following.

- Goal sharing and gainsharing are now viable. These will withstand public scrutiny far better than inflated summary ratings. The answer to the question "Why were those awards given?" used to be "Because it is legal to give awards to people who came to work for another year and didn't screw up." Now the answer may be "Because we met our goal to reduce unit costs by 5 percent."

- An agency could lift its GPRA strategic plan out of the staff office ether and bring it to life for employees very quickly by establishing an incentive scheme where meeting a GPRA (stretch) target could sweeten individual or group awards by some percentage of the amount that would otherwise be granted.

- Ranking techniques and other means of limiting eligibility are generally permissible for distributing rewards. The idea that only the top 15 percent of an employee group will receive awards may be quite sensible; the real issue is how that 15 percent will be identified. As measurement is refined and expanded, those answers may come more easily.

- Peer nomination and award review committees could also be instituted to support a shift to granting larger awards to fewer people.

IMPLICATIONS FOR OTHER PUBLIC ORGANIZATIONS

The lessons the federal government learned through many years of frustration with its performance management system could serve any public organization well. Realizing that credibility and equity are not to be found in standardization, but rather in flexibility and decentralization to the right organizational context, has been the starting point. A need to establish individual accountability for meeting a retention standard can be balanced with an opportunity to establish performance goals that generate commitment and focus energy among the average and good performers that make up the majority of employees. Permitting a variety of performance assessment techniques for individuals, groups, and organizations can create the opportunity to integrate employee performance planning, feedback, and appraisal with an organization's overall performance-oriented management strategy. And establishing credible reward schemes that trigger measured outcomes and results can give those measures meaning and utility for all levels of an organization.

This change from a program focused on enabling managers to deal with poor performers to one that encourages the management of all performers within the context of the goals and strategies unique to each agency mirrors the trend in private sector organizations. Nonfederal government units that have not yet done so need to move in a similar direction. Performance management is too important to the success of the organization to squander on disciplinary problems.

Notes

1. R. B. Bretz and G. T. Milkovich, *Performance Appraisal in Large Organizations: Practice and Research Implications,* Working Paper no. 89–17 (Ithaca, N.Y.: Center for Advanced Human Resource Studies, 1989).
2. National Research Council, Commission on Behavioral and Social Sciences and Education, Committee on Performance Appraisal for Merit Pay, *Pay for Performance: Evaluating Performance Appraisal and Merit Pay,* G. T. Milkovich and A. K. Wigdor, eds. (Washington, D.C.: National Academy Press, 1991).
3. National Performance Review, *From Red Tape to Results: Creating a Govern-*

ment That Works Better and Costs Less (Washington, D.C.: U.S. Government Printing Office, 1993).

4. National Performance Review, Vice President's Report, *From Red Tape to Results: Creating a Government That Works Better and Costs Less: Reinventing Human Resource Management* (Washington, D.C.: U.S. Government Printing Office, 1993).

5. E. A. Locke and G. P. Latham, *Goal Setting: A Motivational Technique That Works* (Upper Saddle River, N.J.: Prentice-Hall, 1984).

6. C. Fay, "The Changing Nature of Work," in H. Risher and C. Fay (eds.), *The Performance Imperative: Strategies for Enhancing Workforce Effectiveness* (San Francisco: Jossey-Bass, 1995).

7. C. G. Thor, "Using Measurement to Reinforce Strategy," in H. Risher and C. Fay (eds.), *The Performance Imperative*, 1995.

8. J. S. Kane and E. E. Lawler III, "Methods of Peer Assessment," *Psychological Bulletin*, 1978, *85*, 555–586.

9. G. P. Latham, C. H. Fay, and L. M. Saari, "The Development of Behavioral Observation Scales for Appraising the Performance of Foremen," *Personnel Psychology*, 1979, *32*, 299–311.

10. W. W. Tornow, "Editor's Note: Introduction to Special Issue on 360-Degree Feedback," *Human Resource Management*, 1993, *32*(2–3), 211–219.

CHAPTER TEN

Merit Pay
Motivating and Rewarding
Individual Performance

Howard Risher
Charles H. Fay
James L. Perry

The most prominent difference between pay programs in the public and private sectors is the emphasis on merit pay. The phrase *merit pay* is widely understood to refer to pay programs that have at least two defining characteristics: rewarding individual performance (rather than group or organizational performance), and rewarding performance differences by granting different increases to base wage or salary (rather than one-time bonuses or other non-base-wage payments). This chapter focuses on merit pay, but alternative forms of pay for performance are also briefly considered.

MONEY AND MOTIVATION

Although some commentators (such as Kohn and Deming) have criticized current merit pay systems as ineffective or counterproductive, it is generally conceded that money motivates human behavior. Early motivational theorists (such as Maslow and Herzberg) who concentrated on needs fulfillment as the primary driver of human behavior and who argued against the impact of monetary rewards on work behavior have been discounted both in theory and practice.

More relevant theory focuses on the process through which people are motivated in the workplace, rather than on any particular set of needs. Four process-related theories have been used to explain how reward systems can motivate work behavior, and each has significant implications for designers of merit (or other performance-based) pay systems.

• *Equity theory.* Equity theory provides the basis for most traditional pay systems. Employees provide labor and other inputs to employers in exchange for a variety of returns including pay. Because it is difficult to determine whether that exchange is equal, employees tend to compare their return-to-input ratio with what they perceive the ratios of others to be. Compensation professionals have developed reward systems that institutionalize these comparisons in an attempt to provide pay equivalent to that of others in the same job working for other employers. Job evaluation systems are meant to build an internal value hierarchy based on comparisons of jobs; merit pay systems are intended to ensure differential pay increases to employees holding the same job based on their merit (usually defined as performance). To the extent that employees feel equitably rewarded, pay satisfaction is increased and turnover and absenteeism are reduced.

Equity theory does not suggest that employee satisfaction is causally linked to employee performance. It does, however, suggest that employers specify which inputs are valued, make sure the rewards for success are explicit, specify relevant comparisons to other organizations, jobs, or persons, specify the process through which rewards are determined, and communicate all these to employees.

• *Expectancy theory.* A different perspective on motivation is provided by expectancy theory. Briefly, it argues that an individual faced with a behavioral choice of effort at work (for example, stay late to finish a project or leave the office on time) considers the probable outcomes of the effort (a completed project and an angry spouse? an incomplete project and a satisfied spouse?). The longer-range impacts of these primary outcomes and their probability are also considered (higher performance rating and subsequent merit increase? breakup of marriage from overwork?). The employee will choose the option which, on the whole, maximizes preferred returns. The theory does not specify what longer-range outcomes are preferred (some may prefer the increase, others a stable marriage). Thus expectancy theory is based solidly on the argument that individuals continually make choices and balance their work efforts in light of expected outcomes.

Employers who accept the validity of expectancy theory will make sure that the linkage between work effort and work outcome is understood by employees, that the rewards linked to desired work outcomes are well known, and that the organization actually does reward performance. In a sense, expectancy theory suggests that employers make sure the rules of the pay-for-performance system are well understood by all employees, and that the organization plays by those rules. The rewards offered by the organization might not outweigh other consequences of desired performance for all employees, but only when employees understand the system and its outcomes can they make rational choices about the effort they will put forth.

• *Goalsetting theory.* Goalsetting theory is less relevant to merit pay than either equity or expectancy theory, but it is reviewed here because it forms the theoretical base for management by objective (MBO) systems and because misunderstanding it has resulted in many failed programs. Briefly, goalsetting theory states that individuals with high, specific, and self-accepted goals will perform better than those with no goals or "do your best" goals. It is not necessary that the goals be participatively set as long as they are accepted by the employee as feasible and commitment to achieve them takes place. Goalsetting does not specifically predict goal achievement, only higher performance. MBO programs typically reward employees for goal achievement rather than performance against standards. Employees who set stretch goals and perform well but fail to achieve their goals are motivated to set more readily achievable goals the following year; soon the system becomes a source of conflict between managers, who try to get employees to set ever-higher goals, and the employees themselves, who understand only too well the "rewards" for doing so.

The other value of goalsetting is that it reminds compensation specialists that rewards encompass much more than money. Feedback and recognition, as well as good performance, can motivate. The goalsetting process and the commitment to goals provide motivation for most employees even if rewards are not explicitly linked to performance.

• *Reinforcement theory.* Reinforcement theory notes the importance of consequences on the repetition of behavior. When a behavior is positively reinforced (that is, when the consequence of the behavior is viewed favorably by the employee) it is more likely to be repeated. Money is usually considered to be a general reinforcer; most employees view it favorably, and it may represent other things of value, such as recognition.

Reinforcement theory has a number of implications for merit pay. The immediacy of the consequence makes it a more powerful reinforcer. It is hard to maintain that a merit increase in March gives much reinforcement for performance last July. The schedule for reinforcement is critical. It is impractical to provide a reward every time good performance is exhibited, although it is under these conditions that learning is quickest. Research suggests that a variable ratio reinforcement schedule is the most powerful in maintaining behavior. This is how slot machines pay off: not every twentieth play exactly, but about every twenty plays on average. Merit plans pay off on a fixed schedule, which is not very reinforcing. Like goalsetting theory, reinforcement theory reminds compensation specialists that things other than money reinforce behavior, some of which may be more powerful for some employees.

CURRENT MERIT PAY PRACTICES

In the private sector merit pay policies are widespread. Heneman[1] reports on a series of surveys showing that more than 80 percent of private sector employees use merit pay plans (p. 8). The 1995 ACA salary budget survey[2] of 3,667 organizations found that more than 83 percent of the respondents had merit pay programs for their nonexempt employees, and more than 87 percent had them for exempt employees. Because respondents include some hospitals, colleges and universities, government units, and nonprofits, these figures understate the prevalence of merit pay in the private sector. The proportion of large employers using merit pay for at least some of their employees is even greater. In the public sector the prevalence of policies providing for merit pay is decidedly less, although adequate survey data are not available. Heneman reports a series of surveys showing that thirty-seven states had merit pay systems in 1989 and that nearly half of all local governments have some form of merit pay (p. 9). Significantly, surveys conducted over the past decade indicate that the emphasis on merit pay policies has increased in corporations.

Realistically, corporate merit pay programs are often no more effective than those in government. Virtually every employee gets an annual pay increase; in the typical corporation less than 5 percent of the staff is denied an increase because of poor performance. However, the philosophy underlying merit policies is almost as important as patriotism or motherhood. The solidly entrenched belief is that workers should earn their salaries and that the best workers should be paid more over time. This belief has been important in the cultural heritage of the United States and permeates many aspects of our lives.

Still, corporations have become increasingly sensitive to the impact of payroll costs as a competitive issue. This has given renewed emphasis to concerns about practices that effectively guarantee pay increases. Companies across the country have acted aggressively to reduce fixed payroll costs. Cost reduction strategies include staff cuts, changes in benefit programs, and the introduction of variable incentive plans. The last of these is one of the most important trends in compensation management.

These trends make any practice that results in entitlement suspect and a focal point for critics. They also increase the pressure for public employers to review their policies and move away from practices that make annual salary increases a right that is difficult for the employer to deny.

THE PRACTICAL SIDE OF MERIT PAY

There is a gap between the philosophy and the reality of merit pay. It is difficult to argue against the ideals of merit principles, but it is also difficult to translate the principles into effective practices. Formal pay policies are only the starting point. The policies are meaningful when supervisors throughout an organization are comfortable making salary increase decisions based on their assessments of individual performance. The supervisors specifically have to know that the organization expects them to recognize that some employees do not deserve a full increase. The denial of increases is always difficult to justify and explain to affected employees; the organization and top management have to make this an important issue or supervisors are likely to grant increases to virtually all employees.

For supervisors, merit pay is a zero-sum game. Salary increase budgets are typically determined as a fixed dollar amount, determined as a percentage of each employee's salary. Over the last few years corporate salary increase budgets have typically been in the range of 4 to 5 percent of covered wages and salaries. Conventional merit practices make it essential to grant increases in each organizational unit so that the total dollars spent during the fiscal year add up to the budgeted amount. Cash flow considerations may complicate the management problem (for example, increases granted at the beginning of the year require more of the budget than increases granted at the end of the year), but above-average increases for some employees generally have to be offset by below-average increases for others.

A common problem is the reluctance of supervisors to deny increases or to grant below-average increases; they do, after all, have to continue working with the employees who are adversely affected by their decisions. Supervisors need to know that the organization is committed to merit pay and is providing adequate ongoing support to facilitate these decisions. Employees need to understand that their compensation depends on their performance and on the organization's financial success. There are typically pockets in any organization where merit pay is perceived as more effective than in others, but it is important to avoid completely ignoring the policy of granting increases for some groups of workers.

The reality is that there are only two possible alternatives to merit increases. One that some companies have begun to adopt is to de-emphasize and reduce the funds available for merit increases, making future pay increases dependent on variable pay incentive plans. Under these plans, payments are made in the form of lump-sum awards, with little or no increase in base salaries. There is reason to anticipate the trend to adopt incentive plans will continue to expand into the future. The other alternative is to grant the same increase to every employee. That can be done with either a general increase or with step increases.

The latter is clearly prevalent in government and in situations where differences in performance either do not exist (such as where performance is dependent on a mechanized process), cannot be measured, or do not matter. Corporations generally are willing to stand behind merit policies even in situations where supervisors and employees know the policies are not effective. Given the pressure from stockholders for increased organizational performance, corporations cannot (or will not) admit that they are not doing everything possible to motivate and reward high levels of individual performance. Public employers have been reluctant to provide the same commitment.

The ongoing problems with merit pay are not new. The period of rapid inflation in the late 1970s and early 1980s helped create a climate in which it was virtually impossible to deny increases. It was during this period that cost-of-living adjustment (COLA) clauses were adopted in many labor agreements. The concern with living cost increases prompted many companies to adopt informal "keep them whole" policies. Although that thinking is now essentially dead in the private sector, it continued for several years after inflation rates declined to the recent 3 or 4 percent level. The experience during this period was largely responsible for the creation of the entitlement mentality that has recently been a focus of concern for those seeking to increase organizational performance through the use of rewards systems.

Unfortunately, no one has conclusively shown that merit-based salary management is important to corporate success. It would be difficult to demonstrate, as very few corporations claim not to rely on the concept. It also would be difficult to isolate the impact of merit pay from other factors affecting performance.

MERIT PAY AND ORGANIZATIONAL CULTURE

Successful merit pay policies can only be understood in the context of the organization, its management style, and its culture. It is also important to appreciate that merit pay is the organizational norm in the United States. Moreover, U.S. culture makes it important to recognize and reward instances of outstanding individual performance. Rewards range from frivolous ceremonial awards with no monetary value to letters of commendation to cash awards. In this broader context, groups that fail to reward good performance stand out to outsiders as unusual and suspect.

The cultural history of the United States includes numerous tales of outstanding individual accomplishments. That history seems to focus on the individual even when it is obvious that the accomplishment involved the efforts of many. Our cultural heroes have been individuals, not teams or groups.

In a corporate setting, the only acceptable reason for ignoring individual performance is the recognition that individuals do not make a difference. This may be the case in work settings where performance is dependent on machines or the availability of materials; thus individual performance can be ignored for some blue-collar and pink-collar jobs. But in almost every other work situation, management will make an effort, effective or otherwise, to assess individual performance.

Merit pay also has a powerful symbolic impact on the culture of the organization. It is a very visible way for managers to control their subordinates. At its best, merit pay provides a manager with a means of emphasizing the importance of performance. In organizations with powerful unions or in government agencies with restrictive civil service rules, merit pay may be the only material consequence a manager can use to influence behavior. At its worst, merit pay becomes a tool to reward friends and punish everyone else.

Merit pay also can be used to signal the outside world that the organization is serious about performance. Both public and private sector organizations have used the implementation of merit pay and other incentive programs to assure stakeholders that a performance culture is the order of the day. Elected officials or senior management can reap the acclaim for developing organizational effectiveness. But if there is insufficient financial or managerial support, managers and supervisors have to cope with implementation and take the blame if the program does not work.

Experience with merit pay has certainly not been universally positive. More than a few managers and supervisors have administered merit budgets poorly. One of the most common problems is the awarding of large wage or salary increases to friends or favorites regardless of performance. When merit budgets are small (most have hovered in the 3–5 percent range for the last several years), it is difficult to differentiate raises for high and low performers. Flat budgets make it difficult to use money as an incentive for much of anything, especially when downsizing places a heavier load on surviving employees. The potholes can be numerous and arise unexpectedly. As a process it has to be planned carefully and with full appreciation for the potential problems. When it works best, it becomes a key to a performance-oriented culture that can be a decided benefit to the organization.

SHOULD PUBLIC SECTOR EMPLOYERS RELY ON MERIT PAY?

This is perhaps the most perplexing problem in defining the appropriate compensation philosophy for the public sector. There is clearly a high level of interest in improving the performance of government agencies; it is manifest in much of the criticism of government and in the widespread support for reinventing it. However, a clear consensus on how to accomplish this is not apparent. If experience in the private sector is meaningful, budget slashing and staff reductions are demoralizing to the remaining employees, which in the short term will adversely affect performance.

Improved performance in any service-oriented organization depends in large part on the efforts of individual employees. A prime and widely recognized example is Federal Express. FedEx has pioneered a variety of high-technology initiatives, from information technology to business process reengineering, to enhance the speed and accuracy of its delivery services while reducing costs for itself and its customers. Nevertheless, FedEx's reputation and success is highly dependent on the efforts of the individuals who pick up and deliver packages. In the public sector as well technology will play a role, and there is undoubtedly something to be gained from meaningful reengineering and process improvement initiatives. But here, too, individuals will always be the focus of any attempts to improve performance. This necessitates changes in the way people perform their jobs and in their ability to work harder as well as smarter.

At the same time the track record for merit pay in the public sector does not augur well for this change in policy. Despite the reliance on merit principles, little more than lip service has been given in the way of commitment to a performance linkage in salary management. To be sure many public employers have merit policies in place and working as well as those in corporations. But a number of prominent public employers, including the federal government, have not made merit pay a reality.

It would be difficult to prove that merit pay contributes to improved performance; no effective basis for determining the impact of such a policy appears to exist. In the private sector the practice is virtually universal, and in other sectors it would require a complicated research strategy to be able to isolate its impact. The evidence is thus largely anecdotal; at any rate the merit increase policy is only one part of an organization's culture. Where merit pay is considered successful, other factors would still need to be considered to fully understand the "action levers" that drive performance. This makes it difficult, if not impossible, to isolate the impact of merit pay on organizational performance.

The importance of an organization's culture and its commitment to performance is agreed upon; some organizations place more emphasis on reaching and maintaining high performance than others. When one has an opportunity to work with a variety of organizations, an easily recognized difference between them is how much emphasis each places on performance and the commitment to succeeding. Some simply want to be the best; this permeates almost every aspect of their operations and culture and is widely shared by the workforce.

Merit pay as an isolated policy is probably not important in this context. It is safe to assume that high-performance organizations—however they are defined—will have a merit pay policy or other ways to recognize and reward the better performers. They make it a focal management issue; they continually identify high performers and high-potential employees and reward them in ways commensurate with their contributions, including with cash but also with promotions and other rewards. Increasingly, such rewards are being shared among a larger percentage of the workforce. All of this contributes to the creation of a performance-oriented culture.

Workers want their value and contributions to be recognized; the value accorded to hard work is an important cultural ethos in this and many other countries. The better performers expect to be recognized and to benefit from their efforts. If they are not so honored over time, questions arise in their minds and in the minds of others who are aware of it. When no differentiation is made between high performers and barely adequate performers, the consequence is likely to be reduced effort. Sooner or later, workers who do not feel their work is adequately appreciated will see no point in continuing to perform at high levels. When there are no rewards the level of effort will taper off to the minimum needed to avoid adverse consequences.

The impetus for merit pay comes, of course, from the private sector. There is evidence that many government employees did not consider money an important consideration when they started their careers; for many it may have been a relatively low priority. Government has the decided benefit of a workforce that is largely committed to public service. Unfortunately, public employers have a tendency to fall back on management practices that diminish such motivations and the commitment to high performance. Policies affecting the pay program, such as budgets for salary increases that are consistently below prevailing levels, contribute to the problem.

The private sector perspective is important to the public sector because the voting public works primarily in the corporate world. Public employers under scrutiny to improve performance will feel pressured to adopt policies and practices expected to accomplish it. Proven private sector practices will need to be considered and accepted, modified to fit the public sector, or explicitly rejected. Politicians will need to be able to defend the decisions they make while in office.

The merit pay theme has innumerable variations; the alternatives are not limited to a single corporate model. The only common theme is that some relatively small group—typically 15 to 20 percent of eligible workers—receives a slightly larger increase than the balance of the workforce and that another even smaller group—perhaps 2 percent—will be denied an increase. As long as the model provides for both eventualities, it can be an effective merit pay system.

Merit pay requires ongoing management support. It has to be introduced as an important management priority, and all subsequent communications on the subject must reinforce its importance. At least a basic effort must be made to make it a component in a performance management process, which requires manager and supervisor training to make the process a reality at all levels; it cannot be seen as simply another requirement of the personnel department.

Dealing with the problems and work needed to shift successfully to a merit pay environment must be balanced against the implications of staying with a step-in-grade or other automatic salary increase concept. Public employers have a reputation for backing an entitlement culture that is contrary to that in most, if not all, other sectors of the economy. There is a widely shared belief that we as a society can no longer afford to maintain an entitlement culture.

Automatic increase policies fail to satisfy both organizational and individual needs; none but perhaps poor performers feel good about the way their salary is handled. If employee surveys are to be believed, government workers tend to be highly dissatisfied with their employers' pay program. Public employers that decide to reconsider a pay program should start by defining those needs and evaluating program alternatives relative to the potential for meeting them.

PERFORMANCE APPRAISAL AND MERIT PAY

The assumption underlying any merit pay program is the existence of accurate employee performance measures. The difficulty of achieving accurate measures is the key shortcoming in many merit pay plans and underlies much of the criticism of pay for performance. This topic is treated in more detail in Chapter Nine. However, it is worth noting a few key points here.

For merit pay purposes it is necessary to have a single performance rating scheme that is applicable to all covered jobs. That is, a clerk who rates 5 (greatly exceeds standards) must be equivalent to a highway research engineer or senior budget analyst who rates 5 in terms of performance against standard. Because performance is multidimensional (an employee may have great technical skills but the interpersonal skills of a rock), it is necessary to distill the value of many performance measures into that single number.

In most private sector organizations the emphasis has shifted from performance appraisal to performance management. Rather than simply keeping score, these organizations work to develop performance plans for individuals and groups and then provide support and feedback to ensure that enhanced performance occurs. In an effective performance management system the appraisal itself is a nonevent because the employees already know how they are doing. Though there is no evidence that merit pay, with its focus on the single performance score, operates against the performance management system in any way, it is critical that the linkages between performance management and the year-end performance appraisal be clear and unequivocal. Similarly, it is critical that the link between performance and reward be apparent as well as real and that employees see the linkage as consistent and fair.

MERIT PAY MODELS

Three merit pay models are in wide use. The simplest is typically found in the public sector: in effect, it is a yes-no decision that provides an increase for everyone whose performance is satisfactory. The amount is normally the step increase provided in the salary schedule; a variation is to provide a two-step increase to a limited number of high performers.

A similar model links each employee's increase to a supervisor's rating of the employee's performance. Typically, permissible salary increases (most often expressed as a percentage of salary) are established for each level of assessed performance. For an organization that recognizes five levels of performance, for example, the ratings and salary increases shown in Table 10.1 might be used.

However, if 80 percent of the employees are typically rated 4 or 5 each year and there is only a 4 percent merit increase budget, giving the increases listed in Table 10.1 would break the bank. By taking into account the expected distribution of performance ratings (there is

Performance Rating	Salary Increase (percent)
5 Outstanding	8
4 Above expected	6
3 Meets expectations	4
2 Marginal	2
1 Unacceptable	0

Table 10.1.   Merit Pay Model: Increase Linked to Rating by Supervisor.

generally a high degree of consistency from year to year), we can specify ratings that will result in a weighted average increase that is roughly
equal to the budgeted amount. A key to successful merit pay policies is
to design the increase schedule so that increases are in line with labor
market trends and with the organization's financial resources.

The third model combines performance rating with position in the
salary range to form a merit matrix. This model is based on the
assumption that the salary ranges are aligned with prevailing market
pay levels according to a specific policy. The most common policy is
to align the salary range midpoints so that they are approximately
equal to average market pay levels for the jobs assigned to each range.
Thus a job incumbent paid exactly at the midpoint is paid at the market level. If we further assume that the market average pay level is for
an average performer, then the company's average performers need to
be paid at the midpoint salary level when they are able to perform at
an average level.

This policy provides higher-than-average increases for employees
paid below the midpoint and lower-than-average increases for those
above the midpoint. The position in the range is defined and tracked
with a *compa-ratio,* which is the employee's salary divided by the range
midpoint. For example, a salary of $44,000 and a midpoint of $40,000
produce a compa-ratio of 1.10. A salary of $32,000 in the same range
means the compa-ratio is .80. In a range with a 50 percent spread from
minimum to maximum the compa-ratios run from .80 to 1.20.

People with little or no experience usually earn close to the range
minimum, and they gradually progress through the range as they gain

experience; the compa-ratio is a simple concept to help track their movement through the range. One can argue that employees low in the range who earn an outstanding performance rating deserve a larger increase than employees with the same rating who are above the midpoint and already well paid relative to market levels. Increases begin to resemble a learning curve pattern as an individual progresses to and then above the midpoint. Table 10.2 illustrates the merit matrix concept.

A variation on the matrix concept is to cap increases within the range based on performance ratings. For example, employees rated 3 (meets expectations) may be made ineligible to be paid more than the midpoint. The logic to this is that competent but average employees should not be paid more than the market average, which is the basis for establishing the range midpoint. Similarly, employees who are rated 4 might be capped at the 1.10 compa-ratio level. On this basis only outstanding, 5-rated employees can expect to reach the range maximum. This effectively strengthens the pay-performance linkage.

The merit matrix is probably the most prevalent policy in larger companies. The actual matrix will depend on the company's pay-performance philosophy, the width of the ranges, and the performance rating scale. The format depends on the number of levels in the performance rating scale and the width of the ranges. (The concept is not feasible with a broad-band structure, because organizations that use it tend to manage against actual salaries rather than against compa-ratio or place in range.) The actual percentage difference in increases for high performers low in their range to marginal workers who are in the upper end of their range reflects the organization's philosophy; with some matrices high performers can expect increases four or five times greater.

When salary increase budgets were larger, some companies added a third dimension to the matrix concept: timing of the increase. The better performers who were low in their range were eligible for increases more frequently (sometimes as often as every six months), and the poor performers had to wait eighteen to twenty-four months. The combination allows better performers to make out significantly better than poor performers over time. As budgets have been cut back over the past few years, use of this variation has diminished.

Limits on salary increases reflect a different philosophy than what is common in the public sector, stressing the viewpoint that good per-

Compa-Ratio

Performance Rating	.80–.90	.91–1.00	1.01–1.10	1.11–1.20
5 Outstanding	10–11	8–9	5–6	3–4
4 Above expected	8–9	6–7	4–5	2–3
3 Meets expectations	6–7	5–6	3–4	0
2 Marginal	4–5	3–4	0	0
1 Unacceptable	0	0	0	0

Table 10.2. Merit Matrix Model.

formers need to make out better over time than poor performers. As salary increase budgets are always constrained, the intent of limits is to force the allocation to benefit the better performers. In most corporations the salary structures are reviewed and adjusted annually (or biennially), which means that the range minimums, midpoints, and maximums are increased to keep pace with labor market trends. These adjustments reduce the relative position of individual salaries in the ranges and the associated compa-ratios, meaning that employees are eligible for at least a modest increase. That pay increases should depend on individual performance is still a well-established belief.

ALTERNATIVES TO TRADITIONAL MERIT PAY POLICIES

Several new merit pay concepts have been introduced in the past few years. The intent of most is to strengthen the linkage between performance and pay increases. One idea that fits the government environment is to establish a separate budget line to be used only for increases for outstanding employees. The amount may be only 1 percent or less of aggregate salaries; the balance of the normal merit budget is available for general increases or for more evenly distributed merit awards for other employees. The objective is to reduce the zero-sum aspects of the typical merit policy. When structured as a separate budgeted amount, granting large increases to better performers does not mean taking money away from individuals whose performance is more modest.

Perhaps the most widely used alternative is to cap salary increases at the former range midpoint. If the midpoint is close to the market average, this makes it possible to progress to the going rate but with further increases possible only when the midpoint and the cap are adjusted. Some organizations provide for lump sum increases once an employee reaches the cap.

Lump sum increases can be used with any merit pay policy. An often unexpected benefit to this is that supervisors seem more comfortable making large lump sum payments than in adding the same dollar amount to an individual's salary. The reason may be that an implied message goes along with lump sum: the employee has to earn the amount again next year because it is not an annuity that will come automatically until retirement or termination. Regardless of how the lump sum payments are structured, they serve to hold down fixed costs and future payrolls.

An idea that may work in lieu of standard merit increases is the use of lump-sum award opportunities for high performers. In an environment where there is inadequate support for merit pay it may make sense to introduce a self-nomination policy under which an employee can announce the intent at the beginning of the year to accomplish something beyond the norm within the work group. Self-nomination makes it difficult for employees to blame anyone but themselves if they are not considered for awards at year's end. The selection of individuals for awards can be delegated to an employee task force that would need to evaluate the track record of individuals within their department. If each department has its own budget for this purpose (perhaps 0.5 percent of the department's payroll), department heads can structure the process and the award criteria to meet their own needs. For example, one department head might want to reward all the members of a team or teams at year's end; another might prefer making quarterly awards to only outstanding employees. This concept makes the award mechanism a tool that can be managed within the department, not just another personnel system.

PROBLEMS WITH MERIT PAY

Undoubtedly the most prominent critic of merit pay was W. Edwards Deming. He focused on the linkage between performance appraisal and merit salary increases, proclaiming it to be among the deadly diseases of management. To Deming's way of thinking, this linkage creates several problems:

- It destroys teamwork, because most appraisal systems and merit increases depend exclusively on individual performance.
- It implicitly encourages mediocrity by rewarding employees for meeting but often not exceeding performance expectations.
- It creates an incentive to improve short-term performance and effectively deemphasizes longer-term issues.
- The zero-sum aspect of the typical merit policy generates counterproductive competition for salary increase funds.

These criticisms have not prompted many corporations to terminate merit pay, but they have created a high level of interest in new ideas and variations on the traditional policies that are more compatible with Deming's thinking. The shift to skill- or competency-based pay, with its future orientation, is one idea prompted in part as a response to Deming, as was the move to three-level rating scales. The 360-degree appraisal system is also more compatible with his philosophy than the conventional approach. Deming did not have a meaningful alternative for organizations that wanted to follow his teachings, but he has had a significant impact on the way organizations think about merit pay.

Salary programs send important messages to employees about management's priorities and expectations, and the messages flowing from a time-in-grade policy clearly do not provide an incentive for improved performance. However, merit pay practices can also result in counterproductive messages, as Deming argues. For example, when completing the appraisal form is little more than a fifteen-minute compliance task at the end of the year, it sends clear messages about the importance of performance management. The problem is not, however, inherent in the concept of performance management; rather it is evidence of management's priorities and lack of concern with performance improvement. An analysis of the messages is often a useful first step in assessing the effectiveness of these practices.

Conventional merit increases compound over time (that is to say, each year's increases are calculated as a percentage of the prior year's salary). Although it is not widely understood, the conventional concept effectively rewards employees for last year's experience for as long as the worker is actively employed and even into retirement. The difference in the increase for an outstanding employee and an average employee might only be 3 percent, but over a period of years the difference adds up. For an employee whose base salary is initially $20,000, a 3 percent differential received for outstanding performance translates into an extra $9,000 over 15 years, even if no further increases are received! If further increases do come, they are calculated against the larger base; furthermore, because the worker's final pay at retirement usually is used to calculate the pension amount, the impact of that 3 percent differential increase lasts long past retirement. If the worker could see the total difference in earnings over all payments through the final pension check, it would provide a strong incentive to secure the outstanding rating.

This, of course, is also a problem with automatic increase models: long-service employees are paid more than those with short service. With compounding, any criterion that drives pay increases over time will result in significant differentials. When organizations shift to a more performance-oriented philosophy, it raises questions about differentials related to job tenure.

Realistically, there is enough question about the use of rating scales to be concerned about equity. Research evidence shows that raters can agree on who deserves to be rated as outstanding—typically 15 to 20 percent of the workers in an organization—and those who are performance problems—less than 5 percent of the typical workforce. The problem is with the people in between. Supervisors do not always agree on who deserves to be rated 3 or 4; some would rate an employee a 3 while others would categorize the same person as a 4. When those differences of opinion are factored into increases and the increases are compounded each year, it can and should be a cause of concern.

None of these problems, however, sufficiently justifies the termination of merit pay. Falling back on traditional tenure-based salary increases is simple to do, but in the current environment it would clearly send the wrong message. Moreover, the consequences to the organization are serious; inevitably employers who continue to rely on step-in-grade or similar policies are going to have problems caused by feelings of entitlement among employees and growing resistance among voters. Certainly it is difficult to maintain an effective performance management and merit pay policy, but the problems can be overcome, and the argument for some form of merit pay is difficult to deny.

THE ROLE OF NONCASH REWARDS

Organizational rewards are surprisingly diverse. They range from a simple pat on the back or smile from a supervisor to special privileges to public recognition that can take almost any form. The now classic book *In Search of Excellence*[3] includes frequent references to company practices that publicly recognize examples of outstanding performance. One organization cited in the book rewarded outstanding workers with a golden banana carved out of wood.

The ceremonial occasions can become hokey and may become a focus of derisive comments, but if employees are offered the choice between a hokey ceremony or no recognition of commendable performance, they will typically choose the ceremony. People enjoy ceremonial occasions; they like to have fun and socialize with coworkers. They also like to be involved with and take part in events that recognize the successes of their friends.

People want to make a contribution to their work group's success, and they want to have that contribution recognized. They want to feel they will benefit from their efforts. They start their government careers with high aspirations; many have a strong commitment to public service. Employees do not start their careers with the goal of being marginal performers! If motivation is a problem, it is typically related to a failure to reinforce the importance of good performance. This represents both a challenge and an opportunity for the organization.

A key is for supervisors to make a concerted effort to monitor performance and to regularly initiate some form of recognition to reward good performers. The form of the reward is decidedly less important than the act of recognition. Some organizations use dining or merchandise certificates; others use extra time off. Whatever the form or value, it is important to set aside equivalent funds for each department and to make sure the funds are used for this purpose.

Too often supervisors are not comfortable with selecting recipients for special awards. Where this is so, it may make sense to delegate the selection to a group of coworkers; they generally will take the task quite seriously. Another common problem is that supervisors may decide that saving award money will benefit them. They need to appreciate that the intent is to reinforce commendable performance and that shortsightedly saving the few dollars devoted to it kills any potential for improvement. It may be necessary to require the full allocation of budgeted increase funds.

IBM used to create policies and practices that had an underlying intent to make as many plan participants as possible feel like winners. Rather than having one employee of the month, it recognized or made special awards to quite a few employees. Every employee would like to feel like a winner. If the awards have a nominal dollar value, the benefit to the organization in terms of employee reaction undoubtedly offsets the cost.

A noncash reward alternative from the culture of another not-for-profit sector, health care, is the practice of allowing employees who contribute to the organization to help design further improvements. Just as outsiders who make sizable donations get a plaque on the wall or other forms of recognition, employees or teams who identify ways to reduce expenses or develop improved work systems create value that is worth as much as a donation and thus warrants the same level of recognition. It may make sense to give the employee or team some input into how a portion of the savings might be spent to improve the individual's or the department's equipment or work area. Perhaps half of the savings could be spent for new computer equipment, for example. This may not be as motivating as a true gainsharing payout, but most employees will certainly react very positively to the recognition.

BUILDING ORGANIZATIONAL SUPPORT FOR MERIT PAY

The shift to merit pay represents a significant organizational change and should be planned for as such. It is doomed if rolled out as a simple change in policy. The planning needs to account for all major stakeholders and to anticipate the sources of opposition to the change. The actual implementation will require two or more years to build support, give supervisors the skills needed to make the decisions, manage related concerns such as performance management, and possibly pilot test the new program.

One of the earliest steps is to obtain goal agreement at the highest possible level. Gaining consensus or, if that is impossible, getting all objections on the table may well be the most important step in the process. The consensus also needs to cover the problems with current policies or systems that are prompting the change. These discussions may represent a political statement if they start, as they most often do, in an early period of a new administration. Unfortunately, political considerations may turn this into a motherhood-and-apple-pie argument that makes it difficult to define problems and goals in the specific terms necessary to best communicate expectations and plans.

If the impetus for change arises from a political goal to shake up the bureaucracy and thus gain political advantage, the suggested new policy may quickly develop a very negative reputation in the governmental agencies. This will almost certainly cause it to fail; lip service may be granted to the new policy at senior civil service levels, but managers and their subordinates are going to resist the real impact of the change, if only subtly. Before they give it the support needed to make it work, they have to see a practical benefit to their agency.

Building support necessarily has to include estimates of the cost and time needed to get the new system up and running, including the full cost of related steps such as supervisory training. These analyses could conclude that there is no direct cost in terms of additional dollar outlays; instead the new policy might result in a reallocation of budgeted funds. It is critically important that these facts be understood.

The change cannot realistically be planned behind closed doors; that could doom it even before initial approval. The level of trust of both senior administrators and supervisors has to remain high at all times, which means a communication strategy should be one of the first considerations. It may be important to hold open meetings so that there is a forum for debate. And as the conclusions reached in these sessions will get to the workforce anyway—the grapevine will make sure of that—it makes sense to manage the communications to ensure that the information is accurate.

Still, there is a definite need for certain high-level closed-door planning sessions. When federal pay reform was being planned in 1988 and 1989, Connie Newman, director of the Office of Personnel Management in the Bush administration, held open task force meetings with presentations by numerous stakeholders and experts. At the same time she conducted closed-door strategy discussions that, when the planned changes were ready to be submitted for congressional approval, shifted to senator-by-senator and representative-by-representative discussions of what was needed to gain these individuals' votes.

The adage about getting everyone on the bandwagon as early as possible applies here. It will undoubtedly prove to be impossible to co-opt all stakeholders, but the planning process should at least try to minimize their ability to shoot down the change. One way is to involve them in the planning. There is no inherent reason to exclude anyone at the planning stage; all stakeholders and interest groups should have an opportunity to state their arguments. At the very least this makes it easier to understand the strength of the opposition. If they have an opportunity for input, it may provide valuable insight to the nuances that may determine the policy's success or failure. Merit pay in particular can generate strong emotions, and people need the chance to express them.

Other strategies to get people on board are to conduct an initial test or demonstration study involving selected work groups or to manage the new process for the first year or so without linkage to the pay program (that is to say, salary increases would still be granted under the old policy). The purpose of both is the same: to iron out any problems and to provide a showcase where stakeholders can see how the policy will affect subgroups of employees. This should help allay anxiety.

When the combination of step increases and range adjustment increases is compared with the typical merit budget in the private sector, it will probably show that the increases received from public programs are reasonably competitive. (This is not to suggest that actual salary levels for public employees are fully competitive.) Thus only a few poor performers can expect to lose under a merit pay policy. Once employees understand and believe this, they may be more willing to acquiesce to the new policy.

MERIT PAY EVALUATION

When an organization establishes a merit pay program, it is important to evaluate its outcomes to determine how effective the program has been and how it can be strengthened. Ideally, the evaluation approach should be established during the program design phase and closely tied to the program goals.

Two aspects should be evaluated. The first part of the evaluation should cover the workings of the program. At the least, this part of the evaluation should answer the following questions:

• Do specific performance measures trigger rewards?

- Are the performance measures linked to organizational and unit goals?
- Do employees who perform at higher levels get larger increases? (It may be necessary to take into account place in range or compa-ratio here.)
- Are program schedules followed?

The second part of the evaluation should cover other important issues, including the following:

- Does the system signal to employees important organizational, unit, and individual behaviors and outcomes?
- Do employees understand the system and accept it as fair?
- Have employee behaviors changed along the lines intended? (That is, has individual performance improved?)
- Has organization and unit performance improved?
- Does the value of the increased performance exceed the costs of the program?

SUMMARY

The most likely private sector incentive practice to gain wide acceptance in public sector organizations is merit pay, and in fact many public organizations already have some form of it in place for at least some employees. In spite of insufficient merit budgets, inadequate performance measures, lack of a good performance management system, and the tendency of many managers to use merit pay to reward things other than performance, most corporations rely primarily on merit pay systems to align the behaviors of employees with organizational goals and to reward performance.

There is risk in moving to merit pay; it can be disruptive and adversely affect employer-employee relations for several years. But there is no inherent reason to expect that, nor to avoid the change because of the possibility. When the transition is planned and managed successfully, agencies stand to benefit, and high performers—the ones who should be recognized under any circumstances—will begin to believe that their efforts are appreciated. Other employees may decide that the potential payoff for extra effort is warranted.

Notes

1. R. L. Heneman, *Merit Pay: Linking Pay Increases to Performance* (Reading, Mass.: Addison-Wesley, 1992).
2. *Report on the 1995–1996 Salary Budget Survey* (Scottsdale, Ariz.: American Compensation Association, 1995).
3. T. J. Peters and R. H. Waterman Jr., *In Search of Excellence* (New York: HarperCollins, 1982).

CHAPTER ELEVEN

Gainsharing in Government

Group-Based Performance Pay for Public Employees

Ronald P. Sanders

T hink about the ideal compensation strategy, one that energizes and engages employees, focuses them on bettering the bottom-line performance of the organization, and links at least part of their pay directly to that performance. Such a strategy brings a work group together as a team, mobilizes its members to increase productivity and improve quality, and encourages them to motivate and manage themselves toward that end—without the destructive competition that often accompanies other forms of merit-based pay. Does this ideal exist? It may, in the form of something called productivity gainsharing (PGS), a compensation strategy that rewards employees on the basis of the productivity of their work group.

Gainsharing quite literally shares the tangible monetary results of productivity increases with the employees who achieve them, a classic example of the kind of strategic pay that focuses and aligns individual efforts in furtherance of the organization's bottom line.[1] Though gainsharing has been around for decades in the private sector (where it goes by other names as well: Scanlon, Improshare, and others), it has not been widely embraced by public employers, its attendant "rules of engagement" seemingly too problematic for government work. However, its application in the public sector has far too much potential to ignore, especially in an era of chronic austerity and citizen-customer dissatisfaction. Experience suggests that with sufficient stakeholder support, careful planning, and the right kinds of resource management policies and support systems, gainsharing can be adapted to government. As a result the performance of government organizations and their employees can be improved dramatically. But before any of this can happen, public employers need to know where to begin.

That is the purpose of this chapter: to introduce public managers to the concept of gainsharing and to offer them some practical considerations as they contemplate the application of this unique performance-based compensation strategy to the government organization. It begins with a working definition of PGS (as well as some of its variations) and a simple hypothetical example of how it operates. Then, after a brief review of its history in the public sector, the chapter will turn to our principal focus: what it takes to make PGS work in government. We will examine these requirements in detail, considering some of the political and practical complications that are unique to the public sector and offering suggestions (not necessarily solutions) about how to best deal with them. It should be noted that this is not intended to be an exhaustive treatment of the subject of gainsharing. For example, it does not address the work measurement and cost accounting applications essential to a successful PGS effort. Rather, our emphasis here is on the policy and practical considerations that determine whether a public organization is willing (and able) to even consider the notion of gainsharing; the details of design and implementation are left to more specialized texts.

DEFINITION

Simply put, gainsharing is a performance-contingent reward system,[2] a group incentive that directly translates increases in employee productivity into financial rewards (*gainshares*) for the employees who contribute to those increases. It can employ any number of means to measure productivity, from outputs and outcomes to cost savings and quality, but its overriding emphasis is on the tangible and quantitative: at its best, gainsharing establishes a clear, predictable linkage between organizational performance and pay. Goalsharing, a relatively recent variation on the theme, rewards employees when their work unit accomplishes more global or qualitative performance objectives.

Usually distributed equally among the employees involved, gainshares are a form of variable pay—that is, compensation that is at risk and not treated as part of base pay except under certain circumstances.[3] It is not a piece rate; it does not focus on the output of individual employees but rather on their aggregate, the output of an organization or group. Nor is it a form of profit sharing, which is based on a whole host of factors such as market conditions and exchange rates that may be paper profits not necessarily reflecting increases in employee productivity. However, gainsharing may take into account all of the various factors that do affect such output, including investments in capital equipment and automation that result in a net increase in productivity or decrease in labor costs.

Here is how it works. Suppose that a government claims processing agency employs five hundred people, with a total annual payroll (excluding benefits for the sake of simplicity) of $12.5 million in its baseline fiscal year. In that baseline year, the agency processes 125,000 claims, for a gross unit cost of $100 per claim and a per capita output of 250 claims by each employee. Now suppose that agency adopts a productivity gainsharing plan, and under its terms employees increase their total annual output to 150,000 claims (a per capita increase of 50 claims a year). This represents a productivity increase of 20 percent. It now costs $83 to process each of the agency's 125,000 claims, for a savings of $17 per claim (a total of $2,125,000). If this were a typical gainsharing plan, half of those savings would revert to the agency's treasury and the remaining half would be divided equally among all of the employees involved, for an individual gainshare payout of $2,125.

But here is where public sector gainsharing becomes problematic. If our example involved a private company, the company's half of those savings could be used to employ more workers (it could afford about forty-two more), increasing the productive and revenue-generating capacity of the firm and the overall value added by the gainsharing program. However, public sector PGS is often a zero-sum game. Productivity increases may mean that the agency's budget is subsequently reduced by the amount of savings generated—after all, it can now process the same amount of claims at lower cost. If that lower unit cost of labor remains unchanged, the budget reduction taken in the next fiscal year (after the gainsharing payout, one hopes) would mean that the agency could then afford to employ only 415 workers, a net loss of 85.

Even from this simple definition, it should be apparent that productivity gainsharing in the public sector is as promising as it is problematic. In the private sector, where costs, output, and productivity are part of the firm's bottom line, gainsharing is relatively easy to implement. It is likely a more challenging prospect for the public organization, where output and outcome measures can be unclear, and where, as in our example, the public budgeting process sooner or later translates productivity increases into smaller resource allocations and fewer employees.

However, these challenges can be overcome, and if implemented correctly, gainsharing can dramatically improve productivity and generate substantial savings for the public. Employees can also gain a tangible "equity stake" in the organization, providing a powerful means of rewarding them for doing the very things that the taxpaying electorate wants them to do. In sum, gainsharing is worth the trouble, most especially in government.

HISTORICAL SUMMARY

PGS has a spotty history in the public sector. In the private sector as many as 2,200 firms have reported active gainsharing programs,[4] and a number of them have achieved well-publicized success; Motorola, for instance, has made gainsharing an integral part of its employee compensation strategy. However, gainsharing has not been widely attempted by government entities—the research literature contains only a few references to the topic,[5] suggesting a relatively small number of government gainsharing experiments. Where they have occurred, the results have been mixed, largely because of nuances unique to public employ.

Most of this experimentation has occurred in the U.S. federal government, where the Office of Personnel Management (OPM) has actively encouraged gainsharing. In the Department of Defense (DOD), gainsharing has been attempted with some success in a number of its large industrial operations, and in several cases it has been subjected to considerable scrutiny by practitioners, auditors, and social scientists. In addition, the Internal Revenue Service (IRS) has effectively applied gainsharing to white collar work: the processing of various tax documents. These efforts emerge as the principal source of data (anecdotal and otherwise) regarding the efficacy of public sector productivity gainsharing, and though these cases are by no means exhaustive, they offer at least some basis for an assessment of its prospects and potential for public organizations.

Private employers have experimented with various forms of gain-sharing for many years.[4] Its roots can be traced back to vintage Scanlon and Rucker plans, which became popular in the 1930s, and more recent "Improshare" schemes. Scanlon and Rucker plans linked labor costs to such global performance measures as company sales volume and inventory; both emphasized worker involvement (unfortunately, sometimes in an attempt to ward off union organizing attempts) through in-plant committees that reviewed and implemented suggestions for productivity improvement, and they shared productivity gains—typically determined by comparing labor costs against overall sales volume—between workers and the company. Improshare plans, which emerged in the 1970s, placed less emphasis on worker involvement, focusing more mechanically on the value of increases in units produced over time as a basis for determining gainshares. All three types of plans, along with a number of customized variations, are found in the private sector today[4] and continue to produce positive results.

As noted, the history of public sector gainsharing is somewhat less illuminating. There are few reports of state and local gainsharing experiments. In the federal government gainsharing experiments in the DOD and IRS during the 1980s have been the most widely publicized and evaluated. The Air Force's Pacer Share demonstration project, involving some 1,500 employees in a distribution depot at McClellan Air Force Base in California, has been perhaps the most notable and far-reaching, largely because it featured union partnership in design and operation and involved the waiver of various federal civil service laws that were thought to impede organizational performance. (For more information on this project, see Chapter Twelve.) According to the project's final evaluation report,[6] over $4.8 million in productivity-based savings were generated by gainsharing efforts, with payouts ranging from $59 to $475 in nine of the project's seventeen fiscal quarters of existence. However, these and other performance measures were disappointing, especially when compared to control sites without gainsharing. When a reorganization transferred about half of the project's workforce to another DOD agency, the program was allowed to lapse without much fanfare. Nevertheless, in a

1986 report the General Accounting Office concluded that the proto-type gainsharing efforts at the DOD held a great deal of promise, and it advocated that PGS be adopted by other DOD and domestic agencies as a means of improving the productivity of federal employees.

Several less-publicized but somewhat more successful gainsharing efforts were attempted at a number of Navy shipyards and aviation repair depots, as well as at several Defense Logistics Agency supply facilities. According to Navy figures,[7] gainsharing engendered almost $31.2 million in savings at eight PGS sites; this amount was divided equally between covered employees and the Navy itself. However, an audit revealed major financial management and accounting discrepancies at two of the sites, which resulted in $12.4 million in erroneous overpayments ($3,410 per affected employee). Ironically, the findings were based primarily on the two facilities' failure to comply with the terms of their own gainsharing plans, which were construed as binding contracts between facility management, employees, and (most important) the Navy.

All of these efforts began with high hopes, and their initial promise led the OPM (successor to the Civil Service Commission) to issue a special bulletin[8] encouraging productivity gainsharing throughout the federal government. In 1989, Rep. Frank Wolf (R-Virginia) introduced legislation calling for the federal government to "share savings" derived from documented increases in employee productivity. That legislation did not pass, but gainsharing momentum did not diminish, and in 1993 the concept (retitled federal performance sharing) was endorsed by Vice President Gore in the National Performance Review Report.[9]

These trends notwithstanding, gainsharing seems to be on the decline in the federal government. The IRS initiative continues with apparent success, but DOD efforts have come to a standstill. The Air Force's Pacer Share demonstration project, extensively evaluated by various third parties, yielded mixed results at best. The aggressive Navy gainsharing program, covering some 40,000 employees at its peak, remains on hold despite millions in documented savings—the result of the critical 1992 audit report cited earlier. A substantial Defense Logistics Agency effort has been rocked by the closure and consolidation of a number of its facilities, events unrelated to its gainsharing program but nonetheless disruptive to it. As a consequence, the vice president's strong support for more federal performance sharing has so far gone unheeded, although the savings generated by these aborted gainsharing efforts remains impressive. Difficulties can be traced to technical and procedural issues but not to any fundamental flaw in the concept. At any rate, the cases cited serve a very useful purpose: they are a source of lessons learned.

CRITICAL SUCCESS FACTORS

What do these lessons teach us about public sector PGS? What exactly does it take to make productivity gainsharing work in government? Practical experience and a modicum of empirical research suggest a number of factors critical to successful gainsharing in the government organization:

- First, the effort requires the strong, visible support of the government jurisdiction's immediate political leadership—the elected and appointed officials who oversee the public organization as well as the senior career civil servants who manage it. All these leaders must clearly communicate their support to the organization's members.

- Second, the effort requires support from internal stakeholders: the supervisors and employees (and their union representatives, if any) who will be asked to produce more—who are involved and empowered with the authority and information to effect improvements in productivity and quality.

- Third, the successful PGS program requires something not yet common enough in today's public organizations: a bottom-line orientation, a singular focus on the organization's outputs and outcomes (whether goods or services) and on the customers who receive them.

- Fourth, the gainsharing government organization must ensure that PGS is implemented in a manner that complements the various other means by which it manages the performance of its resources, from individual performance ratings to performance-based budget allocations; that is, as but one part of a larger, integrated system that constantly and consistently reinforces its strategic goals and values.

- Fifth, PGS requires breaking some traditions: it will not work (at least not as well) without changes to the way government organizations have historically managed their financial and human resources. This is particularly so with the perverse logic of the public budgeting process and the well-intentioned but debilitating rigidities of traditional civil service rules. PGS requires a new approach.

For the most part these requirements are not unique to government, but they are complicated by the political dimension: scrutiny by the media, relations with various constituencies and interest groups, the vagaries of elected and appointed leaders, and the interplay of internal and external stakeholders with an interest in the public organization's performance.

PGS is also complicated by the very nature of public organizations, rooted as they are in the traditions of bureaucratic structure and behavior. All of these factors have an impact on the essential politics of public management and bear on the chances for successful gainsharing. Accordingly, each is examined here in greater depth.

The examinations should also make it obvious that, above all, successful public productivity gainsharing requires patience to overcome initial worker suspicions, to teach employees and managers the reengineering and quality management techniques that optimize its chances for success, and, perhaps most important, to inculcate the values (such as group cooperation and teamwork) that are just as important to the effort as new budget rules. In short, PGS means a fundamental change in an organization's culture, and such changes take time and tenacity on the part of the public official who champions the cause.

Top Management Support

As with any initiative that affects the culture and performance values of an organization, the strong, visible support of its senior leadership is essential to the success of gainsharing. In the private sector this means the firm's CEO and principal operating and staff executives and managers. In the public sector it means the civil service analogs: the head and senior career staff of the public works department or tax return processing center, the commander of a military base, the city manager and department chiefs, and the like. It also means top-level political support from the jurisdiction's executive and legislative bodies.

Obviously, this political dimension complicates things. Elected and appointed public officials have different motives, agendas, and time horizons than the career civil servants who run public organizations, and they must be persuaded that gainsharing is in their—and their constituency's—best political interest. This has often proved difficult. Why, if PGS is so promising, would any public official hesitate to endorse it? After all, who could argue against the potential for substantial savings for the taxpayer? The rhetorical answer may be found in the present public attitude toward government: many will assert that civil servants are already paid, perhaps too much, to find the most efficient way of doing public business, and that they should not be offered more money just to do what the public expects of them. Moreover, cognitive dissonance theory suggests that once public employees receive financial rewards for productivity improvements, they will never again make such improvements "for free"—for the intrinsic rewards that may be associated with bettering service to the public. Something like this view was expressed by several senior military officers involved in the Defense Department's various gainsharing efforts, who are uniformed executives with motives and time horizons not unlike those of elected and appointed officials.

But it is the promise of substantial savings without risk that can win these skeptics over, or at least keep them at bay. Whether or not one believes that government employees should be paid to produce more, the simple fact is that often it does take some tangible incentive to encourage them to make the organization work better, especially if they are suspicious of the motives behind any attempt at public productivity improvement and of the consequences of success. You cannot order employees, public or private, to be more productive, nor can you threaten them with the loss of their jobs. Both strategies have been tried without great results. But though punishment and negative reinforcement rarely motivate, money (among other things, of course) can, especially when it is linked to the performance of the entire work unit or organization. And if that organization does not perform, employees get no additional pay, a no-risk guarantee that ought to appeal to any politician. Ideally, that appeal should be translated into unequivocal public support for the gainsharing effort.

Employee Involvement and Empowerment

Under the best of circumstances, gainsharing is likely to be viewed with some suspicion by public employees—supervisors as well as the rank and file and their unions. At a time when most public jurisdictions are confronting severe budgetary constraints, gainsharing is often perceived as yet another "do more with less" scheme, a work speed-up in the classic sense (a senior union official involved in the early Pacer Share discussions used this very phrase to decry the experiment). This reaction is understandable, especially given that savings are traditionally treated as personnel reductions in the public budgeting process: if the organization demonstrates that it can do the same amount of work with fewer, more productive people, budget offices or legislatures are likely to respond by reducing its budget allocation or its authorized number of employees. If gainsharing is to have any chance whatsoever, employees must be convinced that their productivity gains will not backfire on them.

The motivating effects of productivity gainsharing—not to mention its impact on the bottom line—are leveraged when employees and managers are intimately involved in gainsharing design and then empowered to increase productivity by continuously streamlining and improving the organization's work processes. It is no coincidence that involvement and empowerment are classic tenets of the quality and reengineering movements (as well as their many progenitors), and they serve to connect gainsharing with a whole host of complementary organizational strategies that exponentially increase the odds of success.[5]

Employee involvement may be the most important condition precedent in this regard. Involvement is the best way to secure employee buy-in, and it is perhaps the only means of overcoming the skepticism often engendered by gainsharing initiatives. This takes more than just saying that employees are involved; it requires the organization to establish some formal, structured (but preferably non-bureaucratic) employee involvement mechanism, such as a system of in-plant committees, joint labor-management productivity councils, classic Total Quality Management (TQM) steering groups and process action teams, or even a simple suggestion program. And this mechanism cannot be limited to rank-and-file civil servants; it must also apply to the organization's managers and most especially its unions if they are organized. By definition, gainsharing is intended to mobilize and align these organizational stakeholders and the various interests they represent, and it is clear that if they are not formally and intimately involved in all aspects of program design and implementation, they are likely to resist and impede the effort.

Where public employees are represented by a labor union, this kind of involvement may occur first at the bargaining table. In many public jurisdictions gainsharing is likely to be considered a mandatory subject of collective bargaining, effectively giving the union veto power over the effort. For example, the Federal Labor Relations Authority has held that a union proposal prescribing the distribution of an organization's "productivity profits" is negotiable,[10] and this can be problematic where a confrontational labor-management relationship exists. Under such circumstances some form of organizational therapy— training in interest-based bargaining and alternative dispute resolution techniques or more traditional organizational development interventions, for instance—may be in order before gainsharing is even seriously considered by the parties.

Moreover, though collective bargaining may be essential (legally so in some jurisdictions), it does not necessarily guarantee employee buy-in, especially in the public sector where union membership is usually voluntary. For example, in Pacer Share, union participation was extensive, intimate, and widely publicized; however, it involved only a few union representatives, managers, and personnel officials, and as a result employee surveys indicated that rank-and-file workers remained wary of the gainsharing effort during the first two years of its operation;[6] interestingly, those same surveys disclosed similar suspicions among first- and second-line supervisors. Thus those who are most critical to making the gainsharing effort work—the employees and managers who are actually responsible for delivering an organization's products or services—can become disenfranchised or worse if they are not in some meaningful way involved in design and implementation. Obviously, this can be tricky in a unionized environment because labor officials will not lightly concede their exclusive right to speak for employees. But employee involvement may mean just that if the effort is to enjoy the support it requires.

In addition experience suggests that the gainsharing plan must be effectively communicated—even marketed—to employees and managers, especially those who cannot be part of the design effort. Communication must be made early and often. This goes hand-in-hand with visible top management support, first to overcome employees' natural fear of the new and different, particularly when it concerns their pay, and then to constantly reinforce the relationship between organizational performance and gainsharing payouts. Successful gainsharing requires unrestricted information sharing as well; in this regard, employees must be continually informed as to how the organization is doing (bad as well as good), a prospect made easier by modern information technology and networks—indeed, that technology often gives employees access to such information whether their bosses like it or not!

Although involvement and communication are essential, they do not guarantee tangible results in and of themselves. Gainsharing employees and managers must also be empowered. Empowerment is a word that has become hackneyed, but it still succinctly describes the concept: discretion, on the part of both employees and managers, to make improvements in work processes and organizational practices that result in greater quality and productivity. Explicitly and otherwise, employee empowerment was extant in all of DOD's gainsharing initiatives; every one started with quality improvement efforts and either included, or eventually migrated to, gainsharing as a way of rewarding employees for the results of those efforts. Moreover, like involvement, empowerment must be formally sanctioned and structured within the organization. Just saying that employees are empowered is not enough—it requires a clear devolution of authority (and accountability) to them.

Though this may sound like yet another prescription for TQM in public organizations, it is not. Although most of the organizational examples reviewed here implemented some or all of the tenets of TQM as a part of (or along with) the gainsharing initiative, this does not mean that one needs to embrace its dogma to be successful. However, it does mean that if it wants to optimize the effects of this kind of reward system, the gainsharing government should be prepared to involve and engage all of its employees in the productivity improvement effort, from initial planning and design to implementation and evaluation. Indeed, employees will likely demand such participation anyway. This just happens to be characteristic of the quality culture.

Output, Outcome, and Process Measures

The heart of a PGS program is the gainsharing plan itself. The plan serves as a contract of sorts (as noted, the Navy and the Federal Labor Relations Authority both see it as a legally binding one) between employer, employee, and in the case of government organizations, the public. And the singular focus of that plan must be productivity. Thus it should come as no surprise that gainsharing works best in organizations that have measurable outputs: appliances, automobiles, airplanes, ships, even social security checks. The organization's gainsharing plan usually identifies these measures, as well as their baseline level of output; that level becomes the standard against which future output is compared. The plan also includes the formula for translating the output measure or measures into gainshares, thereby establishing the linkage between performance and reward (clearly, the simpler this formula the stronger the linkage, at least from the employee's viewpoint).

However, except for the more obvious examples cited earlier, most public organizations have difficulty identifying their outputs, and often their broader outcome goals—such as enhanced national security or reduced poverty—are even more problematic. Typically, government organizations measure resource inputs (people, dollars) and process activity (throughput). It is not so much that they do not have outputs and outcomes, but that as a practical matter they are rarely held accountable for them—in part because public budgets traditionally are based on input and activity rather than the bottom line. Fair warning: identifying output and outcome measures will not be easy. Even those public organizations that appear to have tangible performance indicators may be focusing on ones that are only surrogates. For example, many law enforcement agencies measure arrests, a throughput measure, rather than convictions, in part because they have less control over the latter.

In gainsharing, the organizational domain of the output or outcome measure may be just as important as the measure itself. If the domain is too large—that is, if the measure represents the combined efforts of too many diverse and seemingly unrelated components of the organization—employees will have difficulty seeing how their individual or work unit efforts contribute to any resulting payout. In other words, the performance-pay linkage gets muddled. The Pacer Share gainsharing experiment apparently suffered from this; surveyed employees expressed some dissatisfaction with the gainsharing initiative, in part because they did not perceive a clear relationship between their performance and the payouts they may or may not have received.[6] But if the organizational domain is too small (a single work group, for instance), the output measure may be too sensitive to factors beyond the work group's control, with similar muddling effects. Moreover, work units in the output domain must be large enough to have enough resources, workload volume, product flow, employee turnover, and the like to allow for meaningful savings and meaningful payouts.

Because of its emphasis on group and organizational productivity, gainsharing is clearly optimized where outputs are the result of interdependent work activities—that is, where all the various employees or work units contribute more or less directly to the output measure. As a corollary, it is also apparent that the group dynamics of gainsharing are further leveraged when work activities have been organized around teams. Nevertheless, gainsharing can be based on an aggregation of individual products (for example, cases processed by individual investigators), its synergistic effects having a positive impact upon workers and work measures that appear to be independent; for instance, where gainshares are based on aggregate individual output, other members of the work unit are much more likely to pitch in to help (or push) those lagging behind. However, in many cases, interdependence is often just a matter of picking the right measure, one that represents group rather than individual efforts; for example, global performance indicators such as customer satisfaction can be used as a basis for goalsharing and group incentives.

All of this emphasis on output measures should not suggest that gainsharing cannot work in organizations that find it difficult to identify them. Input and process measures can be incorporated into a gainsharing formula as well. By definition, fewer inputs, or greater throughputs, mean improved productivity and tangible savings that can be measured and shared. And because such measures traditionally have been used to gauge the performance of public organizations, they may be more readily available. They may not be optimal, but such process measures may have to suffice, particularly where a public organization's program outputs or mission outcomes have been deliberately left ambiguous by governing bodies.

If employed correctly, input and process measures can be important indicators of product and service quality: for example, fewer defects (whether in the repair of avionics or the processing of unemployment compensation claims) mean fewer net inputs per person, a result that can be translated into hard budget savings and gainshares. In this regard, statistical process control and continuous process improvement are central to quality management, and both rely on process measures that can and should be considered in gainsharing. Goalsharing, which does not demand the quantitative rigor of its kin, is another way of encouraging and rewarding improvements in quality and service, especially in such intangible measures as customer satisfaction.

Process reengineering, TQM's heir apparent, is similarly conducive to goal- and gainsharing; such things as reduced cycle time can also be translated into measurable productivity increases and rewarded accordingly. Unfortunately, process improvement (or reengineering) can be a challenge for the public organization, where work procedures are often embedded in law or regulation, the product of micromanaging legislatures and regulatory bodies. However, appearances can be deceiving in this regard; in many cases seemingly intractable process rules are self-inflicted, the natural sediment of bureaucracy ("This is the way we've always done things"), and managers and employees can make dramatic process and productivity improvements if they are willing and able to question these traditions. If these efforts can be linked to and lubricated by gainsharing, they are that much more likely to happen. The group dynamics of gainsharing are especially important here as a way of providing employees a tangible incentive to change.

Integrated Performance Management

PGS can be a catalyst for organizational change on a variety of levels, but its effectiveness in this regard depends on the clarity and strength of its relationship to the organization's larger goals and values. At its root, productivity gainsharing is a form of performance-based pay, and in establishing a pay-performance linkage at the group level it can also influence the behavior of employees and managers in a more strategic sense.[1] By this definition, PGS must be viewed as a performance management system, and as a consequence the gainsharing government organization must ensure that it is implemented in a way that complements other performance management systems. More important, it must ensure that all of those systems, taken together, serve to reinforce its strategic goals and culture.

This is more than just a mechanical consideration. Like any other method of assessing and rewarding performance, the gainsharing plan sends cultural signals to employees, telling them what the organization values. Moreover, though they may not be labeled as such, performance management systems exist in a variety of forms throughout the organization, many of them outside the traditional purview of the organization's human resource (HR) department. For example, the budget process rewards certain kinds of behavior and thus may be construed as a form of performance management (indeed, in many public jurisdictions budgeting has now become explicitly performance based). Great care must be taken to ensure that all these value systems send employees congruent messages regarding their behavior. This raises important design issues on a number of levels.

The most apparent of these involves the individual performance appraisal. In the public sector formal performance management systems typically focus on the individual, and they increasingly feature some form of monetary reward (merit pay) for those who exceed certain performance standards. At their worst such systems can breed competition between employees—one of Deming's "deadly sins" and a result clearly at odds with gainsharing's group effort–group reward linkage.[1] Nevertheless, individual performance-based pay remains the prevailing practice and conventional wisdom in the private sector, and as public organizations are encouraged to become more privatelike, they will not likely abandon such merit pay systems. Indeed, it is often politically impossible to do so.

However, it is entirely possible to craft individual and group-based systems that reinforce each other, by focusing on and rewarding individual performance behaviors that are consistent with the underlying dynamic of gainsharing: group contribution, teamwork, constructive interpersonal relations, problem solving, task cooperation, and so forth. Note here that gainsharing, with its emphasis on organizational rather than individual output as a basis for monetary reward, is perhaps the only form of merit pay that may be acceptable to the TQM orthodoxy. To be sure, that orthodoxy argues against numerical production quotas, an implicit element in many gainsharing formulas, but only because it posits that employees will produce to the quota and no more. However, most gainsharing plans place no limit on payouts for productivity above standard, thus minimizing that risk.

Human resource departments must formulate policy that identifies and deals with individuals at either end of the performance continuum. This is especially the case with truly outstanding employees. No organization can afford to let individual excellence and achievement go unrewarded, and such individual recognition, if based on a credible performance appraisal system, does not necessarily vitiate the team ethic fostered by gainsharing. Poor performers also deserve to be singled out. In theory, the group pressures associated with gainsharing are supposed to be effective, but practical experience suggests otherwise: employees do not like to confront poor performing coworkers any more than their supervisors do.

The Pacer Share gainsharing effort provides an interesting case in point. Its original vision was a Deming-like organization without individual performance appraisals and all their supposedly attendant pathologies. Only organizational appraisals, in the form of productivity measures tied directly to gainsharing, were to be used. However, in reviewing the final terms of the project the OPM insisted that the designers incorporate some mechanism for dealing with poor performers. Banking on the group dynamics inherent in gainsharing, the designers added what later became known as the "snitch provision," a procedure by which group members could identify poorly performing members to their supervisor or union shop steward. As could be expected, employees never used the procedure.

Poor performers diminish the prospects for everybody's gain, and survey data suggest that employees want something done. Those same surveys also indicate that employees miss the feedback, however spotty, that comes with individual appraisals, to complement the information they receive on more global measures of performance. Despite the effectiveness of the group dynamics engendered by PGS, the organization should retain some formal means of individual assessment that identifies and rewards (or removes) outliers at either end of the performance spectrum.

This may also rectify a major flaw of most public sector employee performance appraisal systems today, which focus exclusively on the individual. Designed and managed by the HR department, they typically fail to link the individual appraisal rating to broader organizational performance indices—especially hard output and outcome measures—except perhaps in a visceral sense.

Some public organizations are starting to refocus their appraisal systems toward bottom-line performance, especially when evaluating managers. Productivity gainsharing can bring this same orientation to street-level public employees. Designed correctly, PGS can integrate the group and organizational performance measures that are a necessary part of gainsharing, with the individual performance assessments that are a common (and often politically correct) feature of civil service systems in most public jurisdictions.

Supportive Support Systems

Gainsharing occurs in a larger organizational context, particularly when applied to government. Public organizations are literally embedded in a web of rules that govern how resources are allocated and people are managed. Taken together, these rules comprise the various management systems that operate within and upon the government organization, and it is clear that they must complement the gainsharing effort if the latter is to work. This too is easier said than done, especially when it comes to the traditions of civil service and public budgeting.

Contemporary organizations, public and private alike, must contend with an extremely turbulent, uncertain environment, where change is the rule rather than the exception. Flexibility, particularly in managing the organization's human resources, becomes a survival trait. This is especially true for the gainsharing organization. An organization that can rapidly size its workforce to meet demand for its services and deploy teams of multiskilled and motivated employees will be positioned to thrive in such an environment. And gainsharing is clearly consistent with these characteristics. However, they are at odds with the historical traditions of most civil service systems, with their protracted hiring and separation protocols, complex job evaluation and classification systems, and rigid compensation rules. The good news is that many public jurisdictions, including the federal government, are beginning to contemplate more flexible civil service compensation and employment policies—fewer job classifications, pay banding (see Chapter Two for more on this), longer probationary periods, limited-term employment contracts, and expanded use of on-call or temporary ("contingent") workers across all job categories—with which the advantages to the gainsharing organization should be apparent.

As a general proposition, flexibility is cost-effective, and in the case of the gainsharing public employer, the ability to rapidly size and deploy a flexible workforce to reflect productivity and process improvements as well as fluctuations in customer demand translates directly into more immediate (and hence greater) savings and larger gainshares. This also gives rise to a difficult dilemma for public employees and their unions: in today's fiscally austere public sector, gainshares for some may mean lost jobs for others. However, concentrating lost jobs in the contingent component of the public organization's workforce permits the permanent core of full-time tenured employees to enjoy both gainshares and comparatively greater job security. This was precisely the bargain struck in the Pacer Share experiment, where the union conceded greater flexibility (and less protection) for a newly created category of contingent employees in exchange for larger gainshares and greater stability for the rest of its constituents.

Gainsharing has a profound effect on a public employer's budget as well. Considerable care must be taken to ensure that the design of budgeting and financial management systems is adaptable. Unless modified, traditional fiscal procedures tend to undermine gainsharing efforts. Most experienced public sector managers have long ago learned to "use it or lose it" when it comes to surplus funds, and the implications of this policy to gainsharing should be obvious. Yet this cultural artifact is perhaps the most difficult to undo, inasmuch as it has become embedded in the way governing bodies (legislatures and the like) fund public organizations.

If gainsharing is to work, traditional budget rules must be amended to permit the organization to retain and distribute some portion of productivity-based savings to its employees—easier said than done in a political environment that may construe such amendments as a bureaucratic shell game or worse. Nevertheless, this too is a condition precedent to gainsharing success.

The public organization's governing body and its budget minions must be willing to promise that it will not penalize the gainsharing organization—for example, by reducing its budget—for generating savings that presumably have been induced by the promise of gainshares. To be sure, some of those savings must be returned to the jurisdiction's treasury (although ironically, this is often very difficult in an accounting sense). However, some form of "hold harmless" proviso is essential in order to overcome employee suspicion and avoid by-the-book budget reductions that may vitiate the motivational effects of PGS.

This is no small task, as any public manager knows, because the perverse nature of the public budgeting process tends to allocate fewer resources to organizations that achieve greater efficiency: savings in one year become a debit against the next year's budget allocation simply because the organization has demonstrated that it can operate at that reduced level. This is an understandable, albeit shortsighted, response to the constant political pressure to reduce public expenditures. Public managers and their political leadership must try to strike a delicate balance between the compelling need to reflect productivity-based savings in the budgeting process and the need to credibly convince those who will achieve those savings that they do not put their paychecks and jobs at risk in so doing. This goes to the heart of the political dimension that is unique to gainsharing in public organizations, where a reduced budget is typically the reward for better performance.

Programmatic budget reductions are another matter. Ideally, the gainsharing organization should be able to count on constancy of mission, predictable workload, and a reasonably stable multiyear budget baseline; it is much harder to measure the organization's performance against a moving target. This stability was a key part of early DOD and IRS efforts, and even though workload was substantially reduced later on, an initial period of relative stability allowed sufficient time for the culture of gainsharing to settle in throughout the subject organizations. But public organizations are unlikely to promise fiscal and programmatic stability, and the gainsharing plan must take this reality into account. Up to a point, gainsharing formulas that focus on cost per unit of output are somewhat self-correcting in this regard, but major program reductions or cancellations may stretch these mechanisms to the breaking point. The gainsharing plan must contemplate such contingencies.

Perhaps the best form of insurance is an explicit proviso for flexibility, so that adjustments in the gainsharing plan can be made without arousing the suspicion of employees, auditors, or the electorate. This built-in flexibility was not a part of the Navy and Pacer Share gainsharing efforts, and they both suffered because of it: formula adjustments were viewed as a breach of contract by workers and auditors alike, even though they may have been justified by the realities of mission and workload. A flexible gainsharing formula is particularly important as public jurisdictions experiment with new forms of funding and resource allocation such as user fees, block grants for state and local jurisdictions, and outcome-based performance measures for federally mandated programs.

CONCLUSION

The factors discussed in the previous five sections represent the most fundamental of the various conditions precedent to a government gainsharing effort. There should be no misunderstanding here: the public organization that satisfies these conditions is by no means guaranteed success. These a priori elements merely set the stage, opening the door for the kind of detailed analysis and discussion that will ultimately determine whether PGS is at all practical in a particular jurisdiction; a whole host of other variables, both technical and political, could bear on that question.

Perhaps the most important of these other variables is the least tangible: patience. Gainsharing takes time. For most public organizations, gainsharing, with all of its attendant issues, will represent a dramatic change in organizational culture; it brings with it a new set of values and behaviors for both employees and managers, and every public manager knows how difficult it can be to introduce such things. Conventional wisdom suggests that it may take as long as five to seven years to change an organization's culture and core system of values. That has been the experience in achieving and sustaining a culture that fully supports TQM, and as we have seen, gainsharing is a close kin in this regard. This is at odds with the short time horizon and demand for almost instant gratification that most elected officials bring to the table. Great care must be taken to ensure that early expectations are reasonable. In other words, gainsharing should not be oversold. It will take time to fully realize its potential, and for the public organization that is considering PGS, this means that patience must be accompanied by a healthy dose of perseverance.

Notes

1. E. E. Lawler III, *Strategic Pay: Aligning Organizational Strategies and Pay Systems* (San Francisco: Jossey-Bass, 1990).

2. D. Nebeker, D. Wolosin, and B. Tatum, *A Model of Continuous Organizational Improvement: Integrating Gainsharing and Total Quality* (San Diego, Calif.: Navy Personnel Research and Development Center, 1994).

3. Though gainsharing payouts are a form of variable pay, the Fair Labor Standards Act suggests that they must be included in an employee's base rate for purposes of overtime calculation. For example, an employee earning $12 per hour ($24,000 per year) receives an annual gainshare of $1,200; this equates to an additional 60 cents an hour and increases the employee's overtime rate by 5 percent, from $18 to $18.90 per hour. And the increase is prospective, at least until the next gainshare payout (which may be zero) establishes a new base for the computation. Note that goalsharing, which is not exclusively linked to productivity, may not suffer from this liability. If monetary rewards are tied to more global organizational accomplishments (an increase in market share or, in the public sector, implementation of a major new program ahead of schedule or under budget), they may not be treated as base pay but rather as a one-time-only group incentive award.

The key may be in the degree of regularity and predictability—that is, the extent to which employees can reasonably expect the performance-pay contingency.

4. The Conference Board, *Productivity Gainsharing: A Survey of Current Practice* (Report 967) (New York: The Conference Board, 1991).

5. B. A. Macy and H. Hiroaki, "Organizational Change, Design, and Work Innovation: A Meta-Analysis of 131 North American Field Studies (1961–1991)," in R. Woodman and W. Pasmore (eds.), *Research in Organizational Change and Development* (Greenwich, Conn.: JAI Press, forthcoming).

6. U.S. Office of Personnel Management, *Pacer Share: A Federal Productivity and Personnel Management Demonstration Project: Fourth Year Evaluation Report* (Washington, D.C.: U.S. Government Printing Office, 1992).

7. U.S. Naval Audit Service, *Audit Report: Productivity Gain Sharing* (Washington, D.C.: U.S. Government Printing Office, 1992).

8. U.S. Office of Personnel Management, *Federal Personnel Manual Letter Number 451–6* (Washington, D.C.: U.S. Office of Personnel Management, April 10, 1989).

9. National Performance Review, Vice President's Report, *From Red Tape to Results: Creating a Government That Works Better and Costs Less* (Washington, D.C.: U.S. Government Printing Office, 1993).

10. See *Charleston Navy Shipyard,* 32 FLRA No. 15, 1988.

CHAPTER TWELVE

Paying for Performance

Lessons Learned in Fifteen Years
of Federal Demonstration Projects

Brigitte W. Schay

The federal personnel system, built on the good intentions of founders who wanted to prevent political patronage and corruption, has become a virtual maze of laws, rules, and regulations whose complexity tends to overwhelm both managers and the personnel specialists who assist them.

The most recent attempt to reform the system was made in 1978 when Congress passed the Civil Service Reform Act (CSRA) promoted by President Carter, who had been elected on a promise to reorganize the government. For the purposes of this chapter, the most relevant provisions of CSRA were merit pay for midlevel managers, a job-based performance appraisal system with critical elements and standards for all employees (replacing a system that allowed more subjective trait ratings), and a provision to conduct personnel management demonstration projects under waivers of personnel laws and regulations in order to test more flexible alternatives to the existing personnel system.

The demonstration authority represented the first official acknowledgment by Congress that the federal personnel system had become too rigid to meet the changing demands of agencies that had to accomplish increasingly complex missions. Seven demonstration projects have been implemented since 1980. Changes have been tested in job classification, compensation, performance management, and recruitment methods. This chapter reports on the results of three of these demonstration projects in the area of pay for performance.

CRITERIA FOR SUCCESSFUL PERFORMANCE POLICIES

The concept of pay for performance has considerable support in the abstract and is grounded in a meritocratic personnel philosophy. In practice, however, pay for performance means pay for a supervisory rating, and this is where support begins to decline. Rosabeth Moss Kanter[1] summed up general objections to merit pay as revolving around two essential issues: the amount, and the way the amount is determined. Insufficient funds, subjective judgments and measures, and the reluctance of raters to make meaningful distinctions are the primary causes of the failure of merit pay plans.

The question of whether pay actually motivates and results in higher performance has occupied many researchers and has been a major concern for the federal government since the CSRA introduced merit pay for federal managers. In 1989, after years of discontent with the federal merit pay system, the Office of Personnel Management (OPM) asked the National Research Council of the National Academy of Sciences (NAS) to conduct a study of pay for performance and, if possible, to come up with models that federal policymakers could use in redesigning the Performance Management and Recognition System (PMRS), the merit pay system for federal managers created by CSRA. A committee of national experts reviewed research on pay for performance and in 1991 issued a report that found that the empirical evidence was not sufficient to determine whether merit pay can enhance individual performance.[2] The NAS committee reported that in the private sector merit pay programs were used almost universally for managerial and professional employees.

Support for pay for performance is mainly theoretical and based on expectancy theory that predicts that pay-for-performance plans can motivate and improve employee performance as long as the ideal motivational conditions are fulfilled.

Edward Lawler, a prominent authority on compensation, further spelled out the conditions that must exist for pay-for-performance systems to be successful:[3]

- Significant rewards can be given and tied to performance.
- Information is communicated to employees about how rewards are given.
- Supervisors are willing to explain and support the reward system in discussions with their subordinates.
- Rewards can vary widely, depending on performance.
- Performance can be objectively and inclusively measured.
- Meaningful performance appraisal sessions can take place.
- High levels of trust exist or can be developed between supervisors and subordinates.

The discussion that follows reviews federal demonstration project experience with pay for performance in light of Lawler's seven criteria.

THREE PAY-FOR-PERFORMANCE DEMONSTRATIONS

Federal managers operate in an environment quite different from their private sector counterparts; they have to deal with political as well as bureaucratic rules. The Civil Service Reform Act was the first attempt to implement private sector management practices in the public sector. However, most of these practices did not go very far. The demonstration authority (Title VI CSRA) was designed to permit further flexibility but within the safe confines of a time-limited experimental framework.

The demonstration authority allows OPM, the central federal personnel management agency, to grant waivers of existing personnel laws and regulations for a period of five years to permit agencies to test innovative approaches. Rigorous evaluation of the results is required, and if a project or specific intervention is found successful, permanent legislative changes can be introduced. This process sounds rational in theory, but in practice Congress has been very reluctant to approve governmentwide personnel system changes based on the results of individual demonstration projects. Part of this is due to the inability of any project evaluation to prove beyond a doubt that positive changes were caused solely by the project interventions and that the results are generalizable to other federal installations and agencies. Although demonstration projects employ a quasi-experimental design with comparison groups, they do not take place in a controlled laboratory environment and are affected by many intervening variables, such as changes in personnel and possibly mission at the demonstration sites, as well as changes within the government as a whole and in the economy.

Nevertheless, after fourteen years, Congress in 1994 finally made permanent the changes involved in the first personnel management demonstration project. This action followed after several hearings and numerous legislative proposals, as well as fourteen evaluation reports by OPM that documented the generally positive results. The demonstration project in question was a pay-for-performance project begun in 1980 at two Navy research laboratories in China Lake and San Diego, California.

The second successful pay-for-performance demonstration project, implemented in 1988 by the National Institute of Standards and Technology (NIST), is continuing under extensions granted by OPM for evaluation purposes. A third and less successful project, which tested productivity gainsharing and Total Quality Management (TQM) principles, ended after its five-year statutory period expired.

Navy Demonstration Project

The Navy Demonstration Project, often referred to as the China Lake project, was OPM's first and most widely known demonstration project and was designed to reform both the classification and compensation system. The experiment, implemented in 1980 and made permanent in 1994, initially covered 5,000 employees in two research laboratories, the Naval Air Warfare Center Weapons Division in China Lake and the Naval Command and Control Ocean Systems Center in San Diego. It tested an integrated approach to pay, performance management, and position classification. The two labs pioneered the concept of broad banding (reducing the eighteen-grade federal pay schedule to five bands), introduced generic job classification standards, and extended the concept of pay for performance to all employees, exempt and nonexempt. The combination of pay for performance and broad pay ranges, along with career ladders permitting noncompetitive promotions up to the journey level, made it possible to approach the rank-in-person concept. The labs' main objective was to improve recruitment and retention of high performers by streamlining the personnel system and delegating more authority to managers.

The pay-for-performance system was funded by money previously reserved for step increases, quality step increases, and promotions between grades included in a band. Using historical spending levels as a basis, the Navy labs came up with an annual funding level of 2.3 to 2.4 percent of payroll. An additional 0.8 to 1.0 percent was reserved for cash bonuses. The annual comparability increase was also added to the merit pay pool and made contingent on performance, in contrast to the rest of the federal government where this increase is automatic. The labs used a five-level rating system linked to a system of annual pay increases ranging from 0 to about 6 percent, plus comparability, provided that performance was at least satisfactory. During the 1980s, under this system a high performer could earn annual pay increases of 10 percent, thus meeting the threshold for what was deemed meaningful at the time, 10 to 20 percent.[1] In contrast, the federal merit pay system during the 1980s provided for a maximum merit increase of 7 percent, including comparability.

NIST Demonstration Project

In 1988, the National Institute of Standards and Technology (NIST), formerly the National Bureau of Standards, located in the Washington, D.C., suburb of Gaithersburg, Maryland, and in Boulder, Colorado, adopted interventions for 3,000 employees similar to those of the Navy demonstration. As did their colleagues in the Navy labs, the NIST managers wanted to improve recruitment and retention of high-quality employees and were equally dissatisfied with the lack of flexibility in the federal personnel system. NIST implemented a slightly different broad-banding scheme, as well as simplified classification and pay for performance for exempt and nonexempt employees.

During the first three years of its demonstration project, NIST used the governmentwide five-level rating system to link pay to performance, but subsequent employee dissatisfaction with the forced distribution of ratings and perceived labeling by the five adjectival rating categories led to a redesign. In 1990, NIST came up with the concept of rating employees for pay purposes on a 100-point scale. Any employee rated at or above 40 is eligible for a merit increase. Only two summary rating categories are used (eligible or not eligible for a pay increase), but employee rankings on the 100-point scale determine the size of pay increases. The pay pool at NIST is composed of the same funding factors as Navy's and is currently 2.45 percent of payroll, down from 2.9 percent in the first three years, and a separate cash bonus pool of 1.5 percent. Governmentwide annual pay adjustments are also contingent on performance and added to the pay pool. Individual merit increases can range from 0 to 20 percent plus comparability, depending on the employee's band or position within a band. Larger pay increases are provided in the lower bands and in the lower terciles of each band. Table 12.1 illustrates the funding formulas for the Navy and NIST merit pay systems and includes the former governmentwide merit pay system, the Performance Management and Recognition System (PMRS), as an additional comparison.

NIST also introduced the concept of supervisory differentials, adding 3 percent for team leaders and 6 percent for managers who occupy the same bands as nonsupervisors. As broad banding typically incorporates the dual career ladder concept—that is, pay bands that can cover both supervisors and nonsupervisory technical experts—the designers of the NIST demonstration project were concerned that there would be no incentive for employees to become supervisors.

Pacer Share Demonstration Project

The third demonstration project, Pacer Share, tested a more radical alternative to the federal performance management system by eliminating individual performance appraisal altogether and focusing instead on organizational performance and implementing productivity gainsharing. Pacer Share was conducted for a five-year period (February 1988 to February 1993) at the Sacramento Air Logistics Center at McClellan Air Force Base, California, and covered about 1,500 blue- and white-collar employees in the center's distribution directorate. Pacer Share was the first demonstration project jointly designed with a labor union, the American Federation of Government Employees (AFGE), and involved a redesign of the entire personnel system, including broad banding and job series consolidation.

Pacer Share was guided by the philosophy of the late quality expert W. Edwards Deming, who opposed the concept of merit pay as destructive to employee morale and cooperation. According to Deming, differences in performance are primarily due to the system and not the individual; if nonperformance is caused by the individual, training or reassignment should be considered before a decision is made to separate the employee.

	Navy Demo (percent)	NIST Demo (percent)	PMRS (percent)
Percent of salary payroll for base pay	2.3–2.4	2.45[a]	1.9
Percent of payroll for bonus pay	.80–1.0	1.5	1.15–1.5
1993 governmentwide comparability pay	3.7	3.7	3.7
Total funding	6.8–7.1	7.65	6.75–7.1

Table 12.1.   Merit Pay Pool Funding in Demonstration Projects and the Former Governmentwide Performance Management and Recognition System.
[a]Was 2.9 percent.

Individual performance appraisal was eliminated in favor of measures of organizational performance and statistical process control procedures that would provide performance feedback to all employees; these changes were designed to support a productivity gainsharing system based on organizational performance that required cooperation between work teams. Also, TQM was introduced as a management philosophy.

Under Pacer Share, progression through the broad pay bands was based on longevity and modeled after the General Schedule step system. Annual pay increases were guaranteed and ranged from 1 to 3 percent, depending on position in the band, plus comparability. There was no provision to grant additional quality step increases to high performers or to deny pay increases to poor performers. Pacer Share included a provision for dealing with poor performers that required coworkers to report an employee to a supervisor or union steward for action, involving a preliminary analysis of the problem and possible further investigation by a joint labor-management committee. Statistical process control measures were supposed to be used to determine whether poor performance was due to the employee or the system. This well-intended but potentially complex provision replaced the current federal regulation requiring a performance improvement plan and ninety-day opportunity period.

The productivity gainsharing formula was based on savings in labor costs, which represented 90 percent of the directorate's budget. Cost savings, based on total organizational performance, were to be equally divided between employees and the government on a quarterly basis. The original formula was based on a ratio of hours worked to earned hours credited.

The Pacer Share workforce operated a warehouse with spare parts supporting Air Force bases and commands worldwide. The entire Pacer Share project was designed to enhance organizational flexibility. Job series consolidation created jobs with broader responsibilities, facilitating reassignments as workloads shifted; broad banding expanded pay potential to reward increased skills acquisition; and the elimination of individual performance appraisal was intended to reduce competition and facilitate cooperation. Productivity gain-sharing rewarded improved organizational performance and thus encouraged cooperation between employees across functional areas. Substantial increases in organizational performance were anticipated for the project, and annual payouts of $1,200 per person were projected prior to implementation in 1988.

RESULTS OF PAY-FOR-PERFORMANCE DEMONSTRATION PROJECTS

Evaluation of the three demonstration projects involved the collection and analysis of a variety of data, including annual workforce data (salary, pay grade or band, performance rating, turnover, and the like) and attitude surveys administered at the demonstration and comparison sites to track the effects of the personnel system changes over time. The results cited here are from surveys administered in 1992 and 1993. Most of the survey data provide indicators of Lawler's criteria, and analysis of the results reveals that both the Navy and NIST projects met most of Lawler's criteria for effective pay-for-performance systems, but Pacer Share failed to do so with its productivity gain-sharing system. The results for each of the criteria follow.

• *Significant rewards can be given and tied to performance.* Both Navy and NIST met the threshold for meaningful rewards by being able to offer merit increases of up to 10 percent (Navy) or more (NIST).

Pay satisfaction is generally low in the federal government; in the last governmentwide survey, administered in 1992, 32 percent of federal employees reported that they were satisfied with their pay. However, satisfaction was higher at all the demonstration sites, ranging from 46 percent under Pacer Share to 60 percent for the Navy demonstration in 1993.

Pacer Share never met its original expectation of annual gainsharing payouts of $1,200 per employee. Due to downsizing in the Department of Defense and various reorganizations, the workload dropped and gainshares were realized in only ten of the twenty-one quarters covered by the demonstration project. The total amount over five years was $1,924 per person, not the projected $6,000. Agreement with the survey statement "I will receive more money if I work harder" never exceeded 15 percent during the five years surveyed. Agreement with a more theoretical item assessing the motivational power of money, "More money makes me work harder," was slightly higher, rising to about 25 percent after four years. But throughout the course of the Pacer Share project, more than two-thirds of employees expressed the negative view that financial rewards were seldom related to employee performance. It can, therefore, be concluded from the Pacer Share survey data that employees were not particularly motivated by their gainsharing system.

- *Information is communicated to employees about how rewards are given.* This criterion addresses the adequacy of communication and resulting understanding of how the pay-for-performance system works. Most Navy demonstration employees (82 percent) and NIST employees (77 percent) reported that they understood their pay-for-performance system. Among Pacer Share employees, a minority of 41 percent of survey respondents in 1993 agreed that it was clear what had to be done to earn productivity gainshares, and only 35 percent reported that supervisors shared organizational performance data.[4]

- *Supervisors are willing to explain and support the reward system.* This criterion is closely related to the last one, but there were no survey items to measure it directly. However, unpublished data from site visits and interviews with Navy managers indicate strong supervisorial support for the pay-for-performance system. A NIST survey item that assesses this criterion indirectly, "I understand how pay raises are given in this organization," yielded 68 percent agreement in 1993. Evaluation results from the Pacer Share demonstration project indicate that there was inadequate communication between employees and management about the productivity gainsharing system. Employees in fact expressed confusion and doubt about the calculations upon which the gainshares were based. The original formula was changed after failing to produce payouts during the first year. Twice during the course of the demonstration project, in an attempt to maintain employee morale when no productivity gains materialized, management decided to use the incentive award fund to pay out special awards to each employee. Not surprisingly, though employees appreciated these payouts they also admitted that they added to the confusion about the gainsharing program.

• *Rewards can vary widely, depending on performance.* Under both the Navy and NIST pay-for-performance systems, total merit increases have ranged from 0 to 10 percent for the Navy and up to 20 percent at NIST, depending on the employee's position in the pay range. Pay-performance correlations were carried out for both Navy and NIST and indicate significant variations in pay based on cumulative performance ratings over time.[5,6] Regression models for Navy, in fact, revealed a 44 percent difference in pay over a ten-year period between an average and outstanding performer hired at entry level in 1980. At the comparison sites, the difference over ten years between an average and outstanding performer was 28 percent under the seniority-based civil service system. Top performers tended to be promoted faster.

Many Pacer Share employees expressed dissatisfaction with their pay system, which features increases based purely on longevity and unrelated to individual performance. Productivity gains, when they occurred, were shared equally among all employees. In interviews conducted by external evaluators in 1993, a number of employees were bothered that those who had not worked hard received gainshares equal to those of everyone else.[4]

• *Performance can be objectively and inclusively measured.* Because individual performance is evaluated by supervisors who are human, there is always some degree of subjectivity in rating performance, and it is doubtful that it will ever be eliminated even by using multiple raters. The quest for the holy grail—that is, for a perfect performance appraisal system—is likely to go on forever. But even those of us who have watched rating panels in the Olympics have had cause to question individual ratings.

It is doubtful, therefore, that individual employee performance in the demonstration projects was measured objectively and inclusively by all supervisors. The Navy labs used a modified management by objectives (MBO) system, whereas NIST employed performance plans with weighted job elements and standards. Longitudinal survey data have shown that both systems were an improvement over the pre-CSRA rating systems that permitted trait ratings.[7] When asked about the perceived fairness of ratings, the majority of employees in the Navy (60 percent) and NIST (58 percent) demonstrations reported that their ratings were fair.

Under Pacer Share, organizational performance was measured using industrial work standards already in place. But less than 50 percent of the work could be measured directly by these standards, mostly blue-collar employees. As the workforce was divided almost equally between blue- and white-collar employees, the contributions of white-collar employees were not measured adequately.

• *Meaningful performance appraisal sessions can take place.* About two-thirds of Navy and NIST employees surveyed reported that their supervisors gave them adequate information on how well they were performing. Under Pacer Share, individual performance appraisals were eliminated, but this change was not universally supported. In 1991 (year four), 47 percent of employees agreed that they preferred not to receive an annual performance appraisal; the remainder disagreed or were undecided. The main problem resulting from the elimination of appraisal was lack of performance feedback. Managers who were relieved not to have to perform the onerous task of rating employees also stopped providing performance feedback, and only 36 percent of employees surveyed reported receiving adequate feedback.[8]

Under Pacer Share, statistical process control procedures were supposed to take the place of individual performance feedback, but these measures never materialized to a significant degree, leaving a feedback gap.

• *High levels of trust exist and can be developed between supervisors and subordinates.* Only one of the demonstration projects, NIST, included a relevant survey item: "I have trust and confidence in my supervisor." In 1993, 67 percent agreed with this statement.[6] The question of trust cannot be answered for the Navy or Pacer Share demonstration projects.

Table 12.2 summarizes the results of the demonstration projects in terms of Lawler's criteria. A criterion was considered met when survey data showed agreement by at least two-thirds of the respondents. This may seem arbitrary, but a two-thirds majority is usually needed in Congress to override a presidential veto or approve a constitutional amendment. Because demonstration projects test changes in existing laws and regulations, support from at least two-thirds of the employees should be considered adequate to make a change.

Table 12.2 shows that Navy's pay-for-performance system clearly met five of Lawler's seven criteria; NIST's met six. Pacer Share's productivity gainsharing system failed five of the seven criteria and

	Navy Demo	NIST Demo	Pacer Share Demo
1. Significant rewards can be given and tied to performance.	Yes	Yes	No
2. Information is communicated to employees about how rewards are given.	Yes	Yes	Partially
3. Supervisors are willing to explain and support the reward system.	Yes	Yes	No
4. Rewards can vary widely, depending on performance.	Yes	Yes	No
5. Performance can be objectively and inclusively measured.	No	No	Partially
6. Meaningful performance appraisal sessions can take place.	.Yes	Yes	No
7. High levels of trust exist or can be developed between supervisors and subordinates.	No data	Yes	No data

Table 12.2.   Lawler's Criteria for Effective Pay-for-Performance Systems.

partially met two. Nevertheless, more than two-thirds of employees surveyed in all three demonstration projects supported the experiments. It is interesting that Pacer Share ended with the same high level of support as the other projects before it expired. The evaluation reports indicate that though overall productivity did not improve compared to the baseline or other Air Logistics Centers, intraorganizational cooperation and opportunities to learn new things increased and resulted in improved quality of work life for employees.

For the pay-for-performance systems of the Navy and NIST, the fifth, sixth, and seventh of Lawler's criteria may have been the most difficult to meet. Apart from objective performance measurement, meaningful feedback sessions are critical and reportedly did not occur for one-third of employees. Continuing management training is needed to improve these communication skills. Finally, trust has to exist or develop between supervisors and subordinates for a merit pay system to work. The available data suggest that there is room for improvement. There were no direct data for Navy, but NIST data indicated trust in supervisors by two-thirds of survey respondents. Perceived fairness of ratings, an indirect measure of trust, did not exceed 60 percent at either NIST or Navy, but neither did they at control sites not under a pay-for-performance system. In neither of the demonstration projects did rating appeals increase significantly.

DISCUSSION AND CONCLUSIONS

Implementing effective pay-for-performance systems, especially in the public sector, poses many challenges. Both the Navy and NIST pay-for-performance projects were able to meet most of Lawler's criteria for success; the productivity gainsharing program, tested as part of the Pacer Share demonstration, failed to do so. Lessons learned from these projects follow.

• *Mistrust of merit pay can be overcome by experiencing a system that works.* The initial skepticism about merit pay was clearly reflected in the longitudinal survey data from the Navy demonstration project. Before the project was implemented in 1979, a baseline survey revealed that only 29 percent of employees expressed support for it; it took five years to reach 51 percent support. Support for the project has now leveled off at about 70 percent. Employees were clearly skeptical at first that granting managers complete authority over their pay raises—a standard practice in the private sector—would work in their favor. The Navy achieved its main objective: increased retention of high performers. Turnover among high performers at the demonstration labs has been consistently lower (3.5 percent) than at the comparison sites (5.5 percent) that had no organizationwide pay-for-performance system.[8]

The Navy demonstration also shows that the change from an entitlement culture to a performance culture can be made by changing the system first. After ten years, more than 60 percent of employees present had been hired under the demonstration system. They were clearly recruited to work under a pay-for-performance system, in contrast to most federal employees who know that their pay raises will be mostly based on seniority. It took the Navy five years to convince a simple majority of employees that the new pay-for-performance system was fair, but NIST achieved this level of support in three years.

• *Money does not have to drive performance ratings.* A common problem with merit pay systems is that money tends to drive the ratings and that all such systems have to deal with finite budgets. To make pay increases meaningful for high performers, rating distributions have to approach (although not necessarily match) a normal curve, where the majority clusters around an average and the highest and lowest ratings are reserved for a small percentage of employees. In practice low ratings tend to be considerably more limited than high ratings, mostly because employees have been screened and selected for competence before being hired. Performance rating distributions in the Navy demonstration were found to be considerably more rigorous than those for merit pay employees in the rest of the government. In most years about 50 percent of employees were rated average, and no more than 10 to 12 percent were rated outstanding. NIST rating distributions were more generous; in 1992, only 20 to 25 percent of employees were rated average or lower, and 8 to 10 percent received the top rating.[6] Under the federal merit pay system, which experienced growing rating inflation over the years, the percentage of those rated above average rose to 82 percent in 1991.

Interviews with Navy managers revealed that although they found it difficult to look employees in the eye and tell them that their performance was satisfactory but not above average, they felt it was worth making distinctions based on performance because the pay differences were meaningful enough—0 to 6 percent, plus the governmentwide comparability increase that had to be earned. Most federal managers in the rest of the government felt that differences were not meaningful enough to warrant tough ratings and the accompanying negative reactions from employees.

Another problem inherent with merit pay systems involves employees at or near the top of their pay range. Many of them were denied high ratings because the accompanying pay increase would have pushed their pay beyond the top of their pay range. This engendered a great deal of dissatisfaction, especially among scientists and engineers who valued the high rating more than the money associated with it. The solution to this problem was the replacement of mandatory pay points for given ratings with ranges of points and the combination of bonus and base pay. For instance, if an outstanding rating results in 3 or 4 pay points, managers have the option, first of all, of granting only 3 instead of 4 points and then converting the points to a lump sum bonus or split payout of 1 base pay point and 2 bonus points. Being able to award bonus rather than base pay, even when the employee is not near the top of the range, also serves as an effective cost control mechanism and slows down permanent salary growth.

• *Labeling employees with adjectival performance ratings should be avoided.* Whenever a 5-point rating scale is used to evaluate employee performance, the midpoint is understood to mean average, no matter what adjectival phrase is used to describe it. In the federal government this level is generally described as "fully successful" to make employees feel better. But in the eyes of employees, it is merely a grade of C because there are two higher ratings above it: "exceeds fully successful" or "commendable," and "outstanding." At NIST, even "commendable," the second highest rating, was resented by scientists and engineers who may have been A students in college and excelled in their field before being hired. Many objected to the labeling implicit in the rating, and after three years NIST decided to change the appraisal system by going to a 100-point scale with numerical ratings for pay purposes, but only a two-level summary rating (eligible or not eligible) with those rated at 40 or more points eligible for a pay increase. This cutoff was deliberately chosen so as not to remind employees of academic grading scales.

Employee reactions to the new system have been mostly favorable, but it remains to be seen whether this is a viable system in the long run and whether it is generalizable outside the measurement culture of the National Institute of Standards and Technology. However, the positive results to date may prove that Lawler's seventh factor, trust, is more important than measurement precision. Thus the demonstration projects came up with two different solutions to the problem of labeling employees with adjectival performance ratings. NIST chose to rate performance on a 100-point numerical scale but used only a two-level summary rating (eligible or not eligible for a pay increase). Navy used an MBO-type system where ratings are expressed as "did not meet objectives," "met objectives," or "exceeded objectives." Use of these categories did not provoke criticism that employees felt labeled.

• *Unions resist pay-for-performance systems that are based on individual performance measures.* If pay systems are viewed as based on a continuum with seniority at one end and performance at the other, Pacer Share's base pay system clearly fell on the extreme left end of the continuum, and the governmentwide system would be closer to the middle, as step increases can be granted or denied based on performance. NIST's and Navy's pay-for-performance systems would fall closer to the performance end. Pacer Share was jointly designed by labor and management, and the new pay system, broad bands with annually guaranteed step increases based purely on longevity, clearly expressed the preference of the unions. However, the lack of a performance component met with mixed acceptance by employees. Some preferred pay advancement based solely on seniority, but a majority felt that both excellent and poor performance should be reflected in an individual's pay.

To date, unions have only been tangentially involved in pay-for-performance systems. The Navy lab at China Lake had two small unions that represented support employees who agreed to join the project after its success was evident. NIST involved only one union that represented a small proportion of the workforce and agreed to be included in the demonstration project. As the Navy system expands, it is encountering skepticism from unions, and some of the new sites are resisting participation in the system. Clearly, convincing unions that pay-for-performance systems can be fair and effective continues to be a challenge. Agreeing to a pilot test first may be one way to gain support.

• *Performance evaluation should be eliminated, but not performance feedback.* The Pacer Share experience provided two lessons. First, employees enjoy not being evaluated, but still want performance feedback. Second, they do not want to be held responsible for giving negative feedback to their peers; they regard this as the responsibility of management. The well-intended regulation designed to deal with poor performers by requiring analysis of statistical process results was never applied because it required employees to report coworkers to a union steward or supervisor for investigation. Employees referred to this as the "snitch rule." The statistical process control measures that were supposed to replace individual feedback never really materialized under Pacer Share. A self-assessment based on the Federal Quality Institute's criteria of TQM development revealed a low to moderate stage of TQM development after four years. A visiting delegation from Japan, attracted by the TQM features of the demonstration project, once walked through the warehouse at the Sacramento Air Logistics Center, and one member remarked afterwards, "But you are not measuring anything."[9]

Gainsharing requires continuous workloads or backlogs. As employees did not understand the productivity gainsharing formula and as organizational performance measures were not shared with them, they never knew how well they or the organization were doing. The only reliable clue for when a gainshare might occur was workload. During periods of high workload, as occurred during Desert Shield and Desert Storm, significant gainshares were realized.

• *Supervisor training in managing pay for performance is essential.* Training in how to administer pay-for-performance systems is critical and needs to be provided to managers on an ongoing basis. Public sector managers who have become accustomed to rigid civil service systems with prescribed rules and regulations need training in compensation management and have to be prepared to exercise discretion.

• *Cost control factors should be built into the design of merit pay systems.* The individual pay-for-performance systems implemented under the Navy and NIST demonstration projects were part of an integrated approach to job classification, compensation, and performance management. Both projects implemented broad-banding systems, and authority to classify jobs, determine pay increases, and approve promotions was delegated to managers, along with responsibility for cost control. Survey data revealed dramatic increases in supervisory authority without negatively affecting employee job satisfaction.[7] Under these decentralized personnel systems, the Navy labs proved to be more successful in controlling salary growth than NIST, but average salaries rose under all three broad-banding systems when compared to the General Schedule system.

OPM's report *Broad-Banding in the Federal Government*[5] analyzed the results of these projects and identified seven factors critical to cost control: method of conversion to bands, policy on starting salaries, size of salary and bonus budgets, system of performance management, choice of journey-level band, overall position management, and type of funding (an uncontrollable factor). Most federal agencies receive appropriated funds from Congress, but the Navy labs, which were industrially funded, had to earn their money through reimbursable work and were more successful in controlling costs because they had a bottom line.

The Navy demonstration labs showed the lowest cost for their pay-for-performance system, with average salaries about 2 percent higher after ten years than their control sites under the General Schedule system. At NIST, salaries were 4.4 percent higher under banding after five years. The cost differences between the two systems are primarily due to differences in the way the pay bands were designed and the way the pay pools were funded (see Table 12.1).

PAY FOR PERFORMANCE CAN WORK IN THE PUBLIC SECTOR

Although pay-for-performance systems have now operated successfully for fifteen years in federal demonstration projects, Congress has been reluctant to extend them to the rest of the government. So far, only DOD research labs have been granted the authority to implement China Lake–like human resource management systems, and when Congress authorized the expansion in 1994, it required that these systems be run as experiments under an open-ended demonstration authority shared by the Secretary of Defense and OPM. Earlier legislative proposals such as the Civil Service Simplification Act of 1987, which would have extended to the entire government, were opposed by federal labor unions who prefer seniority-based pay systems that limit managerial authority.

The federal demonstration projects have moved toward a decentralized, professionalized service that gives managers more control over hiring, firing, and paying employees. The evaluation results show that increasing managerial authority did not negatively affect employees. Nevertheless, a decentralized public personnel system that increases the power of individual managers poses a potential threat to the concept of a politically neutral workforce. Managers need to be well trained to ensure that these programs are administered in a fair and equitable manner, and they have to be held accountable for the results.

Changing from an entitlement to a performance culture represents a major philosophical shift for public sector employees. Organizational change experts point out that such cultural change can take many years.[11] Their rule of thumb is that for mature organizations the cycle time for creating fundamental, cultural change is twice that needed for introducing a new technology. For the federal personnel system, demonstration projects can be considered new technology. Given that it has taken fourteen years to implement the first successful demonstration project on a permanent basis, it may take another fourteen years for the federal personnel system to succeed in renewing itself.

The demonstration projects have taught us that commitment to change can overcome the absence of preexisting ideal conditions. Both Navy and NIST gradually moved toward a performance culture over time. The survey data show that resistance to change can be overcome if there is a strong, long-term commitment to making the change successful.

Notes

1. R. M. Kanter, "From Status to Contribution: Some Organizational Implications of the Changing Basis for Pay," *Personnel Journal,* Jan. 1987, pp. 12–37.

2. G. T. Milkovich and A. K. Wigdor (eds.), *Pay for Performance: Evaluating Performance Appraisal and Merit Pay* (Washington, D.C.: National Academic Press, 1991).

3. E. E. Lawler III, *Pay and Organization Development* (Reading, Mass.: Addison-Wesley, 1981).

4. J. Shettel Dutcher, J. P. Sheposh, D. K. Dickason, and C. A. Hayashida, *Pacer Share Final Evaluation Report* (San Diego, Calif.: Navy Personnel Research and Development Center, 1993).

5. B. W. Schay, K. C. Simons, E. Guerra, and J. Caldwell, *Broad-Banding in the Federal Government: Technical Report* (Washington, D.C.: U.S. Office of Personnel Management, 1992).

6. D. R. Reynolds and M. Barton, *Fifth Annual Evaluation Report: National Institute of Standards and Technology Personnel Management Demonstration Project* (Washington, D.C.: U.S. Office of Personnel Management, July 1994).

7. B. W. Schay, "Effects of Performance-Contingent Pay on Employee Attitudes," *Public Personnel Management,* 1988, *17*(2), 237–250.

8. B. W. Schay, "In Search of the Holy Grail: Lessons in Performance Management," *Public Personnel Management,* 1993, *22*(4), 649–668.

9. J. Shettel Dutcher, personal communication with the author, June 2, 1992.

10. J. Shettel Dutcher, C. A. Hayashida, J. P. Sheposh, and D. K. Dickason, *Pacer Share Fourth-Year Evaluation Report* (San Diego, Calif.: Navy Personnel Research and Development Center, 1992).

11. R. W. Beatty and D. O. Ulrich, "Reenergizing the Mature Organization," *Organizational Dynamics,* Summer 1991, pp. 16–31.

PART THREE

Public Compensation in Unionized and International Contexts

The legal environment governing labor-management relations is dominated by state statutes and regulations. The National Labor Relations Act and related federal statutes have established a complex body of law governing labor-management relations in the private sector. Those laws mandate a consistent basis for addressing labor relations across the country. In the public sector a much higher percentage of the workforce is unionized or belongs to a quasi union. A number of states have not given public unions the right to bargain on compensation, but labor organizations have relationships with enough politicians to influence the legislative process.

The diversity of state laws makes it difficult to generalize. Although individuals are in a position to develop the expertise to work effectively within a state, only an extremely small number have reason to deal with legal issues in more than one state. Legislation effectively defines the employer-union relationship and the scope of the issues that can be negotiated or otherwise discussed by the parties.

Even in jurisdictions that preclude the unionization of public employees, it is common for employees to belong to associations that work to protect the interests of members. The associations are in some cases national in scope and maintain a central staff that monitors and assists local groups in discussions with local government leaders. Such "meet and confer" sessions sometimes are similar to bargaining sessions.

The interest of unions and employees in the pay-setting process is similar to that of their private sector counterparts. A difference, of course, is that the process is subject to public debate and scrutiny; it is not a confidential managerial prerogative. As the pay-setting process is more open than in the private sector, union representatives commonly argue that they should be involved, to the degree that applicable law permits, in each step in the process. That may mean anything from helping to define the methodology for salary surveys to the actuarial methods used to estimate pension costs.

Union and employee involvement differs also in the need to work with elected officials and legislators who may have a different agenda than the technical staff working on the management side of the bargaining table. Union leaders want to win higher pay levels, of course, but the decision process necessitates a more complex bargaining strategy. It is still uncommon for public employees to have the right to strike or to threaten to walk out, and this changes the dynamics of collective bargaining.

The interest in reinventing government is not limited to the United States; it is essentially a worldwide phenomenon. Moreover, U.S. public pay programs tend to have characteristics similar to those in other countries. One issue in considering options for programs in this country, particularly the federal program, is the nature of program changes throughout the world.

For the purpose of this book we limit the discussion of this topic in Chapter Fourteen to member countries of the Organization for Economic Cooperation and Development (OECD). That effectively covers most of the developed countries across the world, but the chapter is not intended to be an encyclopedia of practices in every country. Rather, it is a snapshot of trends and issues relevant to the status of public pay programs.

A common theme is the need for flexibility. Interestingly, public pay programs have usually been highly inflexible, almost to the point of rigidity. The federal classification system was the model followed for a long time by other public employers. When that system was conceived, the goal was to replace the inequities endemic in early civil service practice. The pressure for flexibility will inevitably reintroduce opportunities for arbitrary and capricious decision making.

Another theme is the interest in finding acceptable ways to link pay with performance. Public employers throughout the world are facing tight budgets and the need to improve performance. A common hurdle is the need for effective performance management practices. There is also the universal problem of preparing supervisors to assume this new role. The United States is not the only country struggling to shift to a more performance-oriented culture.

CHAPTER THIRTEEN

The Role of Collective Bargaining in Public Sector Pay Determination

Bonnie G. Bogue

M̲ost public sector employees at the local, state, and federal levels are authorized to engage in some form of collective bargaining over terms and conditions of work, including compensation.[1]

Since the early 1960s, beginning with the executive order authorizing a modified form of collective bargaining for employees of the federal government, there has been a legislative trend to grant and expand representation rights for public employees. By the 1990s, a great majority of states had de jure or de facto collective bargaining for some or all state and local employees.[2] And since 1978, federal employees have had a comprehensive bargaining statute.[3]

The legislation varies among jurisdictions, ranging from limited provisions that permit "meet and confer" sessions between the governing body and employee representatives to extensive statutes that mirror their private sector prototypes and authorize employees to elect exclusive representatives, negotiate (and in some instances strike), enter binding agreements, resolve contract interpretation disputes through binding arbitration, and enforce statutory bargaining and representation rights through unfair practice procedures before agencies such as the National Labor Relations Board.

The subjects about which employees have the right to negotiate are defined in "scope of bargaining" language in the employment relations statutes. Wages and economic benefits are usually included in the definition of scope of bargaining. Typical of most public sector statutes is California's local government bargaining statute adopted in 1968, which states the following: "The scope of representation shall include all matters relating to employment conditions and employer-employee relations, including, but not limited to, wages, hours, and other terms and conditions of employment."[4]

In contrast, in the federal sector the scope of bargaining is defined broadly as covering "conditions of employment," but the statute then excludes any matter that is "specifically provided for by Federal statute," which has been interpreted to exclude pay because federal employees' salaries are established "by statute."[5]

When wages are included in the scope of bargaining, that generally is assumed to include compensation items other than pay, such as health care benefits, employer contributions to pension plans, deferred compensation arrangements, and so forth. However, some statutes carve out exceptions, such as New York's Taylor Law, which states that terms and conditions of employment means "salaries, wages, hours, and other terms and conditions of employment provided, however, that such term shall not include any benefits provided by or to be provided by a public retirement system."[6]

Many statutes explicitly require approval or adoption by the legislative or governing body of any term in the agreement that requires funding. The Taylor Law, for example, states that any contract provision that requires legislative action to provide "additional funds therefor shall not become effective until the appropriate legislative body has given approval."[7]

PAY SETTING AND THE MERIT SYSTEM TRADITION

Long before the growth of collective bargaining in the public sector, in most state and local governments, as well as in the federal sector, a civil service or merit system governed public employees' working conditions, including compensation.

Initially, civil service systems were developed to ensure fairness in the hiring, promotion, and termination of public employees, so as to insulate them from political patronage and guarantee that employment decisions were based on an employee's merit rather than political affiliation, religion, race, or other nonperformance-related considerations. Over time, the authority of civil service boards or commissions that administered the merit principle extended beyond such selection issues to include job classifications.

A natural extension of the classification of jobs was to determine the appropriate pay that attached to each classification, as well as a process to ensure that promotion to a higher-level classification is based on the employee's meritorious performance. The civil service board, independent from the elected officials that governed the state or local entity, was in a position to determine fair and equitable pay levels for each classification through objective methods such as salary surveys for comparable jobs in the public and private sectors. Detailed pay schedules were developed, with step increases from entry level to top of the scale for each classification. Progression up the scale was dependent on length of service and meritorious performance.

In many state and local agencies, the question of whether employees were being adequately compensated, whether a general pay increase should be budgeted, or whether a particular classification warranted a pay adjustment was determined by the civil service or personnel commission, which would issue a recommendation to the governing body (city or county council, school board, or state legislature) for funding and implementation.

Thus a public sector tradition has developed of establishing pay standards through a semi-adjudicatory process, based on objective criteria such as prevailing pay rates, rate of inflation, and the relationship of job duties to the level of pay for particular classifications. The governing body retains ultimate legislative authority over the budget and appropriation of funds, but the determination of whether any pay adjustments are warranted, and how much and for which job classifications, is purportedly objective rather than based on political or other subjective and potentially biased considerations. Even in public entities without a merit system, pay is often set by reference to prevailing rates as a matter of personnel administration.

Civil service associations, precursors of the modern public employee union, have had a significant role in this process. They make statements and provide evidence at pay-determination hearings, or petition the civil service board to change its survey methodology or to consider various factors in reaching its conclusions. And ultimately, the organizations lobby the governing body to grant pay increases in the pay schedule, either in conformance with or in addition to the civil service recommendation. Traditionally, some occupational associations—notably police and firefighters groups—have a separate agenda and voice their own interests before the civil service or governing body.

COLLECTIVE BARGAINING AND COMPENSATION

The introduction of collective bargaining into the public sector has come gradually. Many jurisdictions began with (and some still permit only) a limited meet and confer model that merely allows employee representatives the right to discuss pay and other conditions of employment before the employer takes action. This model is an incremental movement away from the traditional role of civil service associations in the pay-setting process and toward a true collective bargaining model where the association has a bargaining, rather than a consultative, role.

Over the past thirty years, as public entities have experimented with various bargaining models, pay setting has been a significant area of exploration. Both employee representatives and public employers were sometimes reluctant to give up the predictability of the traditional prevailing rate method in exchange for a new system where bargaining strengths and strategies could dictate pay adjustments and budgetary allocations.

The resulting statutory models have a wide range:

- Models that exclude pay from the scope of bargaining and retain the traditional civil service–legislative system.
- Models that include pay within their scope but dictate that pay be determined by a defined prevailing rate method.
- Hybrid models where prevailing rate surveys are used to establish either a floor or ceiling for increases that can be negotiated.
- Traditional private sector models where prevailing rate and other objective data are merely used by the parties to shape their bargaining positions.

The scope of bargaining may include a proviso that a collective bargaining agreement cannot disrupt the pay relationships between steps on the pay scale that have been set up by a civil service commission or board because that would violate the merit principle embodied in law or ordinance.

Public Policy Concerns and Bargaining Over Pay

Public policy arguments have long been advanced that collective bargaining may not be the best mechanism for setting pay in the public sector.

Basic to these arguments is the fact that employee compensation is a major part of every local or state budget, as the government is in the business of providing public services through its employees. Determining how to divide the budgetary pie is a political decision wherein various interest groups have the right to lobby their legislators or council members to influence the process.

Over the years critics of public sector collective bargaining have contended that granting public employees the right to bargain over compensation distorts the political process because they are granted more influence over those budgetary decisions than other interest groups. Other groups merely have the right to lobby or petition, whereas public employees have both the right to lobby and the right to compel the public employer to meet, confer in good faith, and abide by a binding, negotiated decision granting pay increases. Furthermore, public employee unions traditionally have been well organized and well connected politically, often influencing the election and reelection of legislators, council members, governors, and mayors, giving them added strength when presenting bargaining demands to those same elected officials.

Critics have also contended that public employees, unlike their private sector counterparts, had no need to bargain over compensation because pay scales were already determined and protected against erosion by the merit or civil service system. Such arguments have led in many jurisdictions to the elimination of the civil service board's authority to link job classifications with pay, instead making the matter of compensation a separate issue for represented employees that is to be determined only through collective bargaining.

Another major policy argument against negotiating compensation for public employees is that the public employer has less concern with the bottom line than does its private sector counterpart. The argument runs that a state, city, or school district can merely resort to higher taxes to pay for negotiated wage increases, and thus has less motivation to hold down costs through lower wages or increased productivity.

But as public sector bargaining has matured, these arguments are heard less often; the experiment with public sector bargaining has become the reality of state and local politics. That political reality does not necessarily accrue solely to the public sector unions' benefit as early critics prophesied. Lawmakers are elected by all the taxpayers, of which public employees are a minority, and voters' sentiments may be antibureaucrat and responsive to candidates who propose to hold down the pay and benefits of employees "feeding at the public trough."

Lawmakers' interest in reelection may influence them not to authorize management negotiators to accept union demands for pay increases, as these would require either tax increases or service decreases, both of which have political fallout.

Also, interest groups with political muscle may have a strong concern over the level of service provided. For example, the local parent association may have significant influence on a school board's decision whether to allocate funds for pay increases for existing teachers rather than for more teachers and smaller class size.

Economic and other factors also place restraints on the public employer's ability to fund pay increases. The public purse is not bottomless, as has been illustrated any number of times since the 1960s, when public employee bargaining first took shape. Taxpayers do revolt: witness California's Proposition 13 in 1978 and subsequent voter initiatives around the country that restrict state and local governments' ability to tax. Economic downturns cause budget shortfalls and deficits. Increased demand for certain services (such as from heightened sentencing standards and the resultant increase in the demand for prisons) often is not tied to any increase in revenue to fund the demand. State budget deficits have a direct impact on local government budgets—sometimes a severe impact on local agencies that have a limited ability to raise revenues. Cities, counties, and school districts have declared bankruptcy with increasing frequency.

The effects of such economic and budget problems frequently include cuts or freezes in public employees' pay or benefits, as well as various reduction-in-force measures such as hiring moratoria, early retirement plans, reorganization and elimination or downgrading of positions, and layoffs. The duty to bargain with employee representatives has not prevented public employers from responding with these kinds of measures, although they must in most instances negotiate first in a good-faith effort to reach agreement.[8] The bargaining table can provide a forum for exploring alternatives that may be more acceptable to affected employees, such as brief, unpaid furloughs for all employees in lieu of permanent layoffs of a few.

Furthermore, public employees' self-interest does not necessarily translate only into an increase in their paychecks. Their unions often recognize the political and economic restraints on the employer's ability to raise revenues or reallocate resources, and temper their demands accordingly. Employees may have an interest in forgoing a pay increase to avoid layoffs and reductions in force, not just to protect their own jobs but also to avoid the negative impact that a reduced workforce may have on their own working conditions, including workload and safety.

Employees often have an interest in the mission of their agency and the quality and level of service that the public receives, which will mitigate their interest in improved compensation. For example, teachers' concern with the quality of education and their willingness to forgo or postpone pay increases to ensure smaller class sizes and more school resources is well documented. Likewise, other occupational groups such as social workers, probation officers, and attorneys have been known to press bargaining demands for reduced caseloads in lieu of pay increases. Law enforcement and fire service personnel have concerns about safety and staffing levels that may curtail demands for increased pay that would result in reduced levels of service.

Prevailing Rates and Other Guidelines for Pay Bargaining

These policy concerns and political pressure on the public employer and employee organizations have led to a search for a rational basis for pay determination in the public sector. If the negotiators can show the taxpaying public that the pay increase in the agreement is fair and equitable, based on objective factors and not on political clout or strike threats by public employee unions, the result is likely to be more acceptable politically.

The traditional salary survey methodology has continued to serve a major function in guiding the parties toward an acceptable solution.

As inflation frequently is a principal justification for increasing pay, use of various indicators to dictate pay increases has long been acceptable, particularly in periods of high inflation. In many instances both salary surveys and inflation indicators are utilized. Then, in the event the employer and unions reach a bargaining impasse, the use of a neutral third party to resolve the dispute, using objective and impartial criteria, can serve the need for a rational solution that does not rest solely on the relative strengths of the two parties.

PREVAILING RATE SURVEYS   Use of prevailing rate information in pay negotiations may be mandated by statute or local ordinance, undertaken voluntarily by the employer and employee organization as a joint venture, or be done unilaterally by either party to support their own bargaining position.

In order for the survey results to be considered credible and useful in the bargaining process, some agreement on methodology is essential. If no agreement is reached, the parties may produce different surveys, which increases the cost and decreases the effectiveness of using such data as an aid to bargaining. A decision must be made as to who shall conduct the survey—the employer, an independent agency or consultant, or a joint labor-management committee. And the data that are to be gathered must be defined.

Initially, it must be determined which employers will be surveyed. Should the survey be of the public sector only or a mix of public and private? How is comparability of employers in the survey to be determined—by similarity of employers (should a city only survey other cities?), by size of employer in terms of budget or workforce, by geographic similarity, by urban or rural similarity, by range and type of service provided, by nature of the population served (such as crime rate, school dropout rate), or by comparable tax base?

Also, the question arises of which classifications should be surveyed. If the parties are looking toward an across-the-board increase for all employees in the agency, which classifications should be used as benchmarks—blue collar, professional, supervisory, entry level, or others? How can an appropriate balance be achieved? Should separate surveys be conducted for certain classifications such as police or fire?

Another issue is the type of compensation to be surveyed. Should only wages or salaries be surveyed, or total compensation calculated (folding in cost of health benefits and pension contributions)? Should benefits be surveyed separately? Which benefits—only health and pensions, or others such as vacation and sick leave? What pay rate should be used—median, entry level, or top of range?

Then the issue remains of how to use the data. Charts and tables are often drawn up so that parties at the bargaining table can refer to the same information, to ensure a common understanding and avoid future disputes over implementation. Even if the governing law dictates how the data will be used—to set a mandatory pay increase, or to set a floor or ceiling for permissible negotiated increases—negotiators inevitably find varying ways of interpreting the data, so there is material for negotiations even in a mandatory prevailing rate setting.

For example, negotiators will need to agree whether the wage increase should be set at the average of those surveyed or be granted only if the agency is lagging behind the low end of the survey. If the agency has traditionally been at the top of the survey, should no pay increase be granted until it drops to the mean or low end of those surveyed? Should a specific classification lagging significantly behind the same class in the surveyed agencies be granted a higher increase than the rest of the employees? How will pay increases affect pay ranges and the differential between rank and file employees and supervisory or managerial classifications?[9]

As the employer's ability to pay is always a deciding factor in bargaining, even though the survey would justify (say) a 5 percent raise, negotiations may center on how much of that percentage the agency in fact is able to pay. If inability to pay precludes granting comparability with surveyed agencies, the survey data may nonetheless lend credence to a union demand for a nonmonetary benefit as a trade-off.

COST-OF-LIVING MEASURES   The second frequently used objective measure of appropriate compensation adjustments is the rate of inflation. The most common source is the U.S. Bureau of Labor Statistics' Consumer Price Index (CPI). (Market rates are in the Employment Cost Index and the Occupational Compensation/Area Wage Survey.)

Negotiators put such information to use in a variety of ways. They may propose a multiyear collective bargaining agreement with an annual percentage pay raise (cost-of-living adjustment, or COLA) equal to the percentage increase in the CPI (nationally or locally). Or the parties may negotiate a specific wage increase in the first year of the agreement, and then create a COLA that will peg increases in subsequent years to the CPI.[10] Common variations include the following:

- A minimum set increase each year, with a variable additional COLA if the CPI rises over a certain percent.
- A guaranteed increase but at a lesser rate than the CPI, such as 1 percent less than the percentage increase in the CPI.
- A guaranteed increase matching the CPI, but with a cap at a certain percentage.
- No pay increase (a freeze) unless the CPI rises by a specified amount, then a pay increase pegged to that rise.
- A negative COLA, requiring pay rates to decrease to match a drop in the CPI.
- A requirement that the contract be reopened for wage negotiations if the CPI increases beyond a certain level.

In bargaining the parties attempt not only to agree on the concept of the COLA but also on the specifics of the formula. Sample calculations at the bargaining table can avoid divisive and expensive disputes over application of the COLA during the life of the agreement.

The perceived advantage of escalator clauses is that they allow for pay adjustments to reflect changed economic circumstances of the employees while creating predictability for the employer, without the parties having to return to the bargaining table every year.

IMPASSE RESOLUTION PROCEDURES Some public agencies have mandatory impasse resolution procedures in the event that the employer and employee organizations are unable to reach a negotiated agreement. Others may permit the parties voluntarily to submit a negotiations impasse to an impartial third party.

Three methods are commonly used in the public sector. By far the most common is mediation, where a neutral third party assists the parties to find a settlement but the parties themselves determine the terms of the agreement and the mediator does not dictate the settlement or issue any written findings or recommendations.

A second method—variously termed fact-finding or advisory arbitration—is where the impartial third party hears evidence to support each side's last preimpasse bargaining position. The neutral party (or the majority of a tripartite panel) issues formal findings of fact (such as what the survey data or CPI indicates) and a recommendation for settlement on each issue in dispute (such as a specified pay increase or COLA formula). The parties then have the option of resuming negotiations on those recommendations or accepting them as the terms of their agreement.

A third, and less commonly used, method is binding arbitration, where the neutral third party (or a majority of a tripartite panel) decides the terms of agreement and the parties are bound by it.[11] Each party makes a formal presentation in support of its last preimpasse bargaining proposals, and the arbitrator then crafts the terms of settlement, with the award usually reflecting some compromise between the parties' final offers.

There are variations. One variation requires the arbitrator to select either one or the other party's final offer on all terms of the contract without modification or compromise (called "final offer" or "either-or" arbitration). Another variation requires the arbitrator to select one or the other party's final proposal on each issue in dispute (called "issue-by-issue final offer" arbitration). This latter method, though it does not allow the arbitrator to modify the proposals, does allow the arbitrator to create some compromise by selecting some of each party's proposals.

These final-offer methods are believed to encourage the parties to reach their own settlement without resort to a third party, because in the course of trying to make their final offer seem the most acceptable to the arbitrator they may move closer toward a position that the other party might accept, thus obviating the need for arbitration or at least producing settlement on some issues. In contrast, in standard binding arbitration, the parties are more likely to stick to their initial bargaining positions in anticipation of the arbitrator splitting the difference between the parties' extreme positions when crafting a compromise award. That tendency chills the bargaining process, preventing the parties from moving toward their own negotiated solution because they are reluctant to give up any ground prior to arbitration.

A common criticism of utilizing a third party to dictate the terms of the agreement, particularly economic terms, is that the arbitrator (unlike the elected members of a school board or city council) is not answerable to the voters or taxpayers. Because the arbitrator has no need to set priorities or look at the broader picture, as the governing body must, there is a fear that the arbitrator may not give sufficient weight to budget considerations. Most impasse procedures attempt to offset this perceived problem by including mandatory criteria to govern the arbitrator's exercise of discretion.

Mandatory criteria commonly include the following:

- The employer's ability to pay (which may include projected revenues, budget reserves, the amount of nondiscretionary funding that is not available for pay increases, anticipated nonwage costs such as equipment or property maintenance as well as consideration of pay settlements in other units).
- Prevailing pay standards in comparable agencies (which may be specified in the local ordinance).
- Cost-of-living data.
- Compensation patterns and bargaining history.
- Recruitment and retention problems.
- Internal job and salary comparisons.
- Total compensation, including the value of fringe benefits.

Not only do these criteria give direction to the arbitrator, enabling an informed judgment, but their existence in the impasse resolution procedure also requires the parties to research and consider the factors when developing their bargaining positions, thus leading to more informed bargaining strategies. An added benefit is that they lend to the entire process an aura of reasonableness, which may help the governing body justify the results to the public. The same criteria are common in fact-finding and advisory procedures as well, which likewise can help the negotiators to persuade their constituents (the union membership and the governing body) that the recommended settlement should be accepted with little or no further bargaining.

FUTURE DIRECTIONS FOR PUBLIC SECTOR BARGAINING

Public sector collective bargaining is still relatively new, coming as it did thirty to fifty years after the private sector statutes were adopted, but it is nonetheless undergoing a new period of change in the 1990s.

The change in part reflects the fact that the system is still experiencing its fragmented development. There is less of a norm in public sector collective bargaining than in the private sector versions, so changes are more in the nature of evolution than reform.

The change also reflects what is happening in the private sector—experiments with labor-management cooperation to increase productivity. Finally, the change in part reflects a public sector phenomenon: the push for reinventing government to make it more efficient and responsive to citizens' needs.

Privatization and Productivity

One primary impact that the movement to reinvent government has on public employees is the impetus for privatization or contracting out of services traditionally performed by public employees.

Though getting renewed attention in the 1990s, the concept of private contractors providing public works is certainly not new and in fact formed one of the motivations for the advent of the traditional civil service system. As noted earlier, the civil service system was developed to establish corruption-free, merit-based standards for public service. A tenet in most merit systems is that public service is to be performed by civil service employees unless it can be performed more cost effectively by contracting with a private entity. Another tenet is that the service should not be contracted out if doing so would either undercut civil service pay standards or displace existing public employees. That is not to say that contracting out is uncommon, as outside contractors frequently provide a variety of services for local public agencies, such as food and janitorial services, street and park maintenance, and trash collection.

As these civil service protection principles are set out in state law or local ordinances or rules,[12] public sector unions may attack privatization efforts as violating such protections if the contracts result in positions being cut or left vacant while the work is being done by a private contractor, or if traditional public works are being performed at pay rates below those called for in public sector collective bargaining agreements covering similar jobs.

The forum for this debate may either be in court, in a lawsuit challenging a contract as violating laws governing contracting out, or in political lobbying, where efforts are being made either to strengthen or weaken statutory civil service protections. A mayor or governor may seek legislation authorizing more contracting out in order to trim back the size and cost of government. In response public sector unions argue and have attempted to prove that cost savings achieved by lower pay for outside contractors' employees does not lead to improved public service or decreased costs because of problems with cost and quality control.

The debate may also be joined at the bargaining table, particularly where there is a weak or nonexistent civil service system. The union may seek job protections by negotiating restrictions on outside contracts for any services currently performed by employees it represents, or guarantees that no bargaining unit member will be laid off as a result of a contract. The public employer may seek to negotiate pay or benefit concessions, backing its demand with a threat to contract out and save the taxpayers money, and the union may be willing to negotiate concessions in order to protect jobs of the employees it represents.

Public employers and employee organizations are also using the bargaining table as a forum for negotiating productivity improvements, including pay incentives for improved efficiency or cost-saving suggestions, or pay increases linked to proven merit rather than time in grade. Or saved funds may be kept in the department, rather than returned to the general fund, and employees and managers can devise ways to use the money. Unions also may seek a voice in job restructuring, in a joint effort to make government more efficient or cost effective while protecting their members' job security.

Unions strongly and traditionally resist pay or benefit cuts, but in the face of a budget shortfall they may be more receptive to two-tier pay, health insurance, or pension plans allowing new hires to receive lesser compensation packages than current employees. The plan may create a new, separate pay schedule with lower entry-level wages as well as lopping off the top step or steps in the existing schedule. It may create a new pension category or health care plan, with lower employer contributions in order to reduce the cost of the benefit package. As the second tier does not affect current employees' compensation and in fact may enable the parties to maintain or improve benefits for existing employees, it is a cost-cutting pay package that is likely to be ratified by union members.

Recurring budget crises in recent years have provided ample opportunity for such joint responses to cutting costs by public sector employers and employee organizations.

Labor-Management Cooperation

Recent pressures on public employee-employer relations have not necessarily led to more adversarial relationships; to the contrary a movement is under way to adapt various labor-management cooperation models that are emerging in the private sector to fit public sector interests.

A notable example of this movement has occurred in California, where the Public Employment Relations Board began a training experiment in the 1980s among public school employers and unions in an effort to improve particularly contentious labor-management relationships. Based on the Harvard Negotiation Project's work, the approach emphasizes interest-based bargaining.[13] By all accounts, the efforts are succeeding.[14] In the process those involved have created a movement toward labor-management cooperation that is extending beyond the schools into other parts of the state's public sector and has received nationwide attention.

Initially, employee organizations were more resistant to the idea than were public employers, fearing that the methods were an end run around collective bargaining that would displace the union as the representative of employees' interests. With time, many unions have become more receptive. The majority of employee organizations that have participated in the training and in interest-based bargaining report that it has improved their employer-employee relations.[15]

In 1995, the Commission on the Future of Worker-Management Relations (the Dunlop Commission) issued its findings and proposals. Although not directed at the public sector, the commission's report expressly encourages this kind of innovation by calling for the expansion of employee participation[16] and labor-management partnerships, thus voicing a national policy that creates a favorable environment for such efforts in the public sector.

Notes

1. Public employees are expressly excluded from the National Labor Relations Act, which governs private sector collective bargaining. See NLRA Sec. 2 (29 U.S. Code Sec. 152).

2. See B.V.H. Schneider, "Public-Sector Labor Legislation: An Evolutionary Analysis," in B. Aaron, J. M. Najita, and J. L. Stern (eds.), *Public-Sector*

Bargaining (2nd ed.) (Washington, D.C.: Bureau of National Affairs, 1988).

3. Federal Service Labor-Management Relations Statute (Title VII of the Civil Service Reform Act of 1978), U.S. Code Secs. 7101 and following.

4. Meyers-Milias-Brown Act, Cal. Gov. Code Sec. 3504.

5. U.S. Code Sec. 7103(a)(12); E. M. Bussey, *Federal Civil Service Law and Procedures* (2nd ed.) (Washington, D.C.: Bureau of National Affairs, 1990).

6. Taylor Act, N.Y. Civil Service Law, Art. XIV, Part 200, Sec. 203.

7. Taylor Act, Sec. 204–a.

8. The decision to lay off in most jurisdictions has been held to be a management right, outside the scope of bargaining, but the employer may still be required to negotiate on the effects of that decision that do have an impact on negotiable working conditions, such as transfer rights or severance pay. See California Department of Forestry (1993) Cal. PERB Dec. No. 999–S, 17 PERC 24112.

9. Managerial employees under most employee relations schemes are not entitled to bargain collectively, and their pay is set unilaterally by the employer or through surviving merit system provisions.

10. For a how-to examination of COLAs and inflation indicators, see M. Taylor, *Cost-of-Living Escalators in the Public Sector* (Berkeley: California Public Employee Relations Program, Institute of Industrial Relations, University of California, 1978).

11. This method is less common for two primary reasons. Unless authorized by statute, it may be an unlawful delegation of legislative authority for the governing body to grant an arbitrator binding authority to set pay or conditions of employment. Or it may be politically undesirable for the governing body to relinquish such authority even though legally authorized to do so. Binding arbitration is most commonly authorized for safety services, where it is considered an appropriate substitute for a strike by police and fire fighters.

12. Not all states or local public agencies have adopted civil service systems, whereas in others, such as California, the merit system is enshrined in the state constitution.

13. See R. Fisher and W. L. Ury, *Getting to Yes: Negotiating Agreement Without Giving In* (Boston: Houghton Mifflin, 1981); R. Fisher and S. Brown, *Getting Together: Building a Relationship That Gets to Yes* (Boston: Houghton Mifflin, 1988); and W. L. Ury, J. M. Brett, and G. B. Goldberg, *Getting Disputes Resolved: Designing Systems to Cut the Cost of Conflict* (San Francisco: Jossey-Bass, 1988).

14. PERB handed off the program to a private nonprofit organization, the California Foundation for Improvement of Employer-Employee Relations (CFIER). See Chisholm and Tamm, "Does Interest Bargaining Really Work? A Test Using PERB Data," *California Public Employee Relations*, 1993, *101*, 3–7, for a study of PERB and CFIER results.

15. See J. Walden, "Program Participants Rate CFIER's Training in the Public Schools," *California Public Employee Relations*, 1994, *109*, 3–8.

16. Worker participation programs in the private sector fell on uncertain ground after the National Labor Relations Board's ruling in Electromation, Inc., 309 NLRB 163 (1992), which found that it is an unfair labor practice for an employer to support an employee participation group if that group fits the definition of a labor organization in the National Labor Relations Act. A participation group that is concerned with compensation issues most likely would be considered a labor organization and unlawful under the NLRA (absent a statutory amendment) and perhaps under similarly drafted public sector bargaining statutes as well. For discussion of the Electromation doctrine in relation to public sector statutes, see J. B. LaRocco, "Electromation and the Fate of Employee Participation Programs," *California Public Employee Relations*, 1994, *105*, 3–12.

CHAPTER FOURTEEN

Public Pay Programs
in OECD Countries

Anke Freibert

—∿∿—

Increasingly concerned about the growing critique of the public regarding the quality and productivity of public services, over the last decade all Organization for Economic Cooperation and Development (OECD) countries have undertaken great efforts to improve public service, and some have launched far-reaching reform programs. These reform efforts encompass a wide range. Besides programs to reduce the size of the public sector through privatization, contracting out, or similar activities, the reforms usually include changes in public service management and in public service pay structures and wage determination.

Pay issues are emerging as a key element in the wider adjustment and restructuring process. However, it is clear that for the public

---

This chapter is based on information gathered by the ILO in preparing the report *Impact of Structural Adjustment in the Public Services,* 1995, and the findings of the Public Management Committee of the OECD, which have been published in several papers.

employer the prime concern is not public service pay and the underlying pay structure. Reforming public service pay has to be seen in context. It is supposed to serve in responding to budget constraints, in meeting the necessity to curb the growth of public expenditure, and in promoting inter alia productivity, efficiency, and labor market flexibility. Therefore public service pay reforms are not only targeted to reducing the overall payroll but also to changing pay structures in order to adapt them to the new challenges the public service is facing and thus the newly emerging job profiles.

A common theme of current reforms in many countries is the need for more flexibility in public sector pay systems so that they can respond more easily to economic and labor market pressures.

Governments are faced with the challenge of establishing a balance between the use of wages as a tool of economic management and labor market adjustment and as a tool of personnel management. The public service payroll represents a considerable part of the government budget, which necessarily has an impact on taxation and borrowing levels. Moreover, public service pay has an acknowledged impact on private sector pay levels. Both these factors are an obvious incentive to impose restraint. At the same time, government has the responsibility to promote equitable employment practices and to ensure that the public sector can attract and retain the caliber of staff it requires. Other pressures on governments include the need to improve managerial efficiency and to respond to the increasing wage flexibility in the private sector. Although there are no product market forces constraining the public employer's ability to pay, decisions on pay and employment are increasingly taken on market as well as economic, political, and social grounds.

TRADITIONAL PAY SYSTEMS

In the past most public service pay systems, in spite of national and regional variations, shared certain common features, including centrally determined pay structure; across-the-board increases; pay scales based on grade rather than job content, occupational category, or individual merit; and progress up the scale according to seniority rather than performance.

Public service pay was and still is generally based on a grading system that establishes a hierarchy of responsibility and represents the linkage between pay and position. This grading system is directly linked to reward—that is, the pay scale on the one hand and (often to a lesser extent) the position or level of responsibility on the other. There may be different systems for different occupational groups or categories of workers, such as manual and professional staff, but the linkage between grade and pay level remains the governing principle. Most grades, except the highest, have a scale of fixed increments, though their number and value may vary. These are usually awarded automatically, so that moving up the scale simply depends on seniority. The predetermined steps and fixed increments of the public service are designed to ensure transparency in public expenditure and to prevent patronage. The incremental nature of the system also stems from the traditional view of public service employment as a job for life. Even if employees are not promoted and do not change duties, the employer acknowledges their increasing experience. The pay rates at the top of the salary scale represent a target and incentive for those at lower levels, especially new recruits, and a recognition of the experience and seniority of top staff. For this reason a substantial difference between top and bottom rates is often believed desirable. However, a gap that is too wide and a minimum wage too close to the poverty line is both inequitable and demoralizing for those at the lower levels.

This traditional public service pay system has to be seen in context with the system of internal promotion. In many countries the public service still remains a closed shop with only up to four entry levels followed by internal promotion. Promotion—stepping from one grade to the next based on merit—is therefore seen within the traditional system as the main or even the only reward for good performance. Promotion as part of the reward expectations of public servants related to their performance is thus a major motivator. This is increasingly so as even top-level posts are filled through internal promotion. However, where real wages have fallen substantially over time, enormous pressure builds up on the government to use promotion as a way of restoring their value, regardless of the merit of the individual or of the existence of a real vacancy. Moreover, where promotion becomes more or less automatic, negative effects may be observed in the demotivation of workers and a grading structure that is not only top-heavy but mismatched between grades, job content, and responsibility on one hand and reward on the other. Promotion bottlenecks, where opportunities for further advancement become too limited, are also demotivating.

In all countries, including those of the OECD, basic pay represents only part of public service remuneration. Other elements include cash allowances, social security provisions such as maternity benefits and a pension, and noncash benefits such as housing or a car. Allowances are often tied to the cost of living, to family situation, and sometimes to hardship—living in a remote district, for example, or working in difficult or dangerous conditions. Allowances are also paid for certain specialist functions or additional responsibilities. Bonuses and allowances can be a significant part of take-home pay; exceptionally, they can be worth as much as basic pay, thus doubling the salary.

Cash allowances and other benefits have permitted an element of flexibility in what is generally a fairly rigid structure, and increase the room to maneuver in pay negotiations. On the negative side, however, they can reduce the intended transparency of the pay scale, especially where rates of allowances are not published; if paid automatically they can become a new rigidity and may encourage abuse or patronage. Noncash benefits represent a hidden cost that governments do not always take into account. The employee can lose out if allowances make up too high a proportion of income—say, over 20 percent—because security benefits, in particular old age pensions, are usually linked to basic salary.

APPROACHES TAKEN IN REFORMING STRUCTURES

A major concern is to abolish the rigidity of pay structures and to create pay systems that allow more discretion and can thus be used as a flexible policy instrument as well as a system of reward. Sometimes recruitment and promotion mechanisms are reviewed in conjunction with grading and pay. There are variations as well as overlap between countries aiming to simplify or standardize their systems and those promoting pay flexibility. In both cases, merit rewards or performance-related pay are increasingly common features. It is notable that in a growing number of countries current reforms are bringing into question some of the basic principles underlying the traditional structures described earlier: salaries for the same job or occupation are no longer necessarily standard across departments and regions; grade and seniority are increasingly being supplemented by other criteria for setting pay, such as job content, professional experience, or performance; the pay package has more variable and discretionary elements; and job classifications and grading are becoming more fluid. There are also moves to open the closed structure of the public service, allowing or increasing external recruitment at various levels of the service (thus relying less on promotion to fill all vacant posts) and making more use of temporary and contract workers. A common theme of all these measures is the promotion of flexibility in both the structures and levels of pay.

All of the OECD countries have at least made a commitment to introduce some performance-related pay elements in public service pay. However, the gap is wide between such countries as Germany and France at one end of the scale and Australia and New Zealand at the other.

COUNTRY EXAMPLES

To illustrate the general comments given, the country examples that follow show the differences in public service pay determination, in particular with regard to flexibility. They also point out whether pay flexibility is considered in each country as a means to improve the productivity, efficiency, and quality of public service.

Australia

The reform of job classifications and an increase in the flexibility of pay systems, especially the introduction of a more decentralized system, is regarded as a catalyst for productivity improvement and workplace reform.

On the federal level, public service pay is determined through centralized collective bargaining; however, there is a trend toward workplace bargaining. All pay negotiations take place within a framework of wage fixing principles established by the Australian Industrial Relations Commission. All key terms and conditions of employment, excluding superannuation, are subject to negotiations. Pay adjustments now stress efficiency and productivity improvements. Over the last decade the structure of public service pay has become more flexible, in particular as regards the senior management level. Nevertheless, for the majority of staff fixed pay scales still exist whereby the pay awards provide in general a maximum and a minimum pay level for a given position. Some additional flexibility exists in some areas of the public sector through salary packages for senior levels that enable striking an individual balance between salary and fringe benefits, such as cars and the like. Moreover, the annual increments are subject to satisfactory performance, and there are some provisions for accelerated advancement. For the time being on the federal level pay is based on individual skills and performance only for a few categories (mainly the Senior Executive Service). Outside the federal public service, performance pay and other instruments of pay flexibility have been introduced in some state public services.

Canada

Performance-related pay elements have been introduced in order to improve public sector performance. In general, pay determination is governed by private and public sector comparability. The so-called total compensation comparability takes pay, benefits, and hours worked into account and aims to equate similar public and private employees. To serve this goal pay comparisons both inside and outside the public service are used.

The pay at federal levels is set through centralized collective bargaining; regional pay variation exists only to a very marginal degree, both in amount and in employees affected by it. For the management level, pay is set by the ministers of the treasury board on recommendation of an impartial advisory body of private sector executives. The results of both these pay determination procedures need approval by the ministers of the treasury before they can be implemented; government may, for instance, impose servicewide wage freezes or reject the recommendations of the advisory board, both of which have happened several times.

Nearly all pay is based on fixed scales, though of course some allowances are paid. For public employees covered by collective agreements there is very little pay flexibility as servicewide job evaluation systems coupled with collective agreements leave no room to differentiate pay between individuals. Moreover, pay progression for those covered by collective agreements is based on seniority (pay scale increments and promotion). However, poor performance may lead to withholding annual increments.

For most levels of management (totaling about 7,000 executives), though, performance-related pay elements have been introduced. These encompass discretionary in-range increases and bonuses. In general, performance increases may account for about 10 percent of the base salary; for top executives they can be higher.

Finland

Performance pay schemes and some pay flexibility related to other factors such as the labor market have been introduced in public service pay. There is some regionalization of pay related to the cost of living, and special allowances are given to staff in remote locations.

National income policy agreements influence public sector pay issues. Most state sector agreements have income adjustment guarantee clauses and stipulate an allowance for pay increases in the private sector. Market comparisons therefore play an important role in setting public sector pay.

Pay determination procedures are rather differentiated within the central government. Collective agreements cover nearly 70 percent of the workforce, including civil servants, teachers, and defense and health employees. Moreover, there are collective agreements for the 20 percent or so nonestablished workers. For those civil servants who have employer status, about 5 percent, the Ministry of Finance sets the pay. Finally, for the less than 1 percent of personnel who are senior officials and experts, personal agreements are negotiated. None of these agreements is subject to government approval except for those negotiated on establishment or agency level, which have to be approved by the Ministry of Finance. However, the budget has to be approved by parliament before agreements for the established workers can take force.

Eighty percent of pay is based on salary scales, with the rest determined by qualifications, nature of work, conditions, working time, and other factors. There is a certain flexibility; agencies can decide on pay increments. Pay progression is based on various factors: seniority, qualifications, personal performance, and work group performance. Experiments are being made with personal performance pay for officials as well as work group performance pay.

France

Pay schemes based on performance do not exist for the public service. However, senior executives do now have limited discretion to reward good performance through pay increases. Moreover, there exist some minor regional differences in public service pay; depending on the area, the residence allowance may vary between 0 and 3 percent. Allowances paid to civil servants working in ministries are generally higher than those paid in deconcentrated and decentralized administration.

Pay determination for the state civil service involves an extensive consultation machinery. Pay consultations are centralized for the entire public service; the agreement reached in such consultations is submitted to the government in the form of a recommendation. If no agreement is reached, the government may set the pay unilaterally; in any case it is not legally obliged to accept the recommendation. In order to implement the pay raises envisioned by the recommendation a respective finance law has to be adopted by Parliament. Based on this law, a decree regulating the pay increase for the civil service has to be issued.

Basic pay is fixed in accordance with a common pay grid based on a pay index, which takes into account the category, grade, and length of service. This pay grid sets the starting and finishing rates for each grade. Top civil servants are not covered by this grid, as the top management posts are classified in a special lettered pay scale that allows for a maximum of only two seniority increments. In addition to the basic salary various allowances, mainly job-related, may be paid. Depending on the post, such allowances may be for housing, cars, or special responsibilities.

The system allows for limited flexibility by awarding extra index points to some grades, by disposing of an elaborate system of premiums, and by offering the possibility to regrade posts on the basis of changes in responsibility.

In general, pay increments are awarded on the basis of seniority. Nevertheless, it is now possible to value good performance by reducing the fixed time span between two salary increments or by accelerating the advancement to the next grade. The very limited use of performance pay elements in the French pay system can be explained with the fundamental rationale of a career system: good performance rewarded through advancement and promotion.

Germany

For the time being no performance-related pay elements exist in the German public service pay system for either civil servants or non-established public employees. Other means of pay flexibility are also nearly nonexistent. However, the government has now committed itself to introduce some performance-related elements to public service pay. It can be assumed that this scheme will include a certain flexibility in awarding performance bonuses and in creating a linkage between seniority increments and performance.

Civil service pay for statutory civil servants is determined by law. For nonestablished workers in the public service—those working on the basis of a contract—pay is determined through centralized free collective bargaining by collective agreement. Though the pay for civil servants is determined unilaterally by law, consultations with the trade unions and staff associations take place prior to the legal procedure. The pay of civil servants tends to follow the pay agreement reached through collective bargaining for nonestablished public service workers. This is possible because, traditionally, pay negotiations concerning nonestablished public employees precede the pay consultations concerning civil servants. However, in recent years, due to the pressure on the state budget, a certain gap has emerged between the pay levels of the two groups, to the detriment of civil servants.

Pay adjustments take into consideration the general revenue situation, trends in income and prices, and other factors. However, there is no established link between private and public sector pay. Market comparisons are used only occasionally, in particular if structural pay improvements for specific professional groups are envisioned.

Public service pay is based on fixed pay scales that generally provide for seniority increments. Top civil servants are paid according to a lettered pay scale that makes no provision for seniority increments; usually take-home pay consists of basic pay and job- and family-status related allowances.

Until now good performance has been thought of as being valued through performance. The system allows for a very limited regional flexibility through a supplement in the residential allowance in especially high-cost areas.

Regarding the introduction of performance-related pay elements in particular, it may be worth mentioning that civil service pay is not regarded as remuneration for work performed but as an augmentation linked to the status—grade or rank—that the civil servant holds. The intention of this structure is that the civil servant should be provided with enough resources to live at an appropriate standard for the rank and be independent.

Netherlands

Performance-related pay elements have been introduced in the public service pay schemes.

Public service pay is determined through collective bargaining. Since 1993, these negotiations have been decentralized by dividing the public service into eight independent bargaining sectors. The cabinet has to approve the result of the negotiations. Parliament, however, cannot influence the result of the bargaining; still, the minister (of home affairs for central-level bargaining), as the employer, is answerable to Parliament for the results of the agreement. The results of the negotiations have to be embodied in legislation after completion of collective bargaining.

Public service pay is based on fixed pay scales that allow special premiums—for example, for demanding posts or those requiring irregular work. The system allows for a certain pay flexibility by providing the possibility to award labor market related allowances and bonuses to recruit and retain high-caliber staff.

Moreover, on the basis of performance, civil servants can be awarded special bonuses, additional pay increases, and temporary allowances. The new pay scheme also provides the possibility to deny annual increases if performance was not up to standards.

New Zealand

Performance-related pay schemes have been introduced on a large scale. Under the State Sector Act (1988) and the Employment Contracts Act (1991), the pay determination procedures have changed considerably. The State Sector Act devolved most of the government's employer responsibilities to individual departments or agencies while introducing bargaining and pay-setting arrangements similar to the ones used in the private sector. The Employment Contracts Act takes one step further and removes the special status of trade unions. Under this act, employees and employers may choose who will represent them, individually or collectively, in negotiations and may negotiate on whether to have individual or collective contracts. Every employee's terms and conditions of employment are contained in an individual or collective employee contract with their employer.

These negotiations enjoy a certain independence from government. The government sets the policy parameters and the State Service Commission and the employers devise particular strategies to fulfill them. Though ministers are kept informed about the negotiations, they have no direct role to play in the procedure. Pay adjustment takes account of the general fiscal situation and the objectives of the government. Moreover, the expenditure constraint on the department budgets have to be observed, and the coordination of the decentralized bargaining by the State Service Commission is intended to keep the pay settlements down. There are no formal private sector comparability surveys, though private sector comparisons may be used to assess pay policies and structural adjustments for particular occupational groups.

The salary scales contain provisions for ranges of rates as well as some degree of fixed incremental steps. The pay ranges give employers flexibility to determine initial rates and also rules for progression. Thus they offer the possibility to award performance and to take into account recruitment and retention problems as well as location, experience, and specific skills in determining initial remuneration and any subsequent increases.

Since 1988, performance-related pay elements have been introduced for staff at virtually all levels within most government departments and agencies. The departments and agencies are basically free to devise their own schemes. Most schemes, however, still link pay progression to both seniority and performance, whereby the latter is more important with higher-level personnel. Performance agreements between the public employer and chief executives and senior managers have existed in New Zealand since 1988.

Sweden

Certain provisions to include performance-related pay elements in civil service pay are in place. The public sector pay policy is led by the idea that it should follow the private sector and that it should be adapted to the operational needs of the agencies. However, budget constraints are taken into account when fixing public service pay, as the total amount of the public sector payroll is limited by the state's budget allocations. The budget allocations for pay are assigned as a lump sum to each public sector institution and cannot be exceeded.

Public service pay is set through collective bargaining. There are three separate agreements on the central level: public service, public utilities, and defense. The central level agreement sets only the minimums for pay increases and the amount of pay funds for distribution at the local level, but no rates of pay. The local agreements cover mainly the actual distribution of the pay funds accorded in the central agreements in terms of pay increases by individual employers. All groups of public sector employees except senior officials are covered by collective bargaining. The pay of the very top officials (directors general) is set by government; the pay of other senior officials is set either by a special board or the chief executive of the respective agency.

The government has no role in the collective bargaining process except for budget allocations; on the employers' side these negotiations are independently carried out by the National Agency for Government Employees.

The uniform pay system based on pay grades was abolished in 1989. Since then there exist only a few centrally agreed pay scales. In general the pattern is individual and differentiated pay, similar to the private sector. Agencies may, however, agree on their own pay scales. Moreover, a position classification system has been introduced. The new system allows for more pay flexibility. In particular such factors as market considerations, experience, special skills, and performance may be taken into account when determining pay. However, there is no general system of performance pay. The typical feature of allocating the pay funds agreed upon in the central agreement is to use one part for an overall pay increase and to set the rest aside for individual distribution in local negotiations; this may include awarding bonuses for good performance.

CONCLUSIONS

These examples of determination and adjustment of public service pay in OECD countries show the wide range of practices applied in the public service. Following developments over time, it is obvious that even the most classical civil service systems, such as the German and French, are now starting to experiment with certain performance-related pay elements in their public service pay systems. However, considering the historical development and rationale of the classical continental European public service, performance-related pay may never account for a significant part of take-home pay without a complete break with its traditions.[1]

To illustrate this traditional approach, just a few basic principles and guiding ideas will be recalled to facilitate understanding why continental Europe with its career civil service systems may seem so hesitant to move toward greater flexibility in the public service, including flexible or performance-related pay schemes.

- The civil service is still perceived as providing unified life-time career employment. This translates into pay equity and transparency within the service, with pay progression for experience (seniority) and a career path that values performance.

• The transparency of public service pay is seen as an important element to ensure impartiality and pay equity on the one hand and to facilitate the accountability of the government toward legislators and the public at large on the other.

• Pay flexibility—for example, taking into account labor market developments in determining basic pay—is perceived as a disturbance of the pay equity established within the public service through a grading system based predominantly on qualifications and responsibilities. The situation in the labor market may nevertheless be taken into account by offering special allowances that can be abolished if the situation changes.

• Performance-related pay elements contradict two basic assumptions underlying the classical pay system, namely that seniority (experience) improves performance, which is one justification for seniority increments, and that special performance is valued through promotion. That governments are nevertheless opening up to new schemes, however hesitantly, acknowledges that seniority is not necessarily linked to performance and that promotion possibilities are becoming more and more limited.

Summarizing the developments in public service pay in different countries over the last decade, it seems justified to state that countries based on a career civil service are only slowly beginning to introduce some flexibility in their pay schemes. This may be because the limited number of entry levels, often coupled with specific preentry training targeted to public administration, fosters a certain specialization of the personnel in public administration. This leads to the observed difficulties encountered by public service personnel if they attempt to enter or reenter the private sector after having worked in the public service for a certain time. At the same time this closed-shop phenomenon in career civil service may limit the influence of private sector pay and the general labor market situation on public service pay levels. However, countries that always had or have moved to a job system in their public service—in Europe the Nordic countries and the Netherlands in particular—are relying more on outside recruitment for every level of expertise and are thus more exposed to developments in the general labor market. Civil services with a job system, in order to be able to compete in the labor market with the private sector on a much broader scale than services with a career system, seem more obliged to use private sector pay determination instruments.

LESSONS LEARNED FROM EXPERIENCE

Even though acknowledging the enormous efforts undertaken in recent years to reform the public service, in particular the changes that have taken place in human resource management (including pay determination), it should be understood that a rather similar effort was made in many countries in the late 1970s. Comparing those with today's programs, some seem identical, others show changed priorities, and very few seem completely new; some 1970s programs seem to have disappeared.

The assessment of those early efforts in tandem with the recent efforts for reform may facilitate the task of evaluating why certain reforms did not produce the expected results, and of learning if there may be certain means to improve the results or even avoid a new failure. Moreover, it may be possible to point out why certain reforms may work in some countries but not in others.

The central issue for quite a number of years has been to improve the quality and performance of the public service while curbing the public service payroll. There seems to be a common understanding that besides possible structural and organizational changes and improvements such as decentralization, deconcentration, and to a certain degree privatization, quality improvement is predominantly a matter of improving human resource management. This primarily means having the right person in the right place at the right time and in addition improving motivation, adapting skills and qualifications to meet changing requirements, and rewarding good performance.

However, to be able to reward good performance it is of course necessary to evaluate performance. Assessing the past experiences with performance pay schemes, it seems that the way performance is evaluated is the crucial issue in making performance pay schemes work. It is necessary to learn, then, what the prerequisites are for a functioning performance appraisal system and why in the past so many systems seem to have failed.

Various issues and arguments have to be taken into account. However, before discussing systems design it is necessary to consider whether performance evaluation systems as they have been developed for the private sector are applicable to the public service at all. It is argued that perhaps a number of the problems experienced in introducing such schemes into the public service may stem from the very different values and objectives of public employment. In most countries civil servants tend to be older and better educated but less well paid than their counterparts in the private sector. As this is known from the outset, persons who enter the public service may do so because they prefer job stability to competition.

Another argument raised against common performance measurement concerns the work culture in the public service. It is said that to a far greater extent than in the private sector, acting within a public service environment calls for group effort; it is rare, if not impossible, for an individual to perform well in the public service without being supported by a team. Individual performance is therefore difficult to measure, a fact that most existing performance pay schemes seem to neglect. As concerns the difference in objectives between the public and private sectors, one has to be aware that private sector productivity is both measured and paid through increased profit but that such a linkage is neither possible nor justified in the public service, where issues such as efficiency and quality are predominant. In addition the measurement of products and outcomes is more difficult in the service sector, public or private, than in manufacturing. Also, the basic definition of productivity improvement—the increase of output per unit—tends to devalue the human contribution that is one of the essential elements in public service. Productivity requirements may significantly differ from efficiency and quality of service requirements; it may not be possible to bridge the two in performance evaluation systems. Thus there can be a conflict of interest for public servants between meeting performance requirements and the spirit of service necessary to respond to the needs of the public. What is more, the implementation of performance appraisal and reward schemes can be divisive and undermine the very conditions under which staff may work effectively and efficiently in teams or groups.

The Public Management Committee of the OECD has reviewed performance-related pay for public managers.[2] The findings suggest that many of the existing performance pay schemes are facing the following recurrent problems:

• A lack of discrimination in performance ratings, due mainly to rating inflation over time, resulting in fewer than 5 percent of managers rated as less than fully satisfactory.

- A clustering of managers at the top limit of the salary range in merit pay schemes where they are no longer eligible for merit increments.

- Dissatisfaction among staff who are rated equally but who, under quotas and other restrictive guidelines, receive either a smaller performance pay award than their colleagues or no award at all in a given year.

- Relatively low levels of funding for pay schemes, which mean that bonuses are small or limited by quota, with resulting staff dissatisfaction.

Moreover, it seems that many of the schemes surveyed have failed to use performance-related pay to implement corporate strategy or to shape the culture of the organization. At this stage it is still too early to decide whether this is due solely to the design and operation of particular schemes, and therefore could be improved.

In evaluating the design and operation of various systems the difficulty of establishing valid performance appraisal criteria becomes obvious. Such criteria should meet certain prerequisites. They should mirror the objectives of the institution and its mission, which is especially difficult if standardized schemes are used with little flexibility to tailor them to specific organizational needs. Moreover, the indicators selected should be accepted by all parties concerned, including the staff, as being appropriate for determining performance. For example, if the office for social assistance or the police force have appraisal systems based, among other things, on the number of cases processed, prevention through counseling may not be given adequate attention, though in the long run the latter may be of greater value for the society. Changes in objectives, for example a change from law and order policing to community policing, have to entail changes in the performance appraisal scheme. Performance appraisal and performance pay schemes call for regular monitoring and updating, a concern put forward by trade unions who point out the difficulties and costs implied in administering a fair system of performance appraisal for large numbers of staff and who doubt that the results justify such an effort. The degree of subjectivity, in fact the issue of fairness, in measuring performance is a principal concern of staff and unions; both appraisal and reward seem often arbitrary, and the workers increasingly feel that the system is not fundamentally equitable. It is therefore important to pay attention to the validity of performance indicators, the objectivity of appraisal factors, the safeguards for equal opportunities, and the methods by which performance is linked to pay.

Another issue that may have to be taken into account when introducing performance pay schemes is the possible fear of staff and trade unions that pay restructuring and flexibility schemes may serve as an excuse or a disguise for wage reductions. The new flexible pay schemes should strike a balance between wage security and the recognition of seniority on the one hand and performance reward on the other.

OUTLOOK

Performance pay schemes will stay on the agenda in OECD countries. Based on past experience, there seems to be a tendency to involve all parties concerned in their design to improve acceptance. Performance pay may be used more strategically to support and shape corporate values and to implement corporate goals. It is likely that more team and corporate bonus schemes will be introduced in the public sector as such schemes seem to be more adaptable to the way work is carried out in the public service.

In the foreseeable future in most OECD countries and in particular continental Europe, these schemes are not likely to gain a major influence on public sector pay scales, but they may considerably influence the way bonuses and regular wage increments are awarded.

Other means to recompense performance, such as increased independence and responsibility with or without promotion and salary increase, will stay a major factor in the reward system. Fringe benefits in kind, such as housing and cars, have already lost predominant importance over the last decades, and this trend will most likely continue.

Special public service health care and pension schemes, where they exist, are under scrutiny as they often represent a considerable burden to the budget. However, abolishing these benefits would most likely provoke the demand for pay equity between private and public sector, a consequence that may also be undesirable. Still, changes in these schemes are most likely to occur.

Notes

1. It should be noted that public utilities, in particular public enterprises, are not subject to these conclusions; their pay determination procedures have

always followed other principles (that is, they enjoy greater flexibility in wage setting) even in such countries as France and Germany.

2. Organization for Economic Cooperation and Development, *Private Pay for Public Work: Performance-Related Pay for Public Managers* (Paris: Organization for Economic Cooperation and Development, 1993).

Planning for the Future

Howard Risher
Charles H. Fay

———

Aheated debate about the role of government in our society has been ongoing since Bill Clinton was first elected president. If the trends over these few years are projected into the future, the United States will have a very different public sector by the beginning of the next century. As politicians try to redefine and gain consensus on the appropriate goals of government, it is obvious that public employers will have to find ways to become more productive and to meet the needs of society with reduced resources. This means that performance expectations for public employees will be raised, and that will change the work environment across the public sector.

Political leaders generally concentrate on the philosophical issues and the mission of public agencies. Many of these leaders have never had to manage large groups of employees; some exhibit little interest in the day-to-day problems of the managers and employees who are responsible for fulfilling the mission. To be sure, elected office holders are not chosen because of their managerial acumen or technical expertise. Their success in office is loosely tied to accomplishing announced goals, but voters are not asked to complete an appraisal form covering their performance for the year.

The real responsibility for organizing and managing the workforce to accomplish its goals generally falls on the shoulders of career civil service managers. Like managers in other sectors, they need the tools and resources to satisfy their customers' expectations. The do-more-with-less philosophy that is being imposed on government means that public employees are going to have to find ways to become more productive. That, in turn, will make performance management a higher priority and prompt increased interest in policies and methods to improve performance. Pay and organizational rewards are an obvious tool to accomplish this.

COMPENSATION SYSTEMS AS A TOOL IN REINVENTING GOVERNMENT

The role of government and the public's expectations are likely to be in flux for at least the next decade. If the government reinvention bandwagon follows the logic that has driven organizational change in the private sector, first will come quality management and reengineering—aggressive change strategies that are related to the scientific management thinking that dominated work planning over the last century. These initiatives have sometimes resulted in dramatic gains in performance; there are also many examples where changes have failed to generate the anticipated improvement.

One reason initiatives may not meet expectations is failure at the planning stage to address the people management side of organizational change. To be fully successful, organizational improvement initiatives must take into account the need for behavioral change: people must accept new work methods and new work patterns. If initiatives do not live up to expectations, a common reason is the resistance of workers to changes in the way they do their jobs. Workers are not going to change their habits simply because top management announces that organizational changes are planned; they have to believe it will be to their benefit to change. The private sector looks to the reward system as an incentive to trigger desired behavior. Increasingly, reengineering strategies in industry include steps to facilitate change, and pay system redesign is an important strategic consideration.

For this reason compensation systems are referred to by reengineering specialists as "enabling processes." This recognizes that pay systems can energize workers and stimulate desired behavior; it is a new perspective for public employers but one that is an extension of the prevailing strategy in the corporate world. It is all too easy to dismiss the use of pay for this purpose, but that should be balanced with the importance of the changed behavior.

Corporations have moved in this direction because they recognized three needs:

- The need to give managers and supervisors more discretion to organize and assign work to their staff as needed to accomplish operating goals, with significantly reduced scrutiny and control from the personnel function.

- The need to reduce the time and cost of administrative controls, particularly where their added value is uncertain.

- The need to align organizational rewards with desired performance. This is based on the widely shared assumption that pay, if properly managed, can be instrumental as an incentive to improve performance.

The biggest hurdle for the public sector is acceptance by agency leaders and managers of compensation systems as a managerial tool. The transition from traditional government wage and salary programs, where pay is loosely linked to performance, to a more aggressive tighter linkage will require top management leadership and a willingness to "push the envelope."

This transition will require new thinking about employee rewards and about performance expectations; changes in compensation systems are only a piece of what managers and employees are going to have to learn to live with. Employees will have to adopt new ways of thinking about their jobs and their careers. That is the essence of the push to reinvent government. The public will also need to appreciate how changes in their expectations are interrelated with the reasons for changing public pay programs. As most workers in the private sector will also be affected by similar changes, public acceptance may come easier than it would have even a few years ago. This transition will be an important issue affecting employer-employee relations for the foreseeable future.

ARE GOVERNMENT COMPENSATION PROGRAMS WORKING?

The adage argues "if it's not broken, don't fix it." Replacing or modifying a pay program is potentially disruptive. Employees and managers alike will be anxious about the impact of the new program on them as individuals and on their work unit. In the public sector there is also a need to worry about public reaction to the prospect of a new program. There is no inherent reason to expect a new program to increase payroll costs, but it is certainly not unusual (although it can be avoided or managed). Realistically, an organization can live with an ineffective wage and salary program, which makes it politically easier to postpone consideration of a new one.

The federal government, as a recent example, continued to rely on a national salary schedule for years, despite oft-cited expert opinion and solid survey results documenting the existence of significant geographic differentials. The national salary schedule in effect overpaid workers in low-pay areas and underpaid them in high-pay areas. What constitutes overpayment is, of course, a matter of opinion and certainly not a problem for affected employees. In high-pay areas, the government adopted a special rates program to provide higher pay levels where it was difficult to recruit and retain adequately qualified workers. Over the years the number of employees on special rates grew steadily until federal personnel specialists in Washington joked about taking bets on when the number of workers paid special rates would exceed the number who were paid the approved General Schedule rates. The problem was exacerbated by the years of rapid salary increases in the late 1970s and early 1980s, but not until 1989 was the program revised to reflect locality pay differentials.

The traditional criteria for program effectiveness relate to recruiting and turnover. If these measures are up, then it is often argued that the pay program may not be fully competitive. This certainly may be true, but there are also other reasons why employees decide to quit or seek other job opportunities. "Fed bashing" during the Reagan administration and the general criticism of government since then have undoubtedly served to make public sector careers less attractive. The state of the economy and the availability of alternative job opportunities is another obvious consideration.

Another criterion that logically comes before the turnover and recruitment problem is the quality of applicants and of employees. As public sector jobs become less attractive, the more qualified applicants turn to private sector or not-for-profit careers. There is solid evidence that the "best and the brightest" are less likely to choose a public sector career now than a decade or two ago. At the same time, the public sector has always been an employer of last resort for many marginally qualified workers. It would be difficult to document, but at least anecdotal evidence suggests that the quality of government workers has deteriorated over the past few decades. The quality of applicants is directly related to the quality of government service and should be an important public concern. In the past few years one could interpret public sentiment as approval of this trend, as poor performance is another justification for cutting back government operations.

Yet another criterion is the view of managers and supervisors. If they believe an existing program is fully meeting their needs and the needs of their work units, it would be nonsensical to initiate program changes. Although in the public sector this group is seldom asked questions about program effectiveness, they are the customers of the program and are in the best position to assess its effectiveness. When surveys have been conducted at the federal level, managers have consistently shown little satisfaction with the program.

If it were possible to start with the proverbial clean slate, it is unlikely that a system design initiative would result in a pay program that resembles those that have been traditional in the public sector. Current thinking in compensation management has prompted reconsideration of many traditional concepts. Corporations are moving rapidly to introduce new ideas. This is not to suggest that public employers should adopt programs similar to those in the private sector, but when viewed in the context of the broader trend to transform organizations, the reasons corporations are moving to new pay program concepts are directly relevant to government.

When a new program is being developed, it is common to start with discussion of the underlying philosophy and program goals. There should be a consensus on the design parameters of the new program. The only meaningful basis for evaluating an existing program—to determine if it is working—is to find out if it is meeting agreed-upon goals. This makes discussion of program goals a fundamental step in designing or modifying pay programs.

MOVING AWAY FROM A STOVEPIPE PERSPECTIVE

Pay programs have traditionally been treated as the purview of human resources or personnel organizations, and they have been closely controlled and administered by specialists; managers and supervisors in other departments have had little if any involvement in initiatives to develop and implement new programs. They often have not played a role in decision making that affects their own subordinates. The failure to involve people from outside the personnel function means that the program probably adheres to textbook principles but is not planned or administered to fit the organization. In some jurisdictions, only the specialists understand the program or are trusted to change it.

This started to change with the mushrooming interest in quality management, reengineering, and organizational effectiveness. There is now wide recognition that pay programs do not exist in a vacuum. What was a closed-door personnel problem is now often delegated to a task force of people from across the organization. In some organizations the pay program is now seen as too important to be trusted to personnel specialists!

The pay program is often the single largest budgeted expenditure in a public agency; for some, payroll accounts for 60 to 80 percent or more of the operating budget. Funds allocated unnecessarily to the payroll could be spent for other purposes. Still, the wage and salary program affects the way employees view their job and their employer. Bad pay programs can trigger a high level of distrust and anger among employees. Most public employees do not have the same recourse to work stoppages as workers in the private sector, but their anger can adversely affect their performance. From a more positive perspective, the opportunities to progress to higher wage and salary levels are also believed to be a source of motivation. Although there is some debate over the use of money as an incentive, there is general agreement that pay programs have an impact on the way employees perform their jobs.

For both reasons, pay programs even in a period of stability are— or should be—a focus of continuing concern. The history of pay programs in most jurisdictions suggests that elected officials are extremely reluctant to initiate changes in program design. Indeed, the absence of change stands out as one of the most striking attributes of government pay programs. Despite the frequent transfer of power between the two political parties and the associated changes in government operations, public pay programs have been essentially unchanged, in some cases for decades.

In an era of rapid change, traditional programs can be a serious impediment. Although public and private administrative systems are similar, government employers tend to rely on review and approval processes for personnel actions affecting compensation that are dramatically more time consuming and bureaucratic. For wholesale changes following a reorganization, for example, it can easily be months before all the job changes are reviewed and evaluated and individual pay adjustments approved.

To some degree, automated systems can alleviate this problem. With even the best systems, however, supervisors will not be able to avoid spending hours dealing with the decisions affecting individual job changes and associated personnel actions. Under a traditional salary program every reorganization triggers a review of salary grades and individual salaries.

Reorganization also creates a counterproductive level of anxiety among affected employees. They are very much aware that the pay-related personnel actions will result in winners and losers. From the point that the plan to reorganize is announced the work group will be less productive. Thus the pay program can make managers reluctant to initiate needed changes.

Recognition of this problem is one of the reasons for increased corporate interest in the concept of broad banding. Conventional programs, with their emphasis on job measurement, require in-depth personnel involvement whenever jobs change. Banding makes it possible to redefine jobs, at least in minor ways, as often as necessary and to move ahead quickly without the traditional personnel stamp of approval.

Government pay programs have not been designed and managed to be incentive, but theories agree that pay affects employee performance; the only differences of opinion relate to whether the impact is positive or negative. The potential impact needs to be considered in program planning.

In the opinion of the authors, pay programs always affect employee performance. Existing programs have institutionalized performance that is just good enough to get by; employees know they will receive a salary increase if they stay out of trouble. This is not unique to government, but it is a focal issue in initiatives to create performance-oriented environments.

A cynic could argue that the concern with voter alienation supersedes any interest in employee reactions. But that also contradicts the goal of improved government performance. If a public sector employer intends to make improved performance a publicly espoused goal, it will be essential to address work management issues; the compensation system will be either an impediment or a key to success.

The transition from an entitlement environment to one that embraces a true pay-for-performance philosophy will not be easy. It is difficult to argue with pay for performance in the abstract but equally difficult to make it work. Traditional merit pay policies—where annual salary increases depend on the supervisor's evaluation of each subordinate's performance—are almost universal in the corporate world. When employees are asked their opinion of merit pay, it is common for them to state that they would prefer to have their pay increases reflect their individual performance. In that context the question is essentially abstract. But if they are asked if their recent salary increases properly reflected their individual contribution, the results might not provide strong support for the continuation of the policy.

Performance improvement has become a top priority for virtually every organization. Over the past few years the media have focused on story after story of organizational success; this not only demonstrates conclusively that dramatic improvement is possible but makes it almost impossible for managers to avoid taking the steps to hop on the bandwagon.

Experience with organizational change initiatives—and the development of a new pay system has to be treated as a significant change—provides solid support for involving managers and employees other than personnel specialists. The creation of a task force or committee is an essential early step. The new program needs to be seen as a management system and should be designed to reflect the needs expressed by the managers who will have to live with its consequences. Managers from the highest level down need to understand and agree that the new program makes sense.

THE NEW CORPORATE COMPENSATION MODEL

For better or worse, public employers tend to emulate and adopt versions of programs used in other sectors. Both the private and public sectors have tended over the years to differ more in nuance than basic components. A new model for corporate programs is rapidly emerging; it would be shortsighted for government to ignore it and try to develop different types of programs, because program needs in government are not appreciably different from those in other organizations.

The components in the new model have been discussed in previous chapters, but three trends are worth repeating:

- The high level of interest in moving away from rigid, bureaucratic program concepts toward ones that are more flexible and easier to administer.
- The recognition that new pay programs need to fit the organization and its values and support its operating goals.
- The renewed emphasis on ending the entitlement mind-set and establishing meaningful linkages between pay and performance, including attempts to reward employees for their individual performance, the performance of their team or work group, and the success of the organization.

The program changes related to these points have been revolutionary rather than evolutionary. It would not be surprising to see these philosophical issues reflected in every corporate program by the year 2000. Significantly, these changes are not driven by human resource executives; they have the solid support of top executives.

Another trend toward basing salary increases on individual competencies is a human resource initiative: competency-based pay. This is a response to the dramatic organizational changes of the past decade. The concept is completely consistent with a widely shared societal value—that more competent workers deserve higher salaries—and with the need to enhance organizational capabilities. The argument that organizations are moving away from static jobs toward more flexible and frequently redefined roles has not yet been confirmed as an important trend, but it is consistent with prevailing management thinking.

The end of the job as the unit of work would have enormous implications for many human resource policies and program concepts. The interest in competencies is also important to other human resource applications, such as staffing and selection, career management, training program design, and performance management. The dissatisfaction with job evaluation systems is almost universal and could prompt many organizations to look for alternatives.

The competency framework is compatible with the way classification systems have been managed and with career ladders in government. Many of the occupations important to government—for example, those in public safety, education, social services, health care, and information systems—rely on career ladders where promotions are dependent on demonstrated competencies. At each step in the ladder, incumbents are expected to enhance their competency and to be able to carry out more complicated and difficult duties. The employees at each step on the ladder are arguably more competent than those at lower levels.

Corporations have also begun to place more emphasis on aligning their pay programs with prevailing market levels. Until a few years ago many corporations placed more emphasis on internal equity than on linkage to market pay rates. With the former some jobs will inevitably be paid above market levels and others below. Corporations have concluded that in order to control costs they need to do a better job of managing salaries relative to competitive levels. Internal equity is still an issue in assigning jobs to bands, but the traditional quantitative methods for accomplishing this have been replaced by more subjective comparisons. This shift in philosophy would be difficult to sell to public employees accustomed to bureaucratic classification systems.

Another important aspect of the emerging corporate model is the increasing emphasis on cash incentive systems. Current trends suggest that the organizationwide gainsharing or goalsharing payouts will, by the turn of the century, be almost as universal as merit pay. In the past year or two, new incentives focusing on team performance have become hot. Significantly, special incentive arrangements for small work teams violate the traditional philosophy of paying everyone under the same policy. However structured, corporate programs make pay for performance an important goal. Any attempt to emulate private sector practices that fails to take into account cash incentives is seriously inadequate.

RETHINKING THE ROLE OF COMPENSATION PROGRAMS

These trends make it fundamentally important to focus initially on the role of compensation and objectives in planning program changes. A pay system has a definite impact on the organization and its ability to carry out its mission. Solid research evidence shows that pay systems can improve performance. It may be unrealistic for public employers to adopt pay policies similar to those in high-performing corporations, but that does not nullify the importance of this issue. It might be argued that if a new program is not explicitly designed to sustain or improve performance, it is likely to be an impediment.

Base pay levels influence the caliber of job applicants. Job applicants consider other job opportunities, but better-qualified applicants also will consider their prospects for continued career progression and increased pay opportunities. Pay is clearly not the only issue when considering job offers; there was an era when the prospect of public service was an exciting career alternative. Traditional thinking also made the job security and benefits in the public sector important. These issues are important in workforce planning; public employers need to decide if base pay levels are enhancing or deterring their recruiting efforts.

Related to this is the inherent problem of maintaining a single program for diverse occupational groups. When salary increases are essentially the same across occupations, some workers will fare better relative to the market for their skills than others. When this philosophy prevails for an extended period, which has been common in the public sector, some employees will be paid more than their private sector counterparts and others less. That may be acceptable as public policy, but it has implications for recruiting and retention.

Research shows that employees prefer to be rewarded for their performance. People like to feel that they are making a meaningful contribution and that it will be recognized and rewarded. The reward does not have to be cash, but if there are no rewards, or if the wrong people receive them, the effort needed to continue making that contribution will taper off and eventually stop. Corporations that conscientiously manage the reward system have found that they can enhance employee commitment and support high performance.

Organizations that ignore opportunities to recognize and reward performance or that ineffectively manage the process cannot expect to achieve the same results; research supports this. To be sure, intrinsic motivation will drive some employees who truly love their work, but they are a small percentage of the workforce. For other organizations, the failure to recognize and reward performance, or in the worst case ignore it, means that workers can get by with minimal effort. That is becoming increasingly unacceptable as budgets are tightened.

CHANGING THE PERCEPTION OF GOVERNMENT PAY PROGRAMS

Perhaps the biggest hurdle public employers will have to overcome if they want to compete for better applicants is the common perception that government pay levels are not competitive with those in the private sector. This perception has been prevalent for a long time and is deeply entrenched. There was a time when job security and benefits in the public sector were believed to offset lower salaries, and it is still widely believed that the lower salaries are offset by the less-demanding work effort required in government agencies.

There are also people who view government pay as too generous. In part this is attributable to the perception of public employees, their work effort, and the value of their contribution or that of their agency. Also, of course, the voting public's perception depends on its own situation and compensation. Some private sector workers are paid well above average; others are paid well below average. Given the distribution of incomes in the United States, some people will always think public pay levels are too high; but it is safe to say that their views have a life of their own, independent of the facts. In the near term, perception may be more important than reality. Regardless of how fair a pay program is, if many employees think it unfair it will be a cause of friction that can undermine management's efforts to improve performance. Moreover, it is probably inevitable that the views of government workers are contrary to public opinion.

Pay levels for some government workers are doubtless below the prevailing private sector level. However, an often unrecognized aspect of the problem is that many government occupations have no private sector counterparts, so comparisons are impossible because valid survey data simply do not exist. For these occupations there is no "right" pay level.

Another aspect of the problem is that public employers tend to downplay market pricing and the job-to-job pay comparisons that are the focus in the private sector. By relying on policies that ignore or minimize the importance of labor markets, employers lose a credible basis for justifying pay levels.

Yet another aspect is the value of paid time off—vacations and holidays—and benefit packages. These traditionally have had a higher value in the public sector and, arguably, offset lower salaries. There is also the value of greater job security in the public sector, although this is beginning to change. These issues make it very difficult to state with certainty that government employees are underpaid.

SELLING EMPLOYEE COMPENSATION PROGRAMS

The overriding problem, however, is the widespread failure of public employers to communicate their policies and practices adequately. Employees tend to remember the saying "If you don't have anything good to say, don't say anything at all." When their employer fails to communicate information needed to understand the program, they assume the employer is trying to hide something. They further assume it is poorly designed or poorly managed. This may be the view of the voting public as well.

If as we argue the perception of employees is a key to program effectiveness, then it pays to communicate pay issues on an ongoing basis. Employees are adults and understand the reasons that their pay may not be fully competitive. They may not like the message, but even bad news will be better received than no news. With the increasing emphasis on empowerment, it is always advantageous to be open and to keep people informed of events that affect them.

In other not-for-profit organizations, specifically those in education and health care, the culture makes it important for employees to be involved or represented in decisions that affect them. When changes are being planned, it is common to conduct focus groups or surveys or to form committees with affected employees as members and to seek employee input to the plans. In fact, it is not uncommon to delegate some of the program planning responsibility to a committee. If the members of a committee know what decisions are expected and understand the constraints (such as the available budget), they generally take their responsibilities very seriously and make a concerted effort to develop acceptable answers.

Committees do take longer to accomplish assigned tasks, but they also assume ownership for the decisions. As they work through the problems, they naturally keep coworkers informed of progress, hurdles, and the reality of the pay determination problem. They therefore serve as an effective, believable, and understandable communication conduit. Their decisions will also reflect commonly shared values and beliefs. They know they will have to answer to coworkers, so they discuss issues and share ideas as the need for decisions arises. The eventual answers may not fit a textbook model, but the new policies and practices have a high probability of succeeding.

If a committee is involved, management has to communicate its goals along with any important parameters. The members need to understand the limits and the expected end results. If, for example, the goal is to develop a pay-for-performance policy, then the committee has to be given this mandate. The committee members may not fully accept the underlying philosophy, but they will work to develop the best answer that fits the environment.

There is another axiom: "If you hear something often enough, you begin to believe it." The communication problem is best viewed as a marketing problem, with the goal being to establish program credibility. If public employers are to change the perception of pay programs, it will require a concerted ongoing communications campaign. It will be important in this context to manage decisions so that the grapevine reinforces the intended message. Whenever employees hear a contradictory message, it could become a major setback for the campaign.

This is not to suggest that communications in private employers are that much more effective, but corporations do routinely disseminate performance information so that news that normally affects employees is provided well in advance of policy changes. Corporations also are more likely to have articulated compensation philosophies and clearly stated program objectives. Employees certainly may find that they disagree with corporate policies. Corporations that are up-front and honest about the business reasons for a new policy are likely to have employees who will acquiesce to the change if they believe it is necessary.

The communications campaign should focus on program goals and administrative mechanics. The campaign should also cover the underlying philosophy and cultural values. Employees need to know that the program was designed to meet the organization's needs. They also need to understand how the program is going to affect their prospects and what they need to do to achieve their goals. Many employers take the time to develop and disseminate a compensation philosophy statement that provides an overview of the thinking that governed the program's design.

In our media-oriented world, employers should invest in the development of an effective communications strategy. Employees are inundated with sophisticated media messages. Private sector employers have started to get on this bandwagon, reflecting the belief that the workforce is important in gaining competitive advantage. This is an uphill battle in most organizations, but the potential improvement in performance justifies the investment.

Effective communications may also improve the public's perception of government pay programs. Realistically, the differences between public and private sector compensation programs mean that few voters have the experience or knowledge to understand and appreciate how government pay levels are set and increases determined. Voters will probably continue to be skeptical of public pay programs and feel government workers are not properly paid until they are convinced that standards are comparable to those in the private sector. That is a communication problem that government employers have been slow to address.

AN AGENDA FOR DEVELOPING
NEW PAY PROGRAMS

In the private sector it is now "out with the old and in with the new." The traditional model for compensation programs is very much a dinosaur. In part this is a result of the sweeping interest in reengineering and in improving organizational systems. The traditional compensation model has never had truly strong supporters; senior executives have given lip service to it over the years, but that is ending rapidly. Now the only question is how quickly decision makers will become comfortable with new ideas.

Public employers will similarly have to decide if their current programs are "broken." The criteria for evaluating pay programs are not obvious, but most supervisors and managers in the trenches can probably reach a consensus on that decision: they are broken! Still, there are widely divergent opinions on the priorities and goals in considering new alternatives.

One of the basic problems is a fear of the unknown. Public officials have had minimal exposure to the thinking that goes into the new program model. Corporate executives, in contrast, have lived with risk-reward principles and pay-for-performance philosophies for most of their working lives. Public officials also have to be more sensitive to the opinions of stakeholders; they cannot make unilateral decisions to change a pay program. Fear of the unknown is shared by most of these individuals. This makes education and communications fundamentally important to the initial decisions to move to new program concepts.

We recommend that an early step be to assess the opinions of people across the various agencies. This can be done with formal surveys or more informally with focus groups and "town meetings." The era of off-the-shelf or canned programs is dead; the goal now is to develop a program that meets the unique needs of the organization. That involves ongoing input. It will be decidedly advantageous to know which components are perceived as broken and which are still fully functional.

It will probably be worthwhile to consider the needs of each agency as if it were a separate employer. There are real and often dramatic differences between government agencies. A department of education clearly has different pay problems than a department of corrections. Government needs to compete in literally hundreds of labor markets. To argue that a one-size-fits-all pay program will be effective across the spectrum of government operations is to ignore the prospective impact of the program.

There is a high level of interest in giving agencies greater discretion to develop their own programs. The states of Georgia, North Carolina, and Virginia, among others, are all going in this direction. The central "corporate office" establishes the ground rules to make sure agencies are playing on the same field and, to some degree, identifies permissible program alternatives. The resulting programs normally reflect a common philosophy, but there is no reason to live with a mandated program that is ineffective. This is completely consistent with trends in the corporate world, where programs are increasingly fragmented to meet the unique needs of a work group.

Significantly, when the central human resource agency delegates some degree of control over program design, it also forgoes the close control that was typical of traditional programs. That is also consistent with corporate trends, and it translates into new roles for line managers, who then share accountability for the program, and for compensation specialists, who need to develop new consulting skills and work with line managers to design the programs.

One of the basic issues now is the need to understand work processes and work roles. It is important to know how workers interact today and how they may do so in the future. To state the obvious, organizations and work patterns are changing rapidly, and a new pay program needs to support rather than hinder that change. For example, it would be a rare organization that is not creating teams in some work units. The organizational future has important implications for pay programs and should be considered early in the design of new programs.

Undoubtedly the most difficult problem will be the shift away from entitlement to pay for performance, which requires strong management commitment. Successful merit pay policies involve much more than a new appraisal form. Merit policies depend on decision making by managers and supervisors. Public employers need to make sure their supervisors have the necessary skills to manage and assess performance. The commitment to performance management must start at the top of each agency and cascade down tier by tier to first-level supervisors.

The introduction of merit pay is a major organizational change. It cannot be done on a shoestring budget. There has to be adequate funding for salary increases as well as for training and communications. People need to become acclimated to the new environment. It may be advantageous to make the first year under the new policy a trial period to give everyone time to live with the new process.

Significantly, public sector unions seem ready to accept the shift to merit pay. In a recent conversation the president of one of the larger government unions said that his union "had spent too much time and money defending poor performers." He undoubtedly would not make the same statement in public, but as the old saying goes, he sees the handwriting on the wall, and his union has more important problems to address.

It would be decidedly advantageous to shift to a more performance-oriented culture. Perhaps the biggest difference between the public and private sectors is the emphasis on performance and performance improvement. Corporations track an almost endless series of performance measures, some of which generate daily data. Corporate managers are accountable for results, and this is the foundation for the reward system.

Managers in the public sector should be similarly accountable for the achievement of agency goals. Individual performance management and merit pay will not be successful unless they are part of an overall performance planning and measurement process. Deciding to move to pay for performance represents an opportunity to strengthen an agency's goal setting and performance planning. At the very least it sends a useful message regarding the agency's priorities. If merit pay is introduced with little or no top management support and is not tied to overall agency goals, it will be viewed as nothing but more personnel paperwork.

Changes of this magnitude are problematic under the best of circumstances. The change strategy must take into account all stakeholders and should plan for their buy-in. The bandwagon is pulling out, and everyone must get on board.

The involvement of one of the authors as the consultant for federal pay reform proved to be an invaluable lesson in how to gain acceptance of a major change in a government compensation program. The planning session starts with the assumption that a lot of people have to accept and support the change. If elected officials have to vote on proposed changes, they must be approached and considered one at a time. Each stakeholder approaches the situation with an individual bias and needs to be convinced that the change is palatable and in the best interest of government. That may require compromise; at the very least the planners have to understand the points of contention and work to accommodate opposing points of view.

The design of a new pay program involves an endless array of decisions. Salary programs at one time were based on a few off-the-shelf answers, but that era has ended. The design process should involve an ongoing assessment of alternative program concepts. Periodically, program planners must search for answers to these questions: Will the anticipated changes serve government's needs? Will they contribute to better government? Are they consistent with agreed-upon human resource management principles? Will they send the right messages and reinforce desired values? Can we as employers take pride in the planned program?

A new pay program does not have to be designed and installed behind closed doors. Although that may have been the tradition, it would be disastrous in the current climate. But if approached properly, it can be a very positive change. In some public agencies the existing program is so bad that any change will be well received. To be sure, employees will be anxious and skeptical, but this is a natural reaction to change that could affect their careers. It is important to balance the technical program design issues with an ongoing commitment to communicating the goals, the project schedule, and the anticipated outcomes. The program needs to be technically sound and defensible, but unless it is perceived as a good program it has virtually no chance of success.

—ᴡᴠ— Index